Copyright © 2023

CC0

This is the Autobiography of Swami Murugananda by
Swami Murugananda

10 9 8 7 6 5 4 3 2 1

Cover, layout, and design by Nathalie Rukmini Ando, natiando.art

Yogaville, VA 23921

My Journey

The Autobiography of Swami Murugananda

1. So many bridges crossed- Nepal Trek 1998

Dedicated to my beloved Sri Gurudev and all the Holy, kind, and generous teachers I have been fortunate to meet along the way.

2. Sri Gurudev, 1966. I took for Interview for NY Times, unpublished.

3. Last portrait, 2019.

4. Photo by Sri Gurudev.

Contents

9	**Preamble**
	There Is No Real Beginning
13	**The Amble**
16	**A Tribute for Dad on His 100th Birthday**
	December 23, 2009
22	**The Early Days**
23	**A Few Bits of Family History – Plus**
	The Iceman Cometh
	The Radio
	Story of Olga & Saul – An Important Piece of History
	Maternal Grandfather & Great-Grandfather
	To Continue
	A Bit More About Mom
31	**The Path to Becoming a Swami – "Beginnings"**
32	**My Earliest Spiritual Experiences**
33	**A Few Early Ideas**
	Remembering My Best Bud
37	**The Next Step, the Ball Rolls**
	You Make a Choice & Chain Continues to Unfold
38	**College Years**
	The Essential Question
42	**Moving on, "Success", and Important Choices**
42	**Advantages of Good Scientific Training**
44	**The Opening Begins... Ta-Da**
	Synchronicity
	Another Case of Being Protected
	Yet One More Case of Being Protected
	Some Vital Points
50	**Beginning of the Connection**
50	**A Few Words on Hatha Yoga**
	To Continue
52	**Gurudev Story 1**
53	**Gurudev Story 2**
53	**Gurudev Story 3**

54	**The Story of Evolution**
	Inspirational Reading
55	**The Great Adventure – Getting on the Road**
	First Leg
	Yippee
57	**San Francisco Days**
58	**The Persistent Mom**
61	**On to Mt. Shasta**
62	**A Most Wonderful Spiritual Experience**
	One More Adventure
	Hitchhiking, Protected
64	**First Attempt**
65	**Gurudev Story 4**
	Understanding the Guru His Great Teaching & Blessing
66	**Commune Days**
	Starting on Mount Shasta
	Protected Again
	Third Time's the Charm
	AT LAST
71	**Gurudev Story 5**
	Becoming a Disciple, Mantra Initiation
72	**Gurudev Story 6A**
	A Note on My Holy Gurudev
	Interesting Good Karma
73	**Gurudev Story 6B**
73	**On His Infinite Greatness**
	Waves of Gurus Coming to America
75	**Santa Cruz: Part One**
76	**Santa Cruz: Part Two**
78	**Gurudev Story 7**
79	**San Francisco: Part One**
79	**San Francisco: Part Two**
83	**The Very First San Francisco Retreat**
	Many Other Gurus
86	**Gurudev Story 8**
87	**Some Anecdotes in San Francisco**
	Halloween

Siva Ratri
Outside Work Stint
89 **A Great Surprise Visit**
90 **The First Initiation on the Path to Sannyas**
92 **Sannyas Initiation**
Adventure on the Road
94 **Yogaville West**
94 **Gurudev Story 9**
96 **Gurudev Story 10**
Dress Up Dress Down
97 **Gurudev Story 11**
No Job is Below Him
More on Yogaville West
Teaching Yoga to Nuns
100 **Gurudev Story 12**
Departure of Vijay & Shree
Meeting an Exceptional Man Who Became a Good Friend
Selling & Closing Down the Ashram
102 **Santa Barbara Ashram**
105 **Gurudev Story 13**
Plant In, Plant Out
106 **Gurudev Story 14**
The Right Tool for the Job
107 **Gurudev Story 15**
Surprise, Surprise, Surprise
108 **Los Angeles**
A Few Anecdotes About Los Angeles
Visit of Sri Swami Chidanandaji Maharajah
Star Wars & Beyond
111 **Connecticut Ashram**
114 **New York Integral Yoga Institute**
115 **A Couple of Anecdotes**
Driving to Virginia
Dad Passes Away
117 **The Virginia Ashram: Final Destination, at Last**
Some Early History
Evolution & Development

     Venerable & Renowned Visitors
     Short Story About Peter Max
     Other Remarkable People
     Our Most Special Holidays
     The "Great Challenge"—Necessity for Adapting & Innovation

127 **Gurudev Story 16**

127 **Gurudev Story 17**
     On the Spot EMT

128 **All the Wonderful Babies**

130 **Sri Gurudev's Mahasamadhi**
     Abbreviated Version – Diary Entry August 18, 2002

133 **What I Did Over the Years**
     My Hobby

135 **Gurudev Stories 18–22**
     Beginning the Website, Announcement, & Cameras
     Computer Assistance & Much More
     Gurudev – The Consummate Recycler
     A Perfect CD
     Be Careful What You Wish For
     From His Own Hand
     Carry It On

141 **Pilgrimages, Adventurers & Miracles in India & Nepal**
     My First Trip to India – October 1984
     Saved Again

143 **Gurudev Story 23**

144 **Saved Again**
     A Few Coimbatore Events
     Visit to the "Mystic"
     More of Coimbatore
     "Interesting" Aspects of India
     More Things
     Temples

153 **Beautiful Experiences**
     Bede Griffiths
     Palani

154 **Gurudev Story 24**
     Amazing Memory Skill
     Continuation on to Kerala: Katakali Dance & Other Things

      Visit to the Advaita Vedanta Ashram
      Hardwar
      Shankaracharya
      Rishikesh
      Saved Again

162 **Vaishishta Guha**
      Ramana Ashram
      Tea Time
      Small Miracles
      Final Little Miracle
      Kanya Kumari
      Curious Experience

166 **Perur (Mutt) Ashram & Temple**
      Orphanage
      Kovalam Beach

169 **Short Takes**
      The Restaurant Finder

169 **Gurudev Story 25**
      Kaumara Maadam
      Skipping the Taj Mahal
      That Certain Member of the Tour
      Fresh Coconut Joys

171 **Find the Train**
      Small Miracle – Serendipity
      Chennai Beach
      The Local Ice-Cream Place
      The Roots Factory Complex
      Gandhi Kadhi Shops
      Power Outages
      Nature Cure Camp
      Women's Work & Construction
      Tanjavore Artisan Shop
      Note on Hatha Class at the Institute
      South Indian Wedding
      The Glory of South Indian Food & a Special Surprise
      Pondicherry, Aurobindo Ashram
      Jaipur
      The "Great" Departure Experience – Last Trip to India

183	**Nepal & Many Great "Miracles"**
184	**First Minor Miracle**
184	**First Major Miracle**
	Saved
186	**Beginning of Next Major Miracle**
	Kathmandu Beginning
	Common Findings on the Trek
194	**Next Big Miracle Part Two – All Things Linked**
194	**One More Really Big Miracle**
	Saved Again Big Time
	Final Days
196	**The Final Chapter**
	Two More Wondrous Events, Saved
	Flight Home – The Indian Airport Experience
	Finally, HOME AT LAST. My Room, My Bed – AHHH. So Fine.
199	**Epilogue – Postscript**
200	**Appendix I: Spiritual Essays & Brief Ruminations**
	Starters
205	**From My Diaries**
	In Addition
209	**Unwinding the Conditioning – Undoing the Default Setting**
	A Parable
	Fundamentalism
	Jottings
	PAY ATTENTION
213	**Illuminations from Unexpected Places**
213	**Philosophy from an Unexpected Source**
	Encounter on the 22 Fillmore Bus
	Walking Lessons
	A Poem
	Sources of Knowledge
220	**Chanukah Wisdom – The True Story**
	Introduction – Foreword – Prologue
	The History
	The Spiritual/Mystical Purport
	Addendum: Something about Numbers
	A New Translation of the Blessings

227	**Appendix II: A Very Few Movie Reviews**
	Just 4 out of over 400
228	**Birth of a Maven**
	How I Became the Movie Maven of the Western World
	To Continue
	Casablanca
	MMWW
	PPS. Trivia
	Dark Eyes
	Dark City
	After Life
	Atonement
	MMWW
246	**Appendix III: A Bit of Humor**
	Aphorisms Plus
251	**Appendix IV: Story of the Yogaville Library**
	The Beginning: Part One – First Preamble
	The Beginning: Part Two – Second Preamble
254	**Gurudev Story 26**
	The Serious Bits
	The Long Hard Climb
	Great Occurrences
259	**Gurudev Story 27**
263	**The Great Reconfiguration**
265	**Appendix V: The Story of SASTRI**
	The Master Archive of all of Sri Gurudev's Satsangs
266	**Acknowledgements**
268	**Gurudev Story 28**
	The Project Begins
270	**Gurudev Story 29**
	Search Policies
272	**Appendix VI: My Big Book List**
	An Abbreviated List of the Most Inspirational Books in My Life
280	**ADDENDUM**
	Summer Recollections: A Little Memoir
290	**All About the Cover Photo**

Preamble

All that I've done, all the goodness that has come in this life, came through the grace of my beloved Gurudev to whom I dedicate this work and all the work to which my name is attached. He has protected me (many instances cited here), guided me, given unconditional love, kindness, tenderness and many gifts.

This book began as a response to a question from my newly found cousin, Alyssa. At first our only communication was Facebook and a few e-mails until I met her on her visit here. A beautiful, energetic young woman. She asked me a "simple" question wondering why I became a swami rather than a rabbi, as had my Dad had for so many, many generations in his family.

(Sidebar note: There is a book called, Unbroken Chain that traces our family history to 1482. It describes many generations of rabbis, founders of dynasties, founders of yeshivot, heads of village councils [Bet Din], writers and so on. I did not find out about this until relatively recently [25 years ago], so none of this was relevant to me personally. I'd never heard about any of this from my father or family members.).

Upon consideration, it was not such a simple question because what appears to be just the making of one decision, as important as this may be, generally is not birth of its own. There must have been a series of events, conditions and decisions that led up to this. Therefore, it seemed to me that in order to respond properly I would need to give the backstory.

A short note concerning sections labeled as, "Gurudev Stories." Many years ago I started a book entitled "Sacred Stories." This was a collection of stories from my experience, and others, who were direct disciples of Sri Gurudev. The purpose of this book was twofold; firstly it was an account of those who were direct disciples of our dear Gurudev, a perfected Master. Unlike the Gospels of the New Testament which was written 60 to 70 years after the passing of Jesus and were most likely not direct witness accounts. More importantly, it is my contention that many of the greatest teachings were given "off platform" that is to say not in the formal setting of the public talk or satsang. Thus, the stories shared here are not only for the purpose of interesting anecdotes but also for the inherent teachings.

There Is No Real Beginning

Sometimes the most obscure events, or what seems to be the most minor decision can lead one on a life-changing path. Your only option is to go with it and see where it leads. One can never fully know whither a chain of evidence will lead. It is the great adventure, a mystery. But it's worth doing.

All such beginnings are really an arbitrary point, which a writer selects. One may never know in advance the chain of events that may follow. What one thinks of as a "random" event, or "choice" we make in life is but part of a chain that follows preceded by other events. This has been my experience.

There are, in fact, as with most of our choices in life, there are many layers operating here. Two of the concurrent stories operating are the external events or actions we take and there are the inner motivations and reactions. Often the two are woven so that one's external experience influences the internal, which in turn will influence what choices we make in our lives. What in fact is responsible for our reactions to events, or interactions with others, has been laid down well before we could even speak. It is deep in our psyche initially installed by mother and later by father.

This story is just that, a story, not to be confused with the Truth within. Here I speak of those traditions that are imposed on by what one is born into not the sacred teachings from a True Guru.

For each individual on the path this story has its own character, but there are some similar characteristics. It is a process, an evolution of unfoldment as well as peeling away the layers of years of conditioning. This process must keep on; if you think you have arrived to the end, you are dead. It takes courage, one must break away from the past, which may provide a sense of security but also keeps one locked in. That is the problem with old traditions. It is very nice to have that connection, it is very powerful to have those traditions, and it can be very beautiful to be connected. However, that can also be a prison. The more powerful the tradition the more demanding it is of you, the more it insists that you keep all its rules and the less you are able to explore, to question and to really discover for yourself. Therefore, it takes courage to break away. At first, you feel untethered and afloat in a sea of confusion. Here is a danger that many young seekers may find themselves in. I have seen this many times. A confused young person needing such security falls prey to profit-seeking, self-described gurus who take advantage of those people and they are sucked in to a system that may be more restrictive and binding than the place they came from. Of course, this does not apply to the great teachings coming from the true loving master.

This process of evolution is not a straight line but is more like a spiral, as one evolves, often coming to a similar place as before but from a new perspective. It is also multi-layered and multi-dimensional involving mind, emotional body and intuitive self. It is my conclusion, therefore, that one should have trust in one's own experience, one's own understanding of the truth. Along the way I met a genuine and profound teaching given by a true master of the path. Of course, at first the student needs to pay close attention to the teachings. That will be one's touchstone, The Guiding Light in life. That is a starting point. As one progresses on the path one discovers that truth which abides within. That is The Way.

God has no religion, does not take sides. Anyway, the process continues.

Writing biography can be especially daunting and though it is about, what for so many people, is one's favorite subject viz. one's self, it is a challenge to put into a cohesive and interesting form. For what may be so interesting to me may be a massive bore for others. Writing a biography has been asked of me many times. I have thus far refused to answer fully. I call this a "Sacred Story." Thus far, I have never told this journey in this full form to anyone.

I once told a bit of my story to one of our swamis and she said, "I never knew that about you. That is amazing. You should write it down and let everyone know." Well, indeed, this has been an adventurous journey, sometimes filled with very dangerous situations. Somehow, I managed to get out and avoid complete catastrophic failure. I know I have been protected and I attribute all of this to the grace and blessings of my Sri Gurudev. The rather unusual road that I have traveled was another reason for my writing this more completely.

Along the way, I may eliminate certain details. I will not say anything about my very young obsession with my comic books collection or my first foray into private enterprise at age four where I garnered a massive $1.56 in pennies and nickels selling some of my collection of comics which in today's market may be worth $100,000. Well I said it anyway, so there.

5. H.S. Graduation, 1958.

6. Cousin Alyssa's question started this book.

7. Brother Milt (R) & me ages 4 1/2 & 2.

8. Mom, Brooklyn CA, 1925.

9. Milt & me look "surprised", 1947.   10. Our first photo CA, 1945.

The Amble

[I believe it is right for "The Amble" to directly follow the "Preamble".]

We record much in writing during which time we are liable to forget. When, however, we attain realization we will write so that others might not forget.

I should mention that I was born with very poor vision and functionally blind in one eye. This situation has informed most of my life. The condition is known as strabismus or "floating" eye, I had unsuccessful surgery at age 2. From that day on, I wore very heavy spectacles. (Incidentally, my brother had the same situation and we both had cataract surgery within the same week of the same year on the right eye—amazing.). Consequently I was totally rubbish at most sports especially those involving a ball. Furthermore, I was never chosen to be on any team during elementary school years. This apparently minor incident, when repeated over many years that left some very deep scars. Far more significant was the fact that I was unable to drive. I completely failed the initial eye exam for a driver's license. Which was just as well because I could never see traffic coming from the left side. The good thing was that it stopped me from being drafted into the military in 1959.

Another significant event in my early life occurred in around the fourth or fifth grade. I developed a severe lung infection, which I later assumed was pneumonia. Eventually wiped out the lower lobe of the right lung. This put me out of school for the better part of the year. They gave me some abominable medicine that didn't really do much. It had some effect on stamina but not any reduced determination.

I have a younger brother Milton Howard who is 2½ years younger than me. Although we grew up together, we didn't have a strong relationship. That is one of those complex things in life which we do not fully understand.. Later on in our lives, we discovered that we thought about many things in extremely parallel ways. For example we were both movie buffs and we both like and dislike the same movies. He also has a keen sense of humor. He also grew up without ever getting married, and unfortunately retired at a young age and didn't have anything to go to. Consequently, he suffered a long and deep depression. Not taking good care of himself or his home. Back in the mid-60s, he moved to California in the Berkeley area and still lives there to this day in his own home. Around 2010 he suffered a major angina attack and had a quadruple bypass followed by 13 stents [which is a record at San Francisco General.]

Very early on, at about age seven or eight, I learned to do the headstand. No one taught me. Someone just asked one day in summer camp if I could do it and I said, "Yes, of course." Having said so I was obliged to do it. I had no fear, just did it. At another point at that age I was asked if I could do the wheel from a standing position and of course I said yes and just did it. No hesitation. I had no idea that these were part of hatha yoga

Poverty, however, provides one with a certain ruggedness and ability to withstand difficult times. Eventually we climbed out of that and had a moderately good life having a nice small house. However, the daily internal experience was something entirely different. The great portion of my early life was very dark and lonely. There are many levels and expressions of this darkness which are basically not worth going into. As a youth I was also quite rambunctious and more than a bit of a troublemaker. This too is not worth going into detail.

As an aside, it is worth noting that in the 4th grade when they were electing posts such as class president, athlete, secretary and such; I was given the "position" of class-clown. Back then, I memorized jokes and found an ability to tell them well.

I attempted running away from home five or six times at about age 10 or so. This consisted in stuffing my pockets with Mounds Bars or other such finer comestibles, hopping on my 20-inch bike and peddling like mad. My best distance was perhaps three miles.

All this, however, did lead me to the quest of who I really am. That is to say the quest for the highest truth and what my purpose in life is.

As with any autobiography it is obligatory to say a few words about Mom and Dad as they had great influence on my development. The following is what I wrote on the occasion of what would have been Dad's 100th birthday. I know that this is a long section but Dad had a great influence in my early development and I had great respect and love for him.

A Tribute for Dad on His 100ᵗʰ Birthday
December 23, 2009

I have always been fascinated with knowing about my family history. What was it like coming to America? This is the little I can now recall. He did not tell me much about his early life. I am sorry that I never did ask about that. It is a great loss. Knowing one's history is of great value, it puts your life in some perspective. We all have a history. In this article, I focus on Dad because he had a much better influence in my life than Mom. Though I'm sure, she loved us as far as she was capable and in fact worked very hard at being a caring Mom, it is also true that she was very attached to us, created an atmosphere of fear, and impinged on our development..

Born 23, December 1909 Nyirmadja, Hungary a small town in Szabolcs-Szatmár-Bereg County. This is the very northeastern sector of the country He would always joke that he was born "Erev, erev-Christmas." (Eve of the eve of Christmas, erev is Hebrew for evening).

In Hungary, he helped his Dad by driving a horse cart to deliver seltzer water.

Came to America 1929. "I was lucky I came right at the start of the depression." He told me. He spoke no English when he arrived here. At first he got a manual labor job hauling up bags of flour for Ratner's bakery on the Lower East Side.

Of course, this brief memoir does not do justice to who he was or what kind of person he was—no such writing really does.

He had many names; in Hungarian he was *Lajos*, (pronounced *loi-yosh*—a common name in Hungary) Mom called him *Lippe* or *Lajos*, in Hebrew he was *Yonah Yom Tov Lippe ben Moshe Zvi Hersh*. In English, here he was just Leon.

Dad was always very respected by his friends and congregants. He was a man of his word. When he said he would do something you could be sure that he would do it. You could count on him to be there when he said he would. To this day, I lead my life in accord with that principle. It has been a guiding principle of my life. He used to say, "Better to be ten minutes early than a minute late."

Dad taught me many things. He taught me to read when I was four, both Hebrew and English. I got into 1ˢᵗ grade at age four because of that. He also taught me how to blow the shofar. [Ram's horn blown on Rosh Hashanah and Yom Kippur]. I would guess that was at about age 12. I got it right away. However, he never asked me to do it at any service.

He also instilled in me a love for storytelling which I carry on. Dad took me to my first movie ever (Wizard of Oz at age 4 in the Ocean Theater (around 1946). I have loved movies ever since).

He also took me to the chicken market in our neighborhood. This shop was at a large, very smelly but interesting place on Nostrand Ave. (Now an ugly big-box clothing store.) It was like being tossed back a 100 years. There were stacks and stacks of cages. Dad would open one and check to see how fat the chicken was and by some unknown magic, or hidden knowledge, he would pick the right bird. After deploying the proper kosher technique for slaughter he would stuff the bird head first into a conical holder that was attached to the inside of a barrel that had a layer of sawdust on the bottom to catch the blood. After which he would feather the bird and finally turn it over an open flame to singe off the tiny pinfeathers. It was magical.

He taught me a little about cooking too. Just small things like tuna and egg salads I loved doing that. Dad a fantastic memory. He knew all the Hebrew prayers by heart. We had a little game, I would open a Chumash (Hebrew Bible) at random read a couple of sentences and he would quote what followed. I could never trip him up.

He was very perfunctory about performance of all religious observances. We would walk to shul every Shabbat, evening and morning. When we got home for the big meal Friday night he was so happy when we shared challah. He loved singing the zimmreot (tunes) he put his heart into it. I really LOVED when he would tell me stories. His tales were always of saints, sages and miracles. He was a great fount of such tales.

He would be very moderate about drinking. I never saw him drunk. It was not a part of his life.

He did take his tea in a glass, first putting a cube of Domino sugar in his mouth. I never saw him drinking tea out of a cup.

However, he was also a man with a low tolerance for deviation from the norm. (Especially when it came to ritualistic matters. That was, sad to say, mostly rote, without any reference to any mystical aspect.). Eventually all the political wrangling and terrible treatment from the synagogue forced him to resign. He was quite bitter about that. He had served for so many years in so many, many ways, but they did not appreciate him. They did have a fete in his honor. I still have the brochure from that gala.

I loved hanging with him, but it was not until after he was gone that I understood proper respect. Sometimes it happens like that; we do not appreciate our loved ones, our parents, our friends, lovers, brothers, etc., until after they are gone.

What I really **loved** was going with Dad on his special shopping trips when he would get religious supplies; books, the various things for holidays like the Passover wine, the Etrog and Lulav for Sukkos [Festival of the tabernacle], the sachach (reeds that grew by some pond or lake) that was put on top of the Sukkah. Dad was so cool. I especially loved the musty old bookshop, Shapiro's, where he got most of his stuff. It looked very much like the old magic shop seen in the Harry Potter films. There were all sorts of strange, arcane objects piled high in glass cases, loads of old books on creaking shelves and dusty tables. It was, indeed, very magical. Dad always knew just what to get and he always was able to cut a deal. It was from him I tried to learn that art of cutting a deal, but, alas, I did not have that great skill of style and diplomacy. He was the best. Going to the special matzoh bakery for *shmerah matzot* for Passover (specially hand-made round matzot made only for that occasion, they were especially cared for so that it was the most pure, they were thick, round, huge, and delicious *shmerah* means "watched over")—I often wondered what the heck they used the ovens for during the rest of the year. That was a special treat as was going to the winery with their 100 gal. vats of stinky wine.

Alternatively, we'd go to Yona Shimmel for a genuine Knish. Potato or kasha-that was it, none of those fake—blueberry, pomegranate etc.—which are serve these days. I name them "fagels" (fake bagels)Those were the really great rituals. I would love the whole way we set up for Passover. All those smells and foods and the fuss were wonderful to me. Well those were the best things I did then.

It was a wondrous and magical experience going with Dad to buy his new hat every summer. We went downtown and all those hats were piled high and deep in dusky shadows. Older men speaking in strange languages. He would try on various ones for size. I would sometimes offer my own opinions thinking this was a grown-up thing to do. He looked way cool. We would then stop at the pickle stalls to get a few pickles right from the barrels. What a grand aroma wow!! ☺ Nickel a pickle. It was divine. There is nothing like it now.

The best things about these trips was going out for lunch at one of those old restaurants downtown; Ratner's (sadly, now no longer in business) was the place to go. It was basically, a Jewish veg restaurant, but they called it "dairy" (in contrast to meat.). As soon as you walked in you got a basket of *real bread* (no such thing as "gluten-free" then), all homemade, 14 kinds (slight exaggeration) of bread in enormous baskets; black bread, pumpernickel, seeded bread. Not a slice of white bread ever. AND real butter, none of that fake stuff. All this before you would even order. That was a grand place. All the waiters knew Dad. They were all at least 90 years old and tottering. There would be a fantastic banter which was always consisting of one-upping insults. It was all in great fun. It was tradition. I loved the mushroom barley soup. I would have the fake-steak. In orthodox Jewish dietary rules, dairy products are never served with any kind of flesh foods hence the name. It was definitely not health food.

Dad was really cool, but I never knew that then. ☹

Later on when I was much older and we had lunch together in NY I asked him what he liked doing. "I ride my bike to work. (He was about 69 and a lot heavier, his hair had turned all white) and I like some TV."

"Well what do you like on TV?" The only thing I remember was "Charlie's Angels."

Now speaking about the bicycle, this was something of which he was really proud. It was not something you would associate him with, it was like thinking of him as being a master, an Olympic athlete. He got himself one of those heavy bikes with fat tires and learned to ride it. He was proud, justifiably so, of having accomplished this. He just loved going everywhere on that bike. What a strange thing that was. I could not visualize Dad riding a bike.

He loved reading the Jewish newspaper. The Morning Journal was his rag, and not the more leftist Forward, which in its heyday was really rather Socialist. Even though he was a Roosevelt Democrat, he could never go for the far-left side. On Sundays, he would get the special edition with the "roto" (rotogravure) section. That was the all sepia-tone photo section. He loved reading all of it. It was not until several years later, at my insistence that he also purchased the Sunday newspapers like the *Trib (Herald Tribune)* and the *Journal American & Sun*—none of those papers exist today. Otherwise, on a daily basis he'd get either the awful *New York Daily News* or the wretched *Mirror*. Both were tabloid rags. I read them anyway and it was not until years later that I'd get the Times and on Sundays, we'd get the *Journal American* for those fantastic cartoons.

Speaking of the special Sundays; I really believe that we invented the great NYC tradition of getting a pile of papers on Sundays and a bag of real bagels (none of those Fake bagels (I name them *fagels*- cranberry, sun-dried tomatoes, blueberry-feh), lox and real cream cheese. Dad and I would go to Wolfson Brothers deli and Harry would slice up the lox extra thin for Dad. They joked a lot and often gave Dad an extra slice or two. Considering how expensive that stuff was this was a most generous gift. Everyone loved Dad.

One of his little habits, which I never saw anyone else do, was as a memory aid he would tie a little knot in his handkerchief. "This is to remind me to get some butter." Or whatever. I never understood how that little knot would help him remember anything. I do not know anyone who did that sort of thing. Anyway, men no longer carry a handkerchief.

Dad took his privilege to vote seriously. He was a staunch and proud Roosevelt Democrat. His political viewpoint had a strong influence on mine. There were other things Dad taught me. He showed me the left from right shoes; he gave me my first bike lesson on a two-wheeler. That took but five minutes in a local park. It was great. It gave me confidence.

I shall end with my oldest memory and one of the fondest. When we lived in that little hovel in Brighton I clearly remember knowing when he was coming home because I would hear the jingle of his keys as he opened the door. With the greatest anticipation I awaited his entry, often he would have some little gift for my younger (3 1/2 years younger) brother Milt and me. It may have not been much just a cheap tin thing but it was always dear to me. That sound of his keys was the sweetest sound in the world.

I wish I had asked more questions about philosophy, about his early life in Hungary and the US. Wish I had listened more.

Dad passed on July 4th 1982, which was also a special Hindu holiday (Guru Poornima) for which we always do a giant celebration. In his own way, Dad was a righteous man.

11. Dad visits CT Ashram, summer 1980, meets Gurudev. Last photo I have of dad.

The Early Days

We lived what was known as a very traditional orthodox Jewish life and since Dad was the rabbi, I was obligated to attend all services in temple. I must state here that one should not confuse the traditional Orthodox Jewish way with that of the Hasidic sects. That is something quite different. People make a common mistake of conflating the two; when the word "Orthodox" is mentioned. Hasidic sects began around 1760 on the border of Poland & Ukraine. Hasidism is very fundamentalist with their own mode of dress, language (Yiddish) and education. Standard Orthodoxy goes back many 1000's of years. That means, to observe every Shabat (Sabbath), every holiday and to observe every rule and regulation; of which there are 100's. It was a confined, restrictive and, as I would later discover, a most constrictive life. I knew nothing outside this small circle of people all of whom came with similar baggage. What that meant was that one stayed within the scope of a very limited system of belief. What was given by my father to me from his father to him and so on for generations. As was told to me we must believe in this because my father gave it to me and so on so that you must believe only in this and not that. This was very limiting in my developing years.

I accepted and believed in all that was taught to me. In fact, I could not conceive how anyone could not believe in the whole system and totally accept the Old Testament construct of God. That mold of thinking stayed with me for many years after I had left home and the "Jewish way of living." I have observed that is an inherent part of human nature, the deep need to have something in which to believe, something to identify with. On a larger scale that gives one a sense of community, security, and a sense of belonging in a fit place of society. This discussion has been visited in many other books.

A Few Bits of Family History – Plus

The Iceman Cometh

The earliest memory of our living condition was at about age 4. We lived in a dank, forbidden, and broken down apartment that had no bathroom or shower in it. The bathroom etc. was down the hall shared by all apartment dwellers. Mom gave us a bath in a little tub in the kitchen. That was it. Terrible poverty. But, I was very young and did not know better. We had what was known as an "icebox," which was the old way of storing food. It had a section at the top where a big block of ice was put every three or five days. Of course, it had no electricity. Every now and then the iceman came to deliver the ice carried upon his shoulder atop a burlap bag. The ice was cut into the exact shape and size that was needed. He did this all without actually measuring. Brilliant! Now one day my little brother unknowingly turned on all the gas knobs on the stove. Those things had to be lit with a big wooden kitchen match. There was no pilot light. I did not know he had done that. Right then the Iceman came knocking. We were alone, of course. I got up on one of the chairs and turned the lock to let him in knowing that it was okay. The iceman sensing the situation immediately told us to get out and he turned all the knobs off.

I did not realize it at the time but on further reflection I saw that as the first instance of being protected by Divine Grace or one can say by Gurudev and that was before he became a swami.

The Radio

This occurred in the apartment mentioned above. Now there are the Boomers, Gen X, Millennials, Gen Z, etc. but no one mentions my generation, those born just before World War II. I propose we are to be called GEN R. For Radio—that is what we had. That was our main source of information, entertainment, news, etc. We all had a Bakelite encased, big tube saturated box that sat on top of the icebox. I listened to, among other shows, not just The Lone Ranger or Capt. Midnight, but also the wonderfully scary Inner Sanctum, Suspense, The Green Hornet, Gangbusters, FBI in War & Peace, and many more. Dad listened to his special programs all in Yiddish all about some tragic stories, and in the morning we all listened to———The Breakfast Club with Don McNeil. It was a blast especially Aunt Fannie. One day someone broke in to the apartment and stole that radio. It was the only thing he took. That was a sad day.

Story of Olga & Saul – An Important Piece of History

Some stories of family history are worth preserving, this is one such story. This is an abbreviated version of one such story.

Olga was born October 22, 1922 Balkein (Balkany) Hungary close to the town where Dad and his family lived. In that same house one of my father's brothers, Zelig and his wife and four children, rented a room. Another of the older brothers, Saul, would come to visit. Olga was about 14 at that time and Saul was 21. Because her father's business had failed she got a job as a beautician. This was her major skill, one that would keep her and the family going. She was also a top-level seamstress. Eventually she and Saul would go out on a "date." Something like going to the movies. It must be understood, however, that within the very Orthodox family this was forbidden. Young girls did not go out with a man unless chaperoned by a crew of elder family members. That's how it was. In 1944 when the Nazis came to Hungary, all of that ended. Saul was shipped off to work in a copper mine in Yugoslavia and other forced-labor camps. Zelig and his entire family were murdered on the spot. Olga and her little sister Annie were sent off to Auschwitz. Olga did seamstress work there, which saved her life. She also protected her little sister. The rest of her family, mother, father and eight other siblings were taken to the camps and perished.

By 1945 the allies came and liberated all the survivors in the camps. Olga and Annie, who at that time contracted tuberculosis, were sent to Sweden by the Red Cross. How a little girl could survive TB in those days and under those terrible conditions is a great miracle. Now, even though there was no such thing as Internet, no social media or anything at all like that, there was a network that communicated together. So by and by (after four years) some Rabbi sent Olga the money for a ticket to America. Annie had been cured and moved to Israel. Olga went to America, found a room on the lower East side for $10 a month, found a job as a seamstress in a high-fashion wedding dress shop. Unbeknown to her, Saul actually survived and found his way to America. He, his brothers (except my father), sisters and parents all lived in a big house in Brooklyn. Olga knew the family and was in touch with a couple of the sisters. One day she decided to visit in Brooklyn still not knowing anything about Saul. She was in the living room with my grandparents and some of the aunts and uncles when all of a sudden in walked Saul from his dirty factory job all disheveled and messy. As soon as Olga saw him, she jumps him, like "white on rice" with a giant hug. This, of course, sent great shock-waves into the family because that was simply not done. They were conservative, traditionalists. But, the two did not care they were just devoted. They had a brief dating period. After that Saul informs Olga, "Listen, I saved up $200 we can either have a big fancy wedding, or I can get you a ring. Which do you want? She replies, (this is the actual statement she gave me during an interview.) "Well, a wedding is over in just two hours a ring I can have forever."

They had a simple wedding with family and a few close friends. That was it.

To me that is a most fantastic story worthy of a film script. Olga and Saul had two sons and moved to Israel where they both passed on. One of the two sons, whom I never knew, had a daughter, Alyssa. He passed on when his daughter was very young. She was the one who asked the question that set this book going. That is another reason why I include this story.

Maternal Grandfather & Great-Grandfather

It is worth noting that in my family on my Mom's side her Dad was a cantor and a scribe. Mom's family was Levites. Grandpa was a scribe; which means he was the one to write and repair the parchment scroll of The Torah. Which was the most holy item. This was done by hand with a goose quill, and ink made by hand done on parchment made from the skin of a clean calf. Each letter had to be an exact size and shape. I saw my zayde (grandpa) do this. I was later informed that his father was skilled in this as well.

EXTRAS. Those oddly remembered bits I did as a kid that stand out in memory.

1. Going to Bubba's house (grandma) she lived in one of those old walk-up's in the New Lots section of Brooklyn. The apartment building was the sort with little tiles on the landings and metal rails stairway. No such thing as an elevator. I loved her apartment they had one of those giant radios that sat on the floor with the Cathedral dome and 12,002 tubes inside. It was glorious. Plus, they had a giant dictionary that I always opened and read. What I also remember is that peculiar smell that pervaded her place something like musty fungus. I kind of got used to it. She made terrific apple strudel. However, in the 17 years of my life that she lived she never spoke a single to me word even though I could understand Yiddish quite well.

2. Back in my teens, I was just conforming to the fashion that was in style. Therefore, when kids all had "pegged" pants I had them too. Mom would sometimes buy me clothes. One time she got a sports jacket,

it was black & white, in ultra-thin stripes, it was blinding. I did not understand her taste. One time we went to Barney's and I got what is called a Chesterfield coat. It was gorgeous, gray topcoat with a velvet collar. Very posh. I loved it. I had with me all the way to California and ultimately gave it to some street kid in Berkeley. You can't get any of those coats these days.

3. At about age 10 I saved up a bunch of money from odd jobs and bought my first bicycle. It was a three-speed with narrow wheels. I loved it. Rode it all around the area. Then one day my brother borrowed it to take to the library. He didn't lock it. It was stolen. That was very sad for me.

4. Smoking, Jerry Lustig showed me how to do that by the Long Island railroad tracks that was a short walk from home. I was hooked, buying cigarettes at 13, $.25 a pack. Bought Pell-Mell they were super long unfiltered, the best deal. Eventually went to pipes because they were cool and sophisticated. Learned all about various tobaccos and shopped at a special store in Manhattan on Fifth Avenue. Similar connoisseur thing as is coffee today. My mother really liked the idea. She even got me a pipe rack. Imagine that. How could mom possibly know about such a thing? That was amazing.

5. Chocolates. Barton's was a specialty chocolate shop that had a dark chocolate sort of truffle, delicious. Even then, I knew. I never did like Hershey's milk chocolate they were wretched.

6. A few summers we went to Rockaway Beach, rented a very funky little two-room apartment. (toilet was in hallway).One of my favorite things was listening to the radio to shows that were "scary". They were Inner Sanctum and Suspense. I'd sit under the kitchen table and listen to those shows. My brother refused to join me. There is actually an archived site somewhere on the web with all the shows. If you listen now they are really very poorly scripted with inane dialogue.

7. Loved doing acting in elementary school. One time we were putting on some religious play and one of the lead kids was gone, maybe he was sick. They were looking for a replacement. I had memorized the whole thing so I volunteered. Mom made me a beard out of a roll of cotton and I got on. It is beginning of my stage career. I just really liked it in summer camp I would do some kind of improv performance most of it was foolish nonsense.

8. When pizza first came to our neighborhood, it was something completely new. We had never heard of that. It was then 15¢ a slice. Who would've thunk?

9. Coney Island, Brighton Beach: I remember quite well many things. There was the Knish Man, always some poor fat man, no shirt, schlepping two very heavy doubled paper grocery bags in the sand. Broiling hot, selling hot knishes at 25¢. From that, he made a living? We loved the water, the waves and even the sand. Afterwards we would sometimes go to the "snowcone" place and get some shaved ice with some disgustingly sweet syrup poured over it ,we paid 10¢. It was worth maybe a quarter of a penny. As little kids, we would collect Pepsi and Coke bottles (there were never any cans then, only glass bottles). We get the deposit of two cents apiece. Soon we had enough for a couple of ice creams and even more. It was a good deal.

10. The first place I remember living was near Brighton beach in a very decrepit broken down two-room apartment. It was a very wretched neighborhood but what I really liked and remember most was the horse stables that were directly across the street. We had to walk down a number of steps to get to it. It's where I learned to climb steps at age 3. The horses were for the horse-drawn merchant carts. They came around frequently there was, the fruit seller, the rag picker, the flower seller, and the knife sharpener/umbrella repair man. They were all men and they had their own peculiar shouts. It was a different era. We lived in walking distance of the beach and boardwalk. Every weekend they had a tremendous fireworks display that we could see from the boardwalk. I totally loved that. One day, it was probably 1945 I remember a giant parade of military vehicles and soldiers. It is probably VJ day, or something like that, I didn't know what it was at the time. Also very close by on the same block was a public school. I didn't really know what it was I like playing in the yard and going in and out of the building which I would explore. One day I was walking up and down the steps inside and I was locked in I couldn't find a way out I guess I went down to the first floor and found the exit. It was quite scary.

11. One of my very first jobs was on the beach, way out at the subway (in that section "The El") last stop, selling—Good Humor ice-cream. I came to the job all excited. They forced me to put on a pair of pants that was 11 sizes too big and a white shirt, gave me a belt for the trousers. It didn't work. They gave me a big freezer box with shoulder strap filled with ice and ice-creams of all sorts. There I was schlepping along

and "screaming" "Good Humor ice-cream." It was enormously heavy I could barely walk 10 feet and lose my breath even though I was in pretty good shape then. Of course, my trousers kept slipping down so I spent half the time yanking them up to no avail. I gave up after two hours returned the box and the giant trousers , meant for big fat man. But, I was just a kid then no more than 16. I think I made $4 that day.

12. When I was a young lad, I would go to Coney Island for fun. I loved the beach and the ocean. Coney Island had all sorts of fabulous things, for example, the Penny arcade in which most things cost a few pennies, where I played "skee ball." I just loved that. There were many games like that. I found Penny cards of popular Cowboys etc. that I collected. However, what I loved most of all was the bumper cars something I could drive and smash into another car without hurting anyone it was glorious. The one thing, which I did that I did not understand, was riding the Cyclone this was our super roller-coaster. The first time I got on it was exciting but when I got off I threw up I was so nauseous. I tried it again came out super dizzy with my stomach in my brain. Yet with all that, I kept doing it. I do not understand why I kept riding that abomination. Do not understand it why do people think things like that. Well, I did many weird things.

13. As a young lad, I was given a camera. It was a very simple, primitive Kodak Box Brownie. I purchased rolls of film that produced black and white prints about 2 x 4". I would experiment and do "artistic" shots. I was just learning and composition just came to me. Eventually in college I got more interested in this. Purchasing old annual photography volumes from The Strand Bookstore in Manhattan. These were beautiful productions. I asked a fellow about getting a 35mm camera and he suggested some kind of reflex 35mm. Later I met fellow, I didn't know, who turned out to be a cousin. He worked at a camera shop in downtown New York. I bought my first 35mm reflex camera from him. However, he cheated me and gave me a defective used one. I couldn't believe it. I later learned that's the kind of man he was. Eventually I got a proper SLR Yashica–j. I would take many photos and send them out to be printed. I loved doing this. When I worked at Columbia I learned how to do my own developing and printing. There was a German gentleman, who did microscopic photos, he showed me his equipment. It was all top-level Omega enlarger with the best lens. He showed me the whole procedure and all his equipment. I copied everything exactly. Learned all the basics from him in about 10 minutes. I bought all the equipment and did the work in my apartment bathroom in Chelsea. I really loved doing this. Composition just came to me. Eventually when

I had to move to California I sold what I could and gave the rest away a lot of valuable stuff.

14. Frequently when very young, I would go to dad's synagogue, on a volunteer basis, to do various jobs. Mostly office work, doing mailings, using an ancient machine called "Addressograph". I would clean the benches. All that was meticulous detail work, which I loved so much.

To Continue

My day-to-day life was far from **placid**, far from healthy. I had to overcome many illnesses during my formative years. There were also all sorts of battles within the family, between Mom and Dad and with Mom and Dad's family. You may note that Mom was the instigator here for reasons that I would later learn were so trivial that it boggles the mind.

Mom had no respect for Dad, and for some bizarre reason was estranged from all of his family causing a terrible rift. As a result, I never had the pleasure to know those relatives. It was a sad, sad thing. She had much influence on the lives of my brother and me. I know that her extreme anxiety and negativity had a deep impact on my psyche. There was much abuse on many levels that left deep scars in my life.

I must point out, however, that when I joined with Sri Gurudev and severed my affiliation with Jewish tradition that was very painful to my parents. This is something they never saw or expected in any part of their life. When they came to visit me several times with a deep hope of bringing back. It was very painful to experience. I can just imagine the hope that they had when traveling that long distance from New York to California that they could get me back I cannot imagine how much pain they had. It was painful to me as well

A Bit More About Mom

Mom was born Freda Schreiber in Kolagvar, a city in Hungary around 1907. She never actually told us the date but I just figure that out. The city she was born in is now part of Romania [Kluge]. A common occurrence in Eastern Europe was for cities to change borders and countries. I don't know when she came to this country but it was as a teenager or young woman and she took care of our older cousin Gene, who was the son of mom's oldest sister Gizzi. She had a large family we do not know exactly how many sisters she had but she had just one brother Willy. She never told us anything about her life in Hungary but as my guess from observation of her mother that it was not very loving or kind. I would surmise it was from that background that created so much negativity and anger in her. I can tell you that her mom, my grandma, in all the years I knew her never spoke one word to me, even though then I was quite fluent in Yiddish. Strange.

Nevertheless, it was not all dark; she was self-reliant, resourceful and loved to joke around. She could make her own dresses. It is quite remarkable to watch her fashion a dress or two from a pattern.

While she was not a gourmet cook she could still go at it and never ever used a cookbook. She could whip up a batch of blintzes in minutes. That is quite a complex food. After a while I started cooking and would cook for her. It was something I loved to do.

She made friends easily. One could say that it was her hobby to meet people in the most unusual places. I recall quite well when she took me to San Francisco Macy's store and we went to the cafeteria for lunch. All the ladies working behind the counter knew her by name and they all loved her. That was remarkable. Speaking of Macy's another hobby she had was shopping. She didn't actually acquire a lot of stuff she would just buy them and then a few days return them for credit or refund. I could never understand the basis of that but she surely enjoyed it.

I am very sorry that I had never inquired about her early life in Hungary, how she came to America,, what she did, and so on. Somehow, at the time, I never thought of that. I regret that.

She was quite attached to my success and me; and was quite overwrought when I ditched the whole thing for a vagabond life. However, she was quite brave and nothing could get in her way once she made up her mind about something. A trait, which I guess, I acquired. This was the early conditioning that set the pattern in life. It is vital to undo that conditioning for spiritual life. I've written a short piece on this subject entitled, "Unwinding the Conditioning—Undoing the Default Setting," in the chapter of spiritual essays.

She was killed in an auto accident while crossing the street from her home in Oakland, California January 22, 1993. Her ashes are at our memorial grove in Yogaville.

She did meet Sri Gurudev several times and lived for a while at our NY center after Dad died. She, of course, did a lot of cooking there. She also came to visit the SF IYI. Everyone loved her. She was good at spotting people's inner stuff.

I must always remember that they all came to America from seriously difficult conditions, with no skills, no English and not much money. I did not know the circumstances or conditions of her upbringing or how her parents treated her. This is true for all the family I knew. They all came from small towns in NE Hungary, so growing up I was totally surrounded by Hungarians—in fact everyone spoke at least 4 languages, which is how I got quite used to hearing foreign accents and learning languages.

Dad came at the age of 20, in 1929, only to run smack into the depression. One cannot imagine what that must have been like. Mom came a few years earlier also with no English. Somehow, by dint of hard work they all made it. Dad was the only one of his family to rise above a laborer to become a learned rabbi. All his brothers were kind, honest men, who worked their entire lives in some sort of factory. My uncle Joe, had his own butcher business.

The Path to Becoming a Swami – "Beginnings"

One of the leading factors, from an inner psychological perspective, was a sense of alienation, of not belonging to the social order. I think this is a common factor among those who leave the tradition to which they were born. That tradition is not by our choice. It is imposed on us by parents and teachers. I recall back when I was first questioning the whole business of why I should be following all the rules, practices and rituals of that tradition, I asked Dad this question. His response was, "Because that is how it has been done forever, by my father and his father before him," It occurred to me even then that his reply was not a good reason for following all that stuff. Tradition, however, does serve an excellent purpose in that it provides a bond that keeps a culture and society together. Therefore, it serves as an excellent role in giving one a sense of belonging, giving one's culture cohesiveness and proving a well-defined set of guidelines in knowing how to act. In that manner, religions do serve a vital role in society.

I will begin with some of my earliest memories as it relates to education and religious practices, upbringing and experiences. Dad was my first teacher. At the time, of course, I did not know what wisdom he had, what difficulties he had in life to come to America and so on. In other words, I had no proper way of appreciating Dad. He taught me to read and write Hebrew when I was but four years old. Dad also gave me all of my Bar Mitzvah lessons. He did this for many boys and devised a most clever notational system to get the right melody. Naturally, since I grew up in a strict orthodox home (Not Hasidic). I was put into a strict yeshiva at age 4. This was an all-boys school. Later on when we moved I went to a yeshiva with both boys and girls. We later moved to East 28th St between I & J in the Midwood section of Brooklyn where I spent my most formative years. Dad was rabbi at the shul (temple) on Ave. K, Ahavat Yisrael, which is now some super Hassidic temple.

My Earliest Spiritual Experiences

I remember this as if it happened yesterday.

When I was 2–5 we lived in a horrible slum; on West 2nd Street in the Brighton Beach area of Brooklyn. I can say much about this situation. However, what relates to this story is this. We lived next door to an African-American church. One day, on a Sunday, I happened to be in the alley next to the church and I heard their singing. I had no idea what they were saying; I only knew that the sound sent an electric current up my spine. So every Sunday, sitting on bent knees with forehead on ground, I'd hide in the alley just to hear the music and the voices to have that experience. I loved it.

Another occasion was when I was reciting some prayers in temple and in my little mind (I was about 5) I really believed that if I said the prayers right God would hear them. I would put all my effort into really meaning what I said so that "God" would listen just to me. It is quite interesting and a bit surprising that there are so many all over the world who hold to this notion. What is more surprising is that whenever there are two sides in a conflict be it an actual war or even a football game, both sides will have members invoking their deity to bless the outcome for them—invariably one side will lose, does this then mean that God took sides? Perhaps it means that one side did not pray hard enough. Alternatively, it may just mean that there is no one to take sides.

A Few Early Ideas

In my early years, I imagined that I was a puppet and God was the master puppeteer. One of my persistent thoughts was the question of an infinite universe, how can that be so? What is beyond that? I had no idea of a universe without boundaries, which is how one can say we live in a finite universe but it is unbounded and can thus keep on expanding.

In all this time I would say I was not what one would call a "regular average" kid. Whatever that may mean. Instead, I was quite rambunctious and in constant trouble.

I found that quite early on I was questioning authority. I recall that way back then I devised my own form of the classical philosophical question of God's omniscience and foreknowledge vs. man's freewill. The question I proposed at about age 6 was how could God blame Adam and Eve for any misdeed if God knew what was going to happen? Further how could He not know if he was the All-Knowing God? He was God and by definition must know all that comes, ergo (I did not use that word) what He knows must happen and it follows that A & E had no option and therefore could not be blamed. No one, not even Dad, could answer this. Dad thought I was clever to come up with this question. It was the beginning of my skepticism.

Furthermore, how can it be that "This" or "my" religion is right and all others are wrong? How is it that "god" listens only to us, how is it that only we have the "Right Way"? Moreover, no one else does. It is important to point out here that the experiences, opinions and such came out of my own personal life experience. This does not mean that other people's thoughts, opinions are invalid with regard to their religion. There are, no doubt, many aspects of religions that are relevant to those who believe in them. It is, for a large part of society, the binding force that connects people. It keeps them connected on many levels. This is important to remember. This was My Journey.

It may be difficult to believe in this age of instant communication but in those days, there were many things that, amongst the Orthodox, were not just looked down upon but actually not allowed. For example, we were not allowed to say the name Jesus, we were not allowed to draw a cross, not even in making a sort of crooked letter "T". Certain books were not allowed, of course; the New Testament was forbidden. Naturally, even to think of entering a church or having a statue of some deity was pure heresy. To this day, Hassidic Jews and most Orthodox carry on in this practice.

Moreover, what sort of "god" would ask a man to sacrifice his own little son? What kind of thing is that? How can you have a god who gets angry, is jealous, and condones genocide, and so on? This sort of thinking led to my open skepticism. All this can be resolved if you understand the Bible not in the literal sense but as metaphor. On a most elementary level, the Bible contains stories that were told to the masses. However, on a more profound level these stories contain deep mystical symbolism. Within these stories are the most profound mystical teachings. This is a very important point in that one cannot really take the Old Testament stories on the literal level. One can do that but that is quite limited. In Kabbalistic tradition all the stories and teachings of the Torah have a deeper mystical level. It is said that all of this was given by God to Moses but was hidden and lost. Kabbalah teaches that one can find the hidden meanings by deep study and commitment. It is all there. One only has to dive deep into it. This is not known to me at all in my formative years. It is important to note that any further commentary on Torah comes from that early understanding and a criticism of literal interpretation stands.

All along, however, I kept by the faith and all the practices therein. I did not question it actually, and it was mainly because all of us had very tightly insulated lives. All my friends, everyone I knew, came from that enclosed circle. I can therefore see how powerful is the influence of children's parents and teachers. They set the basic tone and development of the child. It is, therefore, a great responsibility to be a parent.

Even then, many doubts and feelings came - briefly, these came because of the many hypocrisies I saw all around me. There was the extreme competitive materialism I saw ("Look at my suit, my car, my house blah, blah, blah) I found it repellent. There were many other things (petty gossiping, open bigotry etc.) perhaps these were just in my social circle but they were enough to put me off. Much of this did not get strong until I got to high school (I was kicked out of yeshiva, but you would have guessed that) where I met people of many backgrounds and religions. I really came to dislike the whole fundamentalist, narrow-minded culture that was imposed on me. That way of life was not my choice. I realized later that this sort of rather parochial, self –important and even bigoted way of thinking is not limited to one culture but can be found worldwide.

I vividly remember one incident that set me off which served as one of those catalysts in life. This happened one year in summer camp, I must have been around nine at the time. Part of the daily schedule was an hour of Torah study. To me that was not something I was in camp for. So instead of attending that BORING class I seated myself near the bunkhouse with one of my fave comic books, (either Batman or Tales From the Crypt) and while sitting there engrossed in that world the teacher saw me and hurled a large piece of wood at my head, making solid contact. That may have started the ball rolling towards giving up the tradition.

I recall one other incident early in life. When I was about ten Mom got very sick and needed surgery. I was sent off to stay with my cousin Libey. During that short stay we went to what is known as a "farbrengen" (gathering) at the Lubabavitcher (a famous Rabbi of the time) rebbe's center. The holy rebbe (I am sure he was a holy man) was there speaking but I could not hear him as I was just a tiny kid and there were 1000's of his followers frantically shoving and pushing. I thought this was rude and mean. From all of the above you can see the direction I was headed. Intense experiences in early childhood can have deep and long-lasting effects.

There was always something missing, or I was missing something in me.

Remembering My Best Bud

Before ending this segment I would be remiss if I did not pay tribute to one of my best friends from high school to past university days—Louis Pelish. The first two years of high school I was sent to a yeshiva that was actually the first school I attended during my first two years of schooling. It was located a long distance from where I lived requiring two buses, about one hour travel time. It was there I met Louie, as we called him then. Louie was born with a disability that was modest when I first met him but became quite serious in later years. We buddied up right away; there was just that easy communication. We even had a little penny-ante card game club. We all had nicknames. Louie was "The Duke", Abraham Lieb was, "The Turk", I was Gomez. I was booted out of that school after two years whereupon I went to the local public high school that was within easy walking distance. We still communicated and remained buddies throughout.

When we were in college, we would go on vacations together. One time we went to New Hampshire and Lake Winnipesaukee. That was quite a lot of fun. Louie was quite brilliant and graduated in computer science. During that time he met this young woman who was on a student visa from Poland. He dated for the first time in his life. After a while, he decided to get married but first he called me to see if it was the right move for him. Of course, I said, yes go ahead. At that time, she was still living in Poland. Later when I had my job at Columbia University Medical Center, he was applying for a government job with the FCC. One day he called me at my apartment and asked if he could come to make a phone call to Elizabeth in Poland. I asked him, "Don't you have a phone?" "Yes, I do but I'm getting a high security government job and I'm afraid the FBI might be checking my phone calls." I said, "Of course, come over, make your call when you like." He did so. After a few years, they did get married and I met them together years later in my apartment on the Lower East Side.

Soon thereafter, I moved to California and lost all contact with my buddy. For many years, I was wondering whatever happened to Louie. Many years later after moving to Virginia and acquiring a computer with Internet I thought, well, perhaps I could look him up in one of the search engines. It was called "Lycos People Finder." Just on a whim I entered his name having absolutely no idea where he lived. By great chance there was only one Louie Pelish in the USA. There was his phone number. I called him up. I said, "This is (using prior name) are you my buddy from high school?" He said, in his usual laconic voice, "I guess so." The conversation we had was as if we just picked up from the last conversation so many decades ago. I had the opportunity to visit him a couple of times in Silver Spring, Maryland. He also came to visit me here. Eventually his disability had become extreme whereby he was obliged to use an electric wheelchair and had a special van equipped for his needs. One day I got a call from one of our mutual friends, Abe Leib. He told me that Louis had gotten pneumonia so they took him to the hospital where they wanted to do a CAT scan but when they put him on the table, he complained that he couldn't breathe. The doctors did not listen. Finally, when they saw he was in distress and he had gone unconscious they had to put him on oxygen but soon thereafter he had to be put on a ventilator. I contacted his wife by which time he was in a nursing home. Turtle, one of my closest friends and a Native American, took me to visit him there and I did not like the place. I knew what a good nursing home should be. That was not it. Louis had lost so much weight, I did not recognize him at all. I had to go out twice to look at the name on the wall to be sure I was in the right room. He was still on the ventilator. A few months later, I got the call that Louie had passed on. On the day of the funeral Turtle and I attempted to drive up to Maryland but there was a powerful snowstorm and we could not make it. Anyway, I had no idea where I would stay. I was sad not to go but I wrote a tribute about our memories as friends. I sent a copy to his wife and two children. One of the children wrote back to me saying he never knew any of those things about his Dad and he was so happy to get that story. Later I spoke to Abie who told me how he had to pack quickly, find the flight to Maryland, and get there overnight. He also said he wished that I were there to deliver the eulogy. He thought I would have done a better job. Abe also told me that he and Elizabeth were cousins. I never knew that.

The Next Step, the Ball Rolls

You Make a Choice & Chain Continues to Unfold

My serious education began in college. Long before college, I had my mind on something in the medical field so I concentrated studies in the sciences where I did rather well. I also enjoyed philosophy quite a lot. Having had some Latin also helped in my biology studies. In philosophy, I had a special affinity for Bertrand Russell; he had a keen mind as a mathematician. On the other hand, he was a strong iconoclast that pleased my way of thinking. It was at this time that I put my mind towards an atheistic bent. This did not happen all of a sudden. Knowing earlier experience given above, the next natural step was to question the validity and purpose of all those stringent rules we had. Many of them made no sense to me. I decided to test a few, one at a time. I took off my hat (wearing a hat is one of the rules for men in Jewish tradition), and amazingly, nothing happened. I also ate on Yom Kippur and was not struck by a bolt of lightning. I tested other constraints and nothing bad happened. I remember well what so many rabbis used to sermonize about—the number one fear, what they constantly would rail against was intermarriage. Good grief, it was like killing your brother. There was such a rigid, hardline, narrow-minded thinking against such things. This coupled with my understanding about science directed my early philosophy in life. That would be modified as I was introduced to spiritual studies and practice.

While on one side was cultivated a skeptical outlook, there was also the intuitive sense that there was more to life than just the pure rational, logical one. I opined that there must be a greater mystery of life, which is not described by science. I further concluded that there must be an infinite "Other" which is beyond simple words. I remember clearly Dad showing me a photo of some uncle of ours, whom I never met and he told me that man was one who knew "metaphysics." I did not know what that meant but was fascinated by the whole idea. I also recall purchasing the famous work by Rambam (Hellenized name Maimonides)—Guide for the Perplexed—after reading which I was even more perplexed—I did not understand a word. (It is a rather difficult book—I later discovered he had done so on purpose.).

In the eighth grade, there is one man who was an early influence on my future life. He was our science teacher, Mr. Joseph Post, who encouraged me to understand and study biology. It is interesting to note what influences early teachers may have on the development and future of young minds.

Eventually it came to me that the substratum of all religions and the need for some all-powerful, all-knowing God who administers due punishment for breaking his rules (here God was always represented as male—which I think is rather strange. The psychology of this was based on two points; first being the human fear of death and not being able to understand that. The essential point to this is the paradox wherein one cannot conceive of what we define as "the self" as not existing. This "self" is the accumulated aspects of our personality. It is our likes and dislikes, what shapes us from the beginning of our consciousness, how we react and interact with all those whom we know. The central point of this paradox is that it is the mind which makes concepts and conceives of things in the mind cannot conceive of itself is not being because it is the mind that is making that concept as well. It is a so-called Catch 22. Since we cannot conceive of ourselves as actually not being or ceasing to exist, humankind therefore has the need for an eternal being.

Second, there is the need to explain the nature of the universe and how it all came to be. There was also a third, not quite as essential, underlying principle, that of having some great judge to maintain the social order; in other words, to keep the masses under control. What better way to ensure such control than by reverting to an absolute authority, which will be swift and harsh in judgment for anyone who should disobey or ignore the "Rules."

Therefore, the imposition of guilt is a most effective method of enforcement. One finds this not only within Jewish tradition but is quite prevalent amongst other religions [not so within the Buddhist tradition, however]. These thoughts formed the basis for me to reject formal religions.

College Years

I had decided early on, as was referenced by my experience in the eighth grade, that I'd pursue a career in the medical field. In high school I took special classes in medical lab technique. In college, I continued this by taking every biology class there was. I was finally in my element. I will never forget what two professors said. The first was my prof in embryology, Dr. Brown—"Isn't that fantastic." YES, it indeed was. In genetics, I devised a proposal for an experiment that I never got done but which was done many decades later—that is to say—in the development of a vertebrate embryo in addition to the nuclear DNA it is known that the yolk also has influence on embryonic development. What would happen if you denunciated a fertile egg and replaced it with the nucleus of a different species (but same genus) on the development. You must know that this was in 1959 and they had just determined the basic structure of DNA.

[Side note: Some years later, I attended a lecture by Stanley Ochoa where he described the first bit of deciphered code of DNA, that is to say, what amino acid a specific triad of nucleotides coded.]

There was also Dr. Ralph Holt Cheney in my physiology class who said, "Report on what you actually observe, NOT on what you expect to see." Thinking more deeply about this apparently simple statement reveals a profound meaning. On one level, it is the direct statement from a teacher to student instructing us to approach our observation with a neutral mind. That means that we should not just try to please the teacher or just "observe" what has been reported previously or what the teacher has told us is the normal condition. This is just to please the teacher not to really learn how to properly observe. Indeed, this tendency to report on what is expected is often carried out in the world of experimental science. The more profound level is to approach all things with the neutral mind in order to understand and observe what is and not what people have been told. This is frequently observed in the spiritual or "religious realm" wherein we adopt the accepted dogma, mode of thinking, community standard teachings of the "faith," or even teaching of the guru, without question. In this manner, we abdicate our own experience or understanding of what is so, what is our truth. I salute Dr. Cheney for this great teaching.

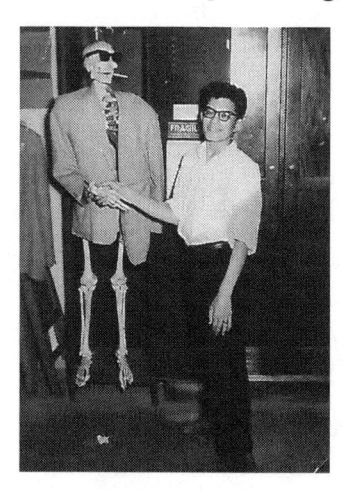

12. Anatomy class goofing (even back then), 1961.

During that time, I was not politically involved, except that I voted as a Democrat as Dad did. While in college, in my history class, one day I was approached by a young man who said I might be interested in the group of which he was a member. He invited me to a meeting. This was during the time right after the McCarthy era. This group was dedicated to opposing the Congressional hearings on exposing the "left wing political groups". That Congressional committee was called House of Un-American Activities Committee (HUAC). The group I was invited to was known as YPSL (pronounced "yipsil." Young People's Socialist League, headed by Michael Harrington (*The Other American*). Their main purpose was action to prevent HUAC from harassing innocent people. Their methodology did not interest me. Therefore, I stopped coming to their meetings.

I became associated with other groups. Out in the section of Brooklyn known as Brooklyn Heights the well-established organization, The Ethical Culture Society had a school and within the organization, they had a college age auxiliary. I joined up with that and found it to be quite interesting. All the young people there were intelligent, talented and very liberal minded people. They had moved away from any standard religious affiliation. It was quite engaging, much of it above my head.

There was also a small group close to home known as, The Liberal Religious League. It consisted mainly of folks who were disaffected with the organized church. There were mostly much older people there, but the conversations were always interesting. Finally, there was the Humanist Society founded many decades before by the brother of Aldous Huxley, Julian. The common direction within all these groups was that they were all exploring the essence of what the self is, or "Who Am I?"

The Essential Question

The essential question within me has always been, "Who am I really? Am I the accumulation of all these anxieties, fears, doubts, etc.? I could not be any of those things. I could not be all those anxieties, doubts, fears and so on that was implanted deep within me so early on that I did not remember how it was done. All such layers upon layers laid down mostly by my Mom, teachers, and friends. I would point out here the influence of teachers upon young children. It is never good to ever shame a child in front of his or her peers. This can have tremendous ill effects upon the child. I would ask, "What is my place in this world? Who am I?"

For all my efforts, all my so-called, "successes," there was always something missing. All those years I had the sense of not belonging anywhere or being left out of society. I felt that there had to be something else. There had to be a way to find peace and contentment. There had to be a way of knowing who I really was.

For it is not enough to simply leave aside one's past or upbringing. One has to go TO something meaningful and deep, to find something that resonates with one's inner soul.

One great influence then was Catcher in the Rye—I read it in 1958, shortly after it came out. It was amazing. It spoke to me of the disillusionment and angst of youth and of the pursuit of an idealized social structure. Many years after, I read it again and found it to be nothing more than the ramblings of a narcissistic, self-absorbed boy. However, then as a 16-year-old lad in college, it was great. During this period, I was also exposed to the early forms of new music. I heard the first electronic music at The Cooper Union. To be there was just a bunch of non-harmonious noise. I also heard the beat poetry in the 50's performed in those, obscure coffee shops of the West Village.

13. College graduate, 1962.

Moving on, "Success", and Important Choices

Upon graduating from college I straight away went to get the one job I wanted (BTW, all during college I had jobs, such as working in a men's slipper factory, microfilming x-rays at a union health center, diagnostic labs in Coney Island hospital, book stores, the college library etc.—I was always industrious). The job I applied for was at the Columbia College of Physicians and Surgeons attached to Columbia Presbyterian Hospital. It was as an entry-level medical microbiologist. It was the only job for which I applied. I got it in one day. The head of the department, my immediate boss, Dr. Paul D. Ellner, must have taken a shine to me; we both had the same prof. in cell physiology. I could also discuss the topics of mutual interest. I really loved the job. I worked with some dangerous pathogens without the proper protective measures that are in place these days. I never got sick.

Soon there was an opening to be in charge of the TB lab, which I took. There I developed methods to eliminate animal testing, to also be able to grow & identify the TB bacteria and distinguish it from similar organisms and do this much faster and efficiently. As a totally unexpected side benefit, this system was also able to grow a fungus [Nocardia asteroides] that causes a terrible lung disease (I recently learned that this so-called "fungus" is actually genetically closer to the TB bacillus.). I eventually wrote all this up and had it published in two specialized medical journals: The American Journal of Clinical Pathology and The American Review of Respiratory Disease. These were also presented twice at the Annual Meetings of the American Society of Microbiology. Subsequently I was then invited to speak at a local convention in N.J. I must have been quite confident, which can often be a good substitute for actual competence. That sometimes helps.

Advantages of Good Scientific Training

There is a certain mindset that comes along with extensive scientific training. It is been a great advantage to me in that it has given me what one may call a mind of discrimination, that is to say an ability to discern what I call flap-doodle from well-done empirical scientific experiments. Indeed, the complexity of so many things often exceeds the time most people have to listen to it all. There is most often a long chain of statements, linked in multivalent, multilevel ways that require one to keep the chain together. That is true for world politics and especially so for most scientific theorems.

Emotional attachment usually clouds the mind to such understanding. One must always distinguish between evidence-based data and mere opinion. Not everything is opinion. Observation and data must be collected and parsed out. It takes patience and time to explain this process. There is hard factual evidence. It is absurd and logically ridiculous to assert that everything said is just "opinion." That is ignorance and dismissive. One must always distinguish between hypothesis, opinion, and data. It is not always easy to explain this as it takes a lot of time to parse out a logical argument.

There's also an awful lot of what may be called junk science, as well as misleading and charlatan "gurus." I have found that this is quite a valuable skill in navigating that ocean of "gurus" that came to America. There were and continue to be many charlatans who take advantage of young people in desperate need of self-affirmation. I must admit, that sometimes in my innocence and desire to find someone to guide me I was sometimes misled.

In this context I was always interested to know what The Truth was, what was The Reality. How was I to find this out? If all that we see in front of us, that dance of life and personality, was not what was real, what then was real? This perplexed me greatly then and I could not understand how to really get that knowledge in the first place. Furthermore, how would I know it when it was presented to me? How would I know what was being told to me was Truth? When you see this as a truly profound question you can see the difficulties that I or, in fact, anyone would have. The understanding of this comes from a different level within one's cognition. It cannot be parsed out by scientific understanding but through the intuitive higher consciousness.

It was at Columbia that I posted my first original joke. I made a poster for my lab saying, "Under optimal conditions, and perfect laboratory environments, organisms behave as they damn well please." It got cheers from the established biologists; the students did not get it.

After a few years at this, for reasons that elude me now, I quit that job but got hired straight way at Mt. Sinai by Dr. Winter to work in Parasitology. He just took me on at the first meeting because he had seen me at the presentations I gave. However, that proved to be exceedingly boring, and most of the people there were as dull as a bent nail. I left that and got a very different job working at a branch of Plenum Publishers where I edited English translations of Russian scientific journals. I did have to learn Cyrillic but not Russian. At that time, I was also in my exploration of pharmaceuticals phase (see below) and could not focus well enough for such details. Thus, for the first and only time ever, I got sacked. I then got a variety of dull jobs as a messenger. I had done this before so I knew my way around the city. Oh, and I did a stint, a rather short one (ONE night—that was quite enough), unloading fruit from a ship at the docks. You had to show up at 8pm. It was brutally hard work. It went until six in the morning. The old timers showed me all the tricks for handling those 50 lb. lugs. The only question the boss asked you at the lineup was, "Do you read English?" I thought that was funny.

During my early days I had opportunities to meet many interesting people; among them was one slightly demented character by the name of Tom Pudney. He was a tall, heavy fellow and lived in a dingy one-room flat somewhere in the West Village. He was writing a book the title of which was something like "What is God?" The unique thing was that he was doing this on loose-leaf paper in three ring binders and in PENCIL. He introduced me to my first electronic music concert and took me around the coffee shops where poets and other like-minded people were. I must've seen many of the Beat Poets but did not know it at the time.

The Opening Begins... Ta-Da

Sound of Trumpets & Tympani

Synchronicity

It was a dark and stormy night..... Oops, someone else already used that. Try again—it was a dark and lonely night. I was in my nice apartment on 93rd St. near Riverside Drive. This was in 1964. At that time, I was paying $94 for a fine 2-room apartment. I had nothing to do that evening, well most evenings were like that, I did not even have a TV and my drinking days were over. I got a copy of the Village Voice to see what was going on that night, preferably what free events there were. Well quite by "accident" or by synchronicity there was a talk by a psychologist, Stanley Krippner on Dreams & Psychedelics. This was 1964 and the whole wave had not yet begun. I went and did not understand a word; it was excessively academic for me.

After the talk, there was this chap, Murray Levy, with hair like Bob Dylan but dressed in a suit and tie, with a giant smile, he was handing out leaflets announcing the "First Psychedelic Art Showcase." This sounded interesting and he seemed to be a genuinely nice fellow. So, we struck up a conversation and it turned out he lived a few blocks from me. I asked him what sort of art would qualify and he said whatever you have. Well at the time I had gotten serious about photography as a hobby, I had not yet gotten my own dark room but I loved taking snaps with my new 35mm camera. I was inspired by the works of the greats like Ernst Haas, Bret Weston and Cartier Bresson. I asked one of my doc friends whom I knew had a dark room if I could use his equipment for a night and he said sure, but he lived all the way over in NJ near the GW Bridge. I took the bus there, for the first time in my life developed, and printed a batch of B&W prints. They all came out perfectly. When I had to go home, I could not find the bus so I walked to the GW. I was literally and metaphorically "crossing the bridge."I was about to enter a completely new realm in life. This was IT.

After some preliminary meetings, we had our opening at some storefront in lower Manhattan. I had my photos mounted and hung them on some burlap supported by a back frame; you must keep in mind we were all a bunch of early hippies not professionals. There I met up with an extraordinary group of people. They were all artists, musicians and just all sweet, gentle people. We would gather in the basement to smoke "stuff." Now I had been smoking since back in '62 when I had my first trip to Mexico and that was just wonderful sitting on the beach at Acapulco—but this was on another level.

From there I got involved with a small group called the League for Spiritual Discovery (LSD) founded by Timothy Leary and Nina Graboi. There I also met Ram Dass who then still was known as Richard Alpert, and Professor Ralph Metzner—these were all associates from Harvard. In addition, many other wonderful spiritual people, too numerous to name, there was Alan Ginsberg & Peter Orlovsky and others. Most memorable of all was Nina Graboi. She was the personal secretary to Leary, she was a most elegant woman from Austria, a fine woman who came from the upper reaches of society, and she was giving up all that high-class life to be among the unwashed, to move beyond the gross material life. In the many Moments of stress, I was always able to go to her nice apartment on University Avenue and she would counsel me. She was an ocean of love. She later moved to California to open an arts shop, she has since passed on. I will always remember her. I recall a few years back, years after Leary passed on she was interviewed on radio and when I heard that voice I felt I knew it and it was not till after the interview (I came in the middle) they mentioned her name—wow.

Richard Alpert (Ram Dass) was a beautiful, gentle soul, so inspiring—always speaking from the heart. I recall him telling us about two saints. For the first one he said, "There is this guy in India who has been keeping silence for 30 years, and he is a very high being, a saint. His name is Meher Baba. He has books you can read." Well I got some of his books; they were indeed inspiring but hard to understand.

I recall the first time I took LSD. There was an artist fellow who had a gallery near Tomkins Square Park, his name was Swedbourg Swede. I don't know if he was actually Swedish. He lived in his gallery with his wife and little child. I don't know how I met him. I was in his gallery one evening and he, said, "Here try this?" He offered me this tiny tablet. I knew what it was and popped it into my mouth. A while later I had to return to my apartment that was all the way over on the west side at 93rd St. near Riverside Drive. I had to take two trains for about a 35 minute ride. I could feel the effects at some point and I wondered how I would be able to navigate my way home, recognize the train stop, walk to the apartment house etc. In my reverie a policeman came by and asked if everything was all right. I said, "I'm all fine thank you, you have a difficult job here don't you?" Clever ploy to divert his attention. I got home just fine and it was a confusing but amazing experience.

The central thesis through all this is to Let Go. That is to say to let go of the comfortable and deeply ingrained ego or identity, the self-created idea of yourself. I found this difficult to do. We are conflicted in that we identify with that false self so much and are so comfortable with it because that is what we have carried around from the beginning of our consciousness. In all the highest spiritual teachings it is given that this so-called self is not the true Self. The same can be said about the pain that we carry about. We know that must be let go of, because the more we put into it the more it becomes real for us. We can say to the guru who tells us to let go of that is not the Truth, "But look, I have nurtured this and carried it around with me for so long. I have put so much energy into it, if I let it go, there will be nothing. And that is very scary." Scary, indeed, that is what it is. And, that's That.

[Digression: When I was a wee lad papa had a succah (the small shed traditionally used for the celebration of the holiday Sukkoth) constructed in the back yard. On the walls of that succah Dad hung a great number of photos of holy Rebbes and Saints. He just loved those photos; so did I. I guess that too influenced me in my later searching].

Many of the people I met were quite a bit younger than I. Somehow, they thought that I knew all this spiritual stuff, which I did not. Anyway we would all get stoned together and meditate or listen to Indian music. One day a few of them came back from a trip to California and they had with them a large supply of LSD. Since they knew I was a scientist they asked me if I could take this and make a dilution to a specified amount. I said sure, no problem. I procured the proper tools and we all sat in my little apartment while I took this little stone into a flask and with a pipette carefully measured some distilled water, measuring, stirring while the music played, as my ability to see the markings on the pipette diminished. I gave them the final product and they "tipped" me with what was essentially a lifetime supply of pure acid.

I also met up with a brilliant chemist, Henry, who produced large volumes of DMT (dimethyl tryptamine), a powerful psychoactive chemical. It's mixed with something like parsley and meant to be smoked in a pipe. He also gave me what amounted to a lifetime supply. In the end I gave it all away.

Another fond memory was meeting up with a fellow named Eric (Not sure of his name). He was a young man working in the advertising business for McCann-Erickson ad agency. He wore a suit and tie. He had kind of a John Denver haircut. Extremely personable, always friendly, smiling and very kind. I remember clearly his beautiful spacious flat and he wanted to show us something saying, "You have to see this. I got a pre-publication copy." What he showed us was the first edition of the Beatles' "Sgt. Pepper" album. Just looking at the cover was amazing. It was the greatest album I had ever heard and the greatest music I had ever heard. He also introduced me to a fellow named Sandy Lehmann-Haupt. He was a genius electronics man who did the sound system for Ken Kesey and The Merry Pranksters bus. That included such luminaries as Neal Cassidy (hero in Jack Kerouac's— On the Road), Stewart Brand (Whole Earth Catalog). So many adventures, so many people—I could never remember all of them.

At that time, I was not vegetarian but there were two restaurants: The Forum & Paradox that were pure Macrobiotic. I'd never heard of that, nor had I ever used chopsticks. It was my good friend, Ruth, one of the artists, who showed me how to use chopsticks. It took me a long time to get the hang of it. In later years, macrobiotics was to become a major movement among the hundreds of different diets to which we were introduced. Whatever diet one was on that was "IT" for people on those specific diets, whether it was Bicher—Benner, Atkins, Paavo Aerola, Swiss, gluten-free, Bieler broth, total wheatgrass. Raw foods etc. Whatever it was and still is, people get to be fundamentalists about their "DIET." It is almost like a religion. I recall years later, when I associated with groups who were fundamentalist macrobiotic adherents, you would often hear conversations such as, "I ate an apple and a banana this morning and became 'Yinned out'." Everyone would nod and smiling knowingly to what he or she was talking about. It was as if they were in the group confessing that they had fallen off the wagon.

Mention should be made of my first trip to Mexico in 1962. It was a cleaner place then. No drug wars. As part of my journey I went to Acapulco. I was actually not much of an adventurer and took a plane from Mexico City to Acapulco. I was a pretty straight fellow then. While on the beach I met up with a man who told me he could get a nice supply of grass at a good price so I took him up on the offer and obtained about 3 ounces for maybe $2. We had a blast. That was a beginning.

Another Case of Being Protected

One time when I was invited to Max's Kansas City, a well-known club on the East Side near Union Sq. that was frequented by the Warhol crowd, I had, prior to arriving, consumed an inordinate quantity of substances and in a not judicious mixture. At one point, the vibrations of the place combined with my ultra-sensitive state found me having to abruptly bound out, which, in the drug-induced time distortion, appeared to take about 2 hours. When I got to the street it was raining and cold, although it was not a far walk to my apartment in Chelsea, I discovered that I had no clue how to get back and I could not trust myself to get a cab as there was no way I could give my address. So I went around the corner and lay down by a subway grating under an awning where I was protected from the rain. I had only shorts and a tee shirt and was quite cold. What madness prompted me to dress that way?Each time a train went by it was like a dentist drill going in my spine. I remember saying to myself—"Who am I? Who am I? Identify, identify, identify." It was scary. Now that was not the safest neighborhood, I had a wallet full of money but no one assaulted me. By morning I was exhausted but the effects of the drugs had worn off enough (about 17 hours) that I knew where I was and could make it home. On the way some Puerto Rican guy stopped me to ask for a cigarette (now this was really BIZARRE) what I did was hug him and say, "I have found something much better than a cigarette." Meaning that I got out of my stupor and was unharmed. I learned from that experience that I was and still am **Always Protected**.

Yet One More Case of Being Protected

Another time I was walking through Tomkins Sq. Park on Ave A. I had been there many times for concerts by the Fugs. That day there was no event. All of a sudden, I was surrounded by a gang of teens. One of them said, "Give us your wallet, we have a knife." Without a millisecond's hesitation, I pushed out my arms straight ahead and said quite forcefully, "Buzz off." (Or some such equivalent statement). I just went. I think they were so shocked they did not dare follow me. PROTECTED.

Many came to our little center (League) in Greenwich Village on the corner of Hudson & Perry. One day it was Liam Clancy (of the Irish singing group—The Clancy Brothers) having paid an extended visit to the old White Horse Tavern [famous old New York pub] who popped in "three sheets to the wind", as they say. I was the only one who recognized him. Then there was Alan Ginsberg and Swami Radha Sivananda, a female disciple of Swami Sivananda. She was from Germany and in her youth was a renowned classical dancer. Then one day a guy came in, totally bonkers telling everyone to read "The Book: On the Taboo Against Knowing Who You Are" by Alan Watts. He was so convincing I invested the full 50 cents to get it and it blew me away. Watts who was once an Episcopalian priest became a Buddhist and was quite brilliant. I would recommend this book to anyone who wants a lucid and quite readable but exposition on spiritual matters from an Eastern perspective. It was a mind turner for me.

Some Vital Points

In those blossoming days we used LSD as a tool for exploring the deeper realms of the mind. There was still something eluding me. That was the pure peace of the True Self. I did not even know what any of it meant. I did know that, even though I was successful in my work, there was something missing. Even a skeptic needs something deeper, something that speaks to the heart, the spirit. I knew it was not any ritual. That is why I felt so connected to the Taoist teachings, which emphasizes being at one with nature. I would attempt meditation but had no clue what that was or how to do it. There is that space within that yearns to be back to our original nature. Not all experiences with LSD were that nice. Some were, in fact, quite scary.

I also had the opportunity to meet the head of the Hare Krishna movement at his original location, a storefront on 2nd Ave. When he spoke, it sounded like he had hot potatoes in his mouth. I saw the whole thing as a fanatical, narrow-minded cult. They also treated the women like chattel. It was appalling to me.

Beginning of the Connection

The next person I met and befriended was a young man, John Rhodes. He had a brilliant mind. He came from a wealthy family, was very well read but a total stoner. We got together frequently to discuss things like the Tao Te Ching and the I Ching. These had great meaning for me. He gave me the most important book I read to date, that being the Patanjali *Yoga Sutras* with introduction by William Butler Yeats. That was the first book I ever read on yoga philosophy. I was intrigued by the concept of Samadhi. What was it? It was John and his little wife who told me about Sri Gurudev—but in those days we just called him Swamiji.

This was in mid-October 1966 and it was just two months or so after He came to America. His center was at 500 West End Ave. The first time I went there was for a hatha yoga class and it was amazing. I just LOVED it totally. I saw this muscular black man near me and he was so agile, I thought, "Now I want to do that. I will do that." That was it. The chanting, which I never heard before in my life was also inspiring to me.

A Few Words on Hatha Yoga

At this point I feel it is necessary to interject a cautionary tale, an "editorial", if you will, on this practice. For many years this was my main practice outside of meditation. As stated, I just loved doing this. Perhaps it was just an ego thing because I became quite good at this and people noticed. I enjoyed every aspect. However, there were at least two critical asanas (headstand and shoulder-stand) that I did incorrectly, owing to being misinformed at the earliest stages of my practice. Demonstrating how essential proper instruction is for beginners most especially with regard to protection from injury. This eventually led to quite serious spinal damage, which to this day has resulted in continual pain and severe limitation in strength and movement of arms, hands, fingers etc. However, that is not the point that I wish to make. In the yoga sutras of Patanjali there is but one

Sutra regarding asana, "Sthira sukham asanam," asana is that which is easy and comfortable. That is it.

Asana keeps the body healthy and supple so that one may do meditation for a long time while sitting in padmasana or an equivalent pose on the floor. This does not mean that one denies all the health benefits of asana. It needs to be pointed out that this must be combined with proper pranayama, yoga nidra and meditation. It should not be for competition or ego fulfillment. These days we have people buying expensive outfits to do asana. They do it in boiling hot rooms, to jazz music or some equivalent. There are dozens of varieties of "yogas," Iyengar groups even sponsor competitions. All this goes counter to the spirit of hatha yoga. Folks forget that and think that yoga means only the physical part. Physical aspect is just one small part. Meditation, meditation, realization.

To Continue

I went to see Sri Gurudev frequently. In those days He would speak twice a week. One evening was for Q&A and the other was for lectures on Raja Yoga. What I saw astonished me. As soon as He entered the room you could feel this energy. It was calm, pure and loving. He would never speak loudly, never preached or admonished. He recommended we read a couple of books, How to Know God by Christopher Isherwood was the main one also Yoga by Ernest Wood. How to Know God was simply a reiteration into more American English of Raja Yoga by Swami Vivekananda. He also gave talks at the Universalist church, an enormous place. On one occasion, which I will never forget, a little girl came up to Him with a bouquet of flowers. He accepted it with such tenderness and love; I'd known many rabbis and none of them had this quality. I thought, "Now here is a real mensch. Mensch is Yiddish for a stand-up guy. Or a really proper, good man." He was the embodiment of saintliness.

Gurudev Story 1

I continued my practices in yoga and study but still I had no clue as to what the goal was. I kept going to His talks. The apartment at West End Ave had one immense room, which was used for classes. When Gurudev spoke the place was always packed full. In those days, none of us knew any of the proper protocol or etiquette in treating a respected guru. His room was a tiny room all the way in the back. So when he came into the big room no one stood up, which is the proper thing to do. When He entered, He just opened his arms, people made room for Him to pass, and said, "Ahh, it's like parting the Red Sea."He never admonished us then, never said, "Oh you people you do not know how to respect a Swami." No. That would not come until years later.

14. 1966 interview (unpublished); only three photos remain of thirty-six. My very first prints.

Gurudev Story 2

At all of those talks there was someone taping them. One evening just at the start of the talk, He turned to the chap running the recorder (in those days all that existed was the old reel-to-reel machines. They had a Webcor brand.) what he said was, "No you first must push that button. You see (to all of us) I must have eyes everywhere." That is to say, He had His awareness everywhere.

Gurudev Story 3

One day, while with some friends, I mentioned Swamiji and what a wise man He was. My friend Avritt Lemon Brown (now how is it I remember this name from 55 years ago but cannot remember where I put my specs just 10 minutes ago? Mystery.) He worked at the NY Times and suggested that we do an interview with Swamiji, perhaps I could set it up and do the photos. What an idea, amazing. We were so young and so without a clue.

I arranged for a time when we could come for the interview and photos. I was quite proud of having what I thought was a fully professional setup with lights and tripod, etc. It all went quite well until I asked my dumb question (I had done this before at one Q&A session with a different question)—right after I spoke I knew it was not the right thing, I was so uninformed and unformed.

After getting all the prints done—they were great—if I do say so—I went back to the Institute, photos in hand to show them to Swamiji, I also thought that I must ask Him to sign a standard "model release form" allowing me to publish the photos. In reality, what I wanted was an excuse to see Him up close again and to show off my photos. When I presented the photos all He said was, "OK" He was not playing my game. When I gave Him the form to sign He said, "Hmm, what is this?" "A release form, sir, allowing me to publish the photos." "It says, 'I, the model.' I am not a model, do whatever you like." That was it. When I left, I shook hands with Him not even knowing the protocol of pranam when meeting or leaving a Master.

The Story of Evolution

Spiritual development is a process, a developmental one. In most cases it is not something that comes on all at once. Therefore, there is first the dissatisfaction with how things are; or, as the Buddha called it, realization of pain in life. There is the leaving of past ways of thinking and lifestyle. Then there is emptiness, there is search for truth, practice of The Way (meditation etc.). Much later comes realization. At first, it all looks like sun and roses, all bright and light. Then comes the real work and you realize that you may have left a whole set of ways behind. However, the underlying mental collection in you remains and that is what needs real examination and cleaning up. Deconditioning. While there really is no magical solution, no one person who is going to lift the veil of ignorance, there is inspiration from great souls and books, there is discipline of the mind gained by practice of mediation. Eventually you get to the place, the place of pure contentment and peace, love and light. The journey can be like a great circle but it is not a closed one, not a straight line—it is an evolving spiral. Finding one's path is like that, a spiral journey.

Inspirational Reading

I will mention a few of the inspirations (among many others. See appendix III). These came from a few of the many books I read. First was Aquarian Gospel of Jesus by Levi. This was very inspiring. I read it during my time on Mt Shasta. The part that struck me most was when Jesus said, "Sell all that you have and follow me." I took this to mean, if you want to become like Jesus you must give everything up. Second were the later books of Thomas Merton a Trappist monk celebrated for his brilliant writings. He lived in the Trappist monastery in Gethsemane, Kentucky. He passed on in 1972. I saw in him such peace and ease in the silent life. That was for me. When I saw a photo of him, I knew straight away that was the way I wanted to be, that was the life I wanted to have. All of that led me to want a quiet, contemplative life. There were also dozens of little booklets that were so-called "channeled wisdom." They were dialogues between Jesus (or some such highly evolved being) and the reader. Each was filled with great light and love.

Finally, there was Raja Yoga by Swami Vivekananda, which is the basic text of Yoga philosophy. [I learned later that this was one of Sri Gurudev's favorite books—this is mentioned in a radio interview in the Tamil Biography written in 1955]. Also influential were the books of Alan Watts and Aldous Huxley's Island. Now, of course, there were many, many more books, many teachers and so on. I'm just presenting this as an outline. (See appendix III, "My List of Most Inspirational Books in My Life".)

One more little story—also how I was protected. Sometime in 1965, I was hanging with a group of politically minded folks headed up by a beautiful man, Robert Snow. They decided to go on the march to the Pentagon protesting the war in Vietnam. I went. When we got there I somehow managed to get to the very front of the crowd, right in front of us was a long line of National Guard with rifles ready and right beside me was a nice looking lad, blond hair and all, putting flowers in the rifle ends. There is an iconic photo of that but I was cropped out. A minute later I observed that there was a giant flatbed beside us (for media) and beyond that was the vast empty space of the Pentagon parking area. I said loudly "Hey, we can go there!" and like a herd of ants people—with me in front—massed over. Within seconds hundreds of army guys came smashing heads with gun butts. My buds and I got away.

Even though I found a great teacher, had spiritual friends and all that I knew I was not ready for any sort of commitment just yet. The Spiritual path, as with any relationship or serious endeavor requires long-term commitment. I had many more things to do. I had long held a vision in my mind of leading a free life, a life in the wilderness where I could get some other lessons. I also had a dream about meeting up with some Native American man who would teach me about wilderness living. I knew I just had to go for the gypsy life for the next leg.

The Great Adventure – Getting on the Road

First Leg

By late 1966 I had moved to a 3 room apartment way down-town on Madison St. by E. Broadway at the exit/entrance to the Brooklyn Bridge. I had also become quite tired of NYC. I was just too sensitive for it. Some years before I had visited San Francisco where my brother lived in Berkley. I really liked the openness and sun and so I made the decision to move there. Problem was I had a lot of stuff and my cat, Krishna, of whom I was quite fond. I gave away most of my stuff and thought it would be interesting and economical to find someone driving west. Therefore, I placed an ad in the papers, saying I'd help pay for the trip. After some rather simple screening I found what

I thought would be the perfect ride. What did I know? The man and car came the next morning. Unbeknown to me this was actually a drive-away, meaning he was just transporting it for someone to California and it was totally packed. There was another problem; soon I discovered that this guy was not just a stoner but someone who could not follow directions, read a map or find his way to the freeway. He was bad news.

After a day or so on the highway I told him, "Now pay attention Melvin, I am going to give you some directions, OK, you do exactly as I say. You will be taking me to O'Hare airport, and that's that." Well we finally got to the airport where I left him, taking my cat and assortment of luggage. When I looked at the flight board I realized, right now I could actually go anyplace in the world. I could. This was the days before credit cards, before security checks. When you could just walk up to the ticket counter get a ticket with no reservation, pay in cash and they would treat you like a human being and you could get hot meals free. For a Moment it occurred to me I could actually go anywhere in the world. That thought departed quickly. What a time. Well I got my ticket to SF, met my brother who had a friend that drove for some hippie cab company. I was home.

This was a magnificent era of our history. There was a cultural revolution in every aspect of the phrase. We had our own style of dress. Our own language, art and symbols, local newspapers, and of course there was the music. That magnificent, spectacular music. Never to be forgotten. Therefore, in all respects it was a culture onto its own. There were communities which were sometimes called communes. It was a transcendental, transforming time—absolutely. The air of this culture persists unto this day. One cannot be hasty in dismissing the importance of this, no less than many other cultural eras.

Yippee

Three weeks or so later the fellow who drove me showed up at my brother's to inform me that it was a good move on my part to split because the car he was driving broke down some place in Colorado and it took a week to get fixed. Cost him a fortune in motel, meals etc. Once again, some divine hand was there protecting me.

San Francisco Days

Eventually I had to vacate my brother's apartment and find one on my own. What followed was a series of serendipitous events. I first found a place with some Sufi chaps. Here is where I met the first of many spiritual guides in California. The Sufis' guru was known as "Sufi Sam." Otherwise known as Sam Lewis. An old Jewish man from New York. He had a large following at small place by Potrero Park in San Francisco. He led what is known is "Sufi Dance." He also gave various talks, none of which made any sense to me. I felt no connection to any of this.

Their apartment was too small, so one day, while having lunch at a nearby macrobiotic place, I struck up a conversation with a fellow next to me (not what I would normally ever do). I asked him if he knew of any places for rent. Turned out he had a room. I followed him to his place. What struck me the most about him was his calm and serene demeanor. I mentioned this and asked him what his secret was. He then showed me some books by his guru, an American named Master Subramuniya (who was later to rename himself as Sivaya Subramuniya Swami—head of a fundamentalist Hindu organization now based in Kauai, Hawaii). His place was much too small for me but I did start taking classes at his teacher's place on Sacramento St. His basic teaching, then, was simply Raja Yoga. His students also gave classes in hatha. I clearly remember after one class going to the teacher and remarking how wonderful the class was, and how calm a person he was. I asked what his secret was. He said, "Practice, practice, always do your practice."I took that as a direct instruction and have followed that ever since. It was that calm centeredness, the peace for which I so longed. It is so beautiful how one teacher can give one simple instruction to a student that can have such a profound, lasting effect.

I eventually found a nice apartment in Oakland. It was actually a large place with 3 extra bedrooms that all needed painting. I did that in exchange for three months' rent. Cool—especially since I knew nothing about painting rooms. Even better, I rented out the extra bedrooms and was thus able to live rent-free for the next nine months. It was here that I became a vegetarian. The way that happened was an interesting story. One of my renters was a pleasant young man from South Carolina. He worked as a gas station attendant. In those days it was called "a Service Station" because they really served you. One day he presented me with a bowl of food that was his own concoction of yogurt, avocado, walnuts, and sliced apple. He said, "Here is what vegetarian food looks like. I even made the yogurt myself." "Really, I said, how do you make yogurt? I do not know about that." He showed me his own homemade technique for making yogurt, which was quite easy. I made yogurt for the first time. From that Moment on I was a vegetarian. It was absolutely no problem. I tested myself one day by cooking some chicken, which I found too horrendous, so I gave it to the cat.

Later on, I moved to an incredible place on Woolsey Street and Ashby Avenue that was run by Michael Haimowitz. He was an artist, carpenter, and fixed his beautiful house up in a most creative manner. Living there were street actors, a group called The Floating Lotus Opera Co. also a musician, Will Scarlet, who played his handcrafted harmonica with Sonny Terry & Brownie McGee.

The Persistent Mom

One day while living in my large single room at that wonderful house there was a knock on the door, when I answered I was astonished to see Mom standing there. How did she find this place? How did she even know how to get here? No doubt she came across the country by bus. She certainly had a lot of energy and gumption. I was astonished and felt put upon that she should intrude without even ever asking ahead of time. I mention this for two reasons. Firstly, this would happen many, many times in all the places that I lived, even as far as the northern isolated mountains in California, the commune in southern Oregon, and two or three of the Integral Yoga Institutes where I lived. She always came without notice with the singular purpose of getting me back to the same old place in New York with that job I had at Columbia. It was the only thing that made her happy. It was the thing with which she identified. She could not accept that I had moved on to a different life. There was nothing I could do that would change that. I did not do well by her. I did not invite her in as I could not empathize with her needs. That was not good, but I felt so put upon, so intruded upon, that I could not appreciate her position. I regret that. She even found Gurudev when he lived in Danbury, Connecticut and went to His few house to tell Him about me, and what I had done. It was so amazing how she was so persistent and so able to do all these things. I did inherit that quality from her. Later I will tell you the story of what happened after Dad died and she came to the New York IYI.

In that period I also had the opportunity to frequent the music/dance places, the Avalon and Fillmore ballrooms, and heard the classic rock groups: Jefferson Airplane, Country Joe, Quick Silver, and many more whose names I do not recall. It was fun. I was a terrible dancer.

During that early time, I also went to San Francisco and hung out with the Diggers, a group fashioned after a political faction in Holland, which gave away free clothes and food. This was founded by Emmet Grogan whom I met in New York. He was an enthusiastic high-energy man who really believed in what he was doing to help others. At the San Francisco Diggers I met Peter Coyote—the actor. At that point he was an aspiring actor getting bit parts with the San Francisco acting company. Later on he was to become a major actor in Hollywood, mostly known now for his voiceover narration's of PBS documentaries.

One day when I was looking for something to do, (there's that "nothing to do" thing again), I found a place in Berkeley called the Berkeley Free Church. This was a sort of hippie hangout run by two defrocked gay Episcopalian priests (interesting combination). I felt at home here. It was here I met my dear friend David Lee, and the young couple Jason Perry and Diane. David was part Native American (Pima). In one of my visions, I felt a strong need to meet a Native American to learn the ways of the wilderness. He was that man.

At the Free Church I started up a free kitchen for the street kids. Somehow, I was able to hustle a 100-pound bag of rice and veggies to make meals every day. One day I got a call from some fellow who said he was from the Berkeley's Oceanic Biology Department and they had a beached whale and would I be interested in 200lb of whale meat. WHAT??? "Oh sure, that's great, will you deliver or should we pick it up?" They delivered. I was a vegetarian and never in my life had even seen whale meat, much less cooked any. Well I made a stew and those hungry kids loved it. I cannot imagine how I got the nerve to do all this.

All along, I kept up with hatha yoga and attempts at meditation as well as reading vast numbers of books. I also made a living by selling a local newspaper on the street, The Berkeley Barb, a sort of weekly Hippie paper with strong leftist civil-rights and antiwar leanings. It was established in 1965 by Max Sherr. Their central office was on Telegraph Avenue close to the University of California in Berkeley. I got good at selling this. All this was made possible by the quality that I described before, strong-willed determination. It was part of the nature in me to overcome the innate limitations. Not giving up and believing that I could succeed are what motivated me and helped me along the way.

I also got into making beautiful little terrariums in fish bowls, which I found to be an exhilarating high form of art. It was an exciting time.

I attended classes with Steve Gaskin, founder of The Farm. He was a brilliant, charismatic man who gathered a large following. His commune has been quite successful and is still thriving in Tennessee. His main teaching was, "Where you put your attention is what creates the energy to make things happen." This is a truism that has many subtle aspects and outcomes. That is how communication works, how partnerships, relationships or communities work. The one in the room who has the greatest power of getting attention is where the energy goes, whose ideas succeed.

I was tight with my friends David, Jason & Diane. David, who knew all there was to know about cars and so many other things, was also a kind man and, as I said, was part Indian, or at least that is what he claimed. Jason was a super-hippy, very with it fellow, and Diane was confused, young and pretty. She had a baby named Noah. We would often take off to a commune up in Occidental, near the redwoods, called Morning Star. This was run by Lou Gottleib. He was former head of the folk music group, The Limelighters. He was actually an accomplished classically trained musician who was financially successful from that and purchased this land in Sonoma County, California. He opened it to all and everyone. His philosophy was that the land belonged to God. When I was there I met Ramon Sender a high-energy Spanish guy who established all sorts of organic farms (he wrote a book on organic farming).We also went to a nearby commune, Wheeler ranch, where I spent a few days.

During that time, I discovered the Ananda Ashram community and retreat where I'd go for a few weeks at a time; a most beautiful and peaceful place founded by Swami Kriyananda, a disciple of Paramahansa Yogananda.. I would go often for retreats and meditation. This is what I wanted. A community, in the country where there was a spiritual practice, with people of like-mind who were kind and generous. Kriyananda, later resuming his original name, Donald Walters, was a gentle, kind man. He has since passed on.

On to Mt. Shasta

Eventually Diane got quite grumpy and complaining, demanding that she go back to the only place she was happy, Mt Shasta. Prior to that, I purchased, for our use, an old bread delivery van for $200. David checked it out and proclaimed it to be in excellent condition. To disguise it from the police I painted it a dark green on the outside, but a beautiful gold inside. We put in a bunk bed with room underneath for supplies, an altar with a Buddha and pictures of saints, we had a Coleman stove and a small cooler, everything but a toilet. It was grand.

When we saw the mountain from a great distance, I thought I was coming to heaven. It was so beautiful and majestic standing there all white with snow. Shasta is an extinct volcano and next to it is Shastina, which is a black cinder "mountain" actually more like a hill, but very steep and made of volcanic glass.

David and I went up the mountain while Jason and Diane remained in town with the baby. The town of Shasta was a strange mix of hippie and loggers. There was the old Society of St. Germaine known locally as the "I Am-ers." There were a slew of venerable teachers all female all much older than us, Sister Thedra who was claimed to be a "channel" for Jesus was most respected and there was Mother Mary a bit batty and others whom I forget. There was also Mrs. Friedman, wife of one of the doctors in town with great wisdom and intelligence. I am sure if I had been more attuned to what she was saying I would have learned much more. I was still very much unaware. Most of these women had been living there for many, many years. They were part of the community, as was the society of St. Germaine. David taught me many practical things about camping in the woods. He fulfilled one of my dreams to learn woodcraft from a native. I will be ever grateful to him for that.

There were many such teachers. I'm sure they had great lessons to impart and I was quite immature then and so was not completely receptive to learning all those lessons. I did get inspiration from the many books that I had been reading.

I learned from all of them. Of course, there were also the resident hippies. Here, I might add that Mount Shasta was a logging town with a paper mill. Half the mountain was owned by Pacific Lumber. The original town residents were hard-working Loggers who did not take kindly to the hippie "invasion." When they realized they were so many living there and so many styles they somehow had to accept that.

One memorable event was I when I was alone at McBride having just a pup tent. It was July so I thought it would be just fine. Well as luck would have it, one night as I lay under the tent it started to snow quite heavily. I had to pack everything as quickly as possible put on my boots, strap on the heavy backpack and walk 3 miles into town in the snow. Luckily, I knew my way around to get to where Jason and Diane were staying and all was well.

A Most Wonderful Spiritual Experience

McBride Springs was the spot we were told to head where the existing campers were. Even though it was April, there was a heavy blanket of snow and it was quite cold. We arrived at night and by great luck found the narrow path going down the steep hill heavily grown with manzanita to the encampment.

There a group of about 10 to 12 people was sitting on logs around a fire. Not a word was spoken. One guy was sitting there apart from the circle, the most striking thing about him was that he had no boots, no socks, no jacket, and it was cold. He was known as "Mountain Jeff." As we sat, they offered us some of the good food. I soon took notice of this gorgeous woman with long black hair sitting a few places to my right holding her infant son. It was beautiful. She indicated by gesture that it would be OK for me to hold her infant. OF COURSE, yes, I was just thinking that. A few Moments later after I handed the baby back. The woman next to me handed me a book and said, "Would you please read." These were the first words spoken that night. I did not even introduce myself, no one did. Well, and this is the truth, the book she gave me was a book of Jewish prayers in Hebrew. I was stunned. At random opened the book and it just "happened" to be the most sacred of Jewish prayers, The Shema. I stood and recited it in Hebrew. Everyone stood. I returned the book and we sat in silence. It was one of the MOST holy experiences of my life.

I stayed on the mountain for the next 5 months with occasional forays to town and a few trips to SF, getting everywhere by hitching. I soon gave away the truck to the Krishna guys I knew. I had now given most everything away, except for a bag of books that I left with this young woman in the town of Shasta. I was down to one big army backpack and my walking stick, which I still have (the stick not the pack). On the mountain there was a small group who traveled together. They would come there for the summer and in winter they'd go to the desert to Joshua Tree. In was a such a sweet group. We would cook together and just hang out, in the latter part of the summer we'd head up to a secret section in Panther Meadows where we would build a sweat lodge out of thick plastic and do a sweat, then hop into the fresh stream fed by the glacier. We had a great time that year.

Shasta is a sacred mountain considered by some to be one of Earth's chakras or power centers like Machu Picchu or The Himalayas. I don't know about it being a "chakra" but I can attest to it having great spiritual energy as do the Himalayas. I would return for short spells over the next five years.

One More Adventure

During this period, I had done a great deal of hitchhiking up and down the coast. It came to be that I knew every town and every perfect spot for hitching. California was my place. I do not recall how this happened but one time when I was going south with David we somehow got stuck in the middle of Highway 1, which is the coast road. It is just a simple 2-lane road. It was getting close to night and with no potential for a ride and no place to go we put our sleeping bags down in a ditch that ran all along the side of the road. There we slept with trucks running not 12 feet away. It was not the best sleep I had. To be perfectly honest it was the worst sleep I'd had in years. I would never do that again. I attribute such things to my youthful insanity. It was yet another example of the crazy things we did in those days. We took chances and learned a lot. There is the great advantage to the audacity, inexperience or you may say ignorance, and courage of youth.

Somehow, we managed to survive. This and all my years of experience with hitching led me to know that—you will always get to where you are headed. That was one lesson that has been with me my entire life. No doubt about it.

Hitchhiking, Protected

Hitching was for me an art form, a way to use the mind to actually attract a ride. There were times when a couple of us were working together and we got into the wrong vehicle. There ensued another bizarre adventure wherein the knowledge that I was protected was quite evident. The short version of this story was that I was with a fellow I met on road to San Francisco. We got into a juiced up fancy sports car. I should've seen that as a sign straight away. The guy sped off down a one lane road. He then came to town and got extremely agitated when a fellow was not moving fast enough. He yelled some derogatory term at him. The other guy stopped got out of his car and challenged the driver of our car. There were a lot of sparks and heat flying and our driver pulled out a knife. We could see that this was a truly dicey situation in which we should depart immediately. We both picked up our heavy backpacks hastened to the freeway ramp and got a ride straight away in a nice pickup truck. Whew.

First Attempt

One day while sitting on a rock by my tent on Mount Shasta I was reading Raja Yoga by Vivekananda coming to the section on Samadhi I thought, "Wow, this is just amazing, it is what I want. But how can I get this? I have no clue. I do not know what path to take, or how to get there. I must find someone who can simply tell me what my path is, who can give me the secret. Yup. Wait, I DO know someone. Swami Satchidananda. I will write to him and ask if we can meet." Therefore, I proceeded to write the letter. The problem was I had totally forgotten the address but I did remember it was on West End Ave. That is what I put on the envelope. Naturally, it was returned. Well I sat there for a while, concentrating, and it came to me in a flash, 500 West End, apt 5D. In a week, I got a reply. He said that He would be in SF on July 16 and I could contact his secretary, Shanti, for an appointment. Wow, cool. Well I got packed, and my girlfriend, Valerie, and I hitched to the city (It's a five hour straight drive and we got there in six.). We got there 3 days early. Valerie was a true city woman so she loved it—I was not comfortable there. I could not stay so I hitched back to the mountain the next day. Missed Him by two days.

Gurudev Story 4

Understanding the Guru His Great Teaching & Blessing

At first, I wanted a guru to give me instructions on how to get to enlightenment or something like that. I had thought that the guru knows everything and can perform some sort of magical insight into my being that needed fixing. That he would give me special personal instruction. He did give me a mantra and some common instruction on pranayama, proper dress, and so forth. There was nothing which I met my preconception of receiving some sort of "magical instruction that would detail my "own path". It was not until sometime later that I realized he was always giving me direct instruction. There were a couple of instances that were worth telling, where instructions were given me in a more convoluted manner. I will give one example. This happened when we were at the first ashram in Northern California, Yogaville West. (See the chapter on that later on.) Among the presenters, during one retreat, was an American swami by the name of Nirmalananda. He had an ashram in Denver and was a disciple of Anandamaya Maa. He was a charismatic, highly intelligent, and entertaining man. He told many illuminating stories about his guru (see chapter on Yogaville West.). This was shortly after we received pre-sannyas initiation. A good number of the men wanted to go study with him (he didn't take women). I also thought it would be interesting to go. After satsang one day, I approached Gurudev quietly and presented my idea. Not having confidence in my own decision, I wanted His opinion. He said, "If I tell you what to do you will do it because I say so. What do you think, that is what is important. You should not just look for my approval." My immediate reaction was that there is no need for me to go anywhere. What he was saying was I should figure it out on my own. I should find the truth on my own then it would be MY TRUTH. I heard the very same words from him several times. It wasn't until many years later that I understood the meaning of this great teaching. It is up to each one of us to discover the answers to any of those questions. That way the truth comes from the source within. It becomes ours.

It is worth noting that the absolute, unconditional love of Gurudev meant that he always accepted us no matter what. This is the absolute unconditional love.

Commune Days

Starting on Mount Shasta

With his pale blond hair, mellow demeanor, and running around naked most of the time, "Prune" looked like an incarnation of Pan or at least one of his close relatives. We hung out a lot. He was a regular denizen of Mt. Shasta. We would sit by the fire cooking rice and beans, I learned a lot about foraging, building fires. I learned the difference between the fire built for heat and one for cooking. I learned the different types of wood and which gave the best and longest fire. We foraged for little edible plants such as fiddle-heads, miner's lettuce and flowers such as penny-royal and manzanita (all quite delicious) for tea..

Shasta is a charmed and holy place. I had learned that if you are not in the Moment, if you do not understand what Aldous Huxley (and Steve Gaskin) said, "Pay Attention," accidents might happen. One such Moment came when I was cutting veggies with my Kaybar knife and I suddenly sliced my finger and back of the right hand. It was a serious cut so Dave rushed me down and we found a doc who gave me stitches without any anesthetic ouch! He did manage to give me a lecture about finding Jesus (I did not even know He was lost). Another time while chopping wood with a hatchet my hand slipped and the hatchet went through the boot on my left foot, missing the foot by just a hair. PROTECTED again. There were many, many such adventures and misadventures.

Each year when I returned for a stay, Prune was there. For all I know he may still be there. One day he told me about a cool commune up in southern Oregon called Sunny Valley. So naturally, I just had to go.

HOWEVER, before doing that I thought I should check out that circus down in Eureka where a guy I met while hitchhiking told me there could be a job at the circus. A crazy idea when you think about it, but I was not thinking much then. There happened to be a little family going directly to Eureka so I got a ride with them. Halfway to our destination the car broke down. This was on a small connecting road. I took this as a sign that I was not meant to go join the circus but must now go to Sunny Valley in Oregon.

Protected Again

Amazingly, I actually got a ride on the lonely road back to Rt. 5 the main N-S freeway in California. I arrived at one of those small California towns, Winters and I did get a ride north and this guy took me about 30 miles when he spotted a car with Oregon license plates, he said maybe I could get a ride with her. I grabbed my giant pack and walking stick, ran up to the car, which was stopped and stuck out my thumb, will full resolve. I got the ride.

When we got to the area of Oregon where the place was it was quite late and we did not know exactly where it was. We stopped by a gas station to ask directions, but to my ears that guy made no sense, in fact it sounded like he was speaking a Martian dialect. After a while of meandering, that lady got frustrated and simply dropped me off on the road. I had absolutely no clue as to where I was. It was quite dark. I moved off to the side of the road to lay out my sleeping bag. I then saw a faint light headed my way. It was a woman with a lit cigarette walking towards me. I asked her where I was. She replied, "I do not know where I am, how the hell am I going to know where you are?" I then saw the lights a car approaching, it stopped about 200 feet in front of me. There was some shouting and then GUNFIRE. Or at least, that is what it sounded like to me. I reacted by bolting up, grabbing the sleeping bag, backpack and my stick and ran like hell up this small path. I went for about ten minutes to what I thought I was far enough. I was exhausted. I found a spot on the side of the path to set up camp. I somehow got enough wood to build a small fire. I tried to sleep. I did not sleep. In the morning totally exhausted and hungry, I walked up the path, having no clue where the road was or where I was and yelled out for help. For some strange reason I had the absurd notion that I was near my destination and all I had to do was walk up the road and yell out. This was, of course, complete delusion. Now, remember, this was a very isolated place. Soon this fellow came up in a car. I flagged him down and asked if he knew where Sunny Valley was. "Sure, hop in." Wow, was I happy to see this guy. Then he proceeded to give me a severe lecture on why I must go to Jesus and give up my wanton ways. Seems like in those days there are a lot of people eager to convert me. I was so grateful for the ride it did not matter what he said. That's a true story.

This brings to mind one of the central guiding tenets of my life, determination. Having been through so many challenging and difficult experiences I found the one thing that got me through it all was sheer grit, determination, call it what you will. I always knew I could get there if I just toughed it out. That and a large good dose of luck or, as some may put it, being watched over by a higher power, or good karma. I really do believe in that. Nevertheless, with all this, despite the natural tendency of thinking one is immortal, or at least impervious, one tends to do stupid things. This is the mark of the young mind.

Sunny Valley was a most interesting place. They had built a giant log building, hexagonal in shape. That served as a central gathering place and kitchen. There were about 20 people there. This was the place that was featured once on the cover of Life magazine. I slept outside. We would go to cut wood, take care of the chickens, and have meals. It was cool. It, however, did not work out for me to live there. So, after a short interim stay at a different commune ("The Mining Claim" the tiny 16 acre commune with a minuscule garden and if you that's. They took advantage of the BLM regulation wherein one can proclaim to and on own 16-acre piece of property as long as they worked it for "mining". They had to put in a certain amount of hours per week or something like that.), I then landed at Magic Forest farm in Takilma, a teeny town in the south-central end of Oregon, about 5 miles from Cave Junction which was 45 miles west of Grants Pass.

Magic Forest Farm was a beautiful organic farm. They had a central meeting and eating house, several cabins, a chicken coop, and goat pen with two goats. Here I learned a lot about farming. I did the composting, took care of the chickens and learned to take care of goats, which I really loved. I did learn all there was about goats, milking and care. The other good thing I learned and loved to do was chop wood. There is quite a difference between the ways you cut oak, pine and madrone, etc. I learned the use of an adz, drawknife (tree bark stripper), tree dogs, peeve, Pulaski, and such things as that. Also, how to sharpen every sort of tool that needs sharpening from axe and snath (scythe), to sickle, etc. These are useful skills. This for me was a very Zen practice, to see if I could slice through a biscuit of wood with one stroke. I also learned to make wooden shakes (shingles) from cedar using a "froe" (special tool designed for making shakes) and mallet. That was my favorite activity. I also dug a giant hole for a 3-seat outhouse using a Pulaski and mattock (specialized digging tools.). The garden had a large variety of vegetables. We learned so much from the local old-timers. This knowledge was of great use in our later ashrams and institutes where I put that to service. It was also at that time that I began my knowledge quest in herbal medicine. I have continued in this study to this day. I have found that it is useful to have such practical knowledge. I loved doing all that. It came in handy under many circumstances. Knowing the healing use of herbs staves off fear associated with diseases, accidents etc. Knowledge is power. In matters of health it is of great value to be one's own advocate.

I worked hard. I also worked hard to please others so that they would like me. This, of course, did not work. I, as usual, was not really happy. I still needed to know, "Who am I?" "Why am I here?"

I knew there had to be something better. Something that was right for me. With all this running around from place to place all the time, something was missing. There was nothing wrong with the outside, I concluded, something was amiss in me. How to mend a broken heart and the broken parts. But it's not really broken, just confused. Truth, beauty, love is there, I just did not know where to find it or, more properly, how to find it. I knew somewhere in my own being that Swami Satchidananda could guide me or even fix it

During this time I would often write letters to Swamiji and send Him packets of medicinal herbs I had picked, I thought He might enjoy that. He did remember me later on, dubbing me "Magic." (After the name of the farm I was living at.)

[Side note digression: You know that bag of books I left with Mary. Well about a year later while back at Shasta from Oregon, I went to her house to retrieve my books, which also had my photographs. She was not home. Now you must know that Mary was well known in that teeny town as not just a stoner but a 24 year old teenage floozy. I just had to get that bag and did not want to wait around so I went round to the side of the house. Not having a clue what I was doing, I found a lose screen window, broke in to the basement and NOT knowing at all where that bag was AND not having a flashlight I actually found the bag. Now that alone would have been amazing. The next thing that happened was more so. I walked with that bag, my backpack and stick to a spot about 11 blocks from the freeway. I knew it would be hard to get a ride from that spot but it was exceedingly far to walk with that heavy load. In about two minutes the sheriff stops he gets out and asks, "Were you just at Mary's house? Did you do a drop off there?"

>"No, sir, I have nothing to drop off (true)".
>"Where are you going?""Grants Pass, Oregon, sir."
>"Well, you'll never get a ride from here, hop in."

He took me right to the freeway entrance. WHEW. Protected.

One day I received a letter from a buddy, Rick Strauss, in Berkeley saying that Swamiji will be in the area next week. Now there happened to be a guy at the farm who lived in the Bay area and who was returning at that time so I arranged a ride with him. When we got to Ashland we stopped for breakfast at some diner. I was in my standard attire for a hippy farmer. As I was finishing my oatmeal I noticed a cop sitting next to me. There was no problem, as I had nothing illegal on my person. But, when we left the diner there were four cop cars and five cops surrounding me (FIVE large guys to take me down at 110 lb. Did they take me for a Kung Fu master?). I was arrested. What for? They said it was the "concealed" weapon I had on my belt in plain sight. (Maybe they didn't have English as a first language). Anyone can tell you that every hippy had such a knife on his belt. It was a tool. Mine happened to be that cool, genuine army surplus Ka-bar. I loved that knife. The cop who took me in was named Cotton. They took me to the station, photos, prints, the whole 9.5 yards. I got out on bail. I got an ACLU lawyer and he had the charges dropped. **[Protected again]** They actually mailed back my knife—amazing. I have since lost that wonderful knife which I've never been able to replace.

Third Time's the Charm

Magic Forest Farm was truly magical. I learned so much. But they were not friendly to my yoga practices. On April 18th 1970 I got another letter from Rick Strauss informing me that the first Earth Day Festival was going to happen April 22 at Davis University, which is one of the agricultural centers of California, making it a suitable place for Earth Day. Swami Satchidananda was going to be there and if I wanted to go I should meet him at his place and we'd go together in his car. Cool. The day came. This time I just packed it up, got a ride to H'way 101 and thumbed my way. There is a secret technique to hitchhiking that I knew well. It requires one to really focus the mind and to put out a strong energy field to get the car to stop. Now you're not going to believe this but when I got to Ashland I got a ride with someone who looked familiar, it was Cotton, the same cop who had me arrested a year before. He did not recognize me, but he was quite friendly. Serendipity.

AT LAST

Well, on the last ride to Berkeley I convinced the guy to take me right to Rick's house AND at the exact Moment I got there he was exiting the door headed to his car, "Come on man, I'm going now, get in." SYNCHRONICITY. I got in and we arrived at the Davis University campus on April 22. There were thousands of beautiful people. It was going to be a grand bash. There was an old buddy from Berkeley handing out his special brownies, there was a little table from the NY IYI with photos of Gurudev. I was overjoyed. He, along with many others, was going to be there the next day. I also met a beautiful woman, Sharon Bryant, who would be my girlfriend for the next year.

Next day, all the teachers came: Sri Swami Satchidananda, Stephen Gaskin, Suzuki Roshi, and many others whose names I do not remember. It was the first Earth Day ever.

Gurudev Story 5

Becoming a Disciple, Mantra Initiation

At that Earth Day celebration many people spoke, I do not remember a single thing that was said. After Gurudev spoke I went right up to Him and said, "May I ask you something, Sir?" He motioned me to wait until the announcements were done. I patiently waited; it had been four years now. Finally, it was time, "I want to be your disciple. Will you take me on?" He replied in that slow calm voice, "Well, there will be an initiation; you must go ask Vijay about it."

Vijay was the wonderful man who, along with his beautiful wife Shree, ran the new San Francisco Integral Yoga Institute. I went straight to the man, explained my situation and he said, "Well, this initiation is for the people who live at the Institute." "Look, I understand, but I have waited four years for this, I hitched 500 miles, this has to happen." Well I guess I convinced him. He then told me the tradition is that you pay something like $18, you wear all white and if you like bring some flowers to give Swamiji." $18?!!!! Wear white??!!!OK, whatever it takes.

Of course, I had nothing white so I went to the reliable old Klein's army-navy surplus on Mission and got a pair of white navy work-pants and a white Chef's shirt. It was a bit on the scruffy side. Well, I thought it was cool. I got to the Institute one hour early perfectly done up. Sri Gurudev finally came down to the front room. It was all set up for the puja, the first of one in San Francisco—April 24, 1970. Slowly He told us what He was about to do, carefully showed us the pranayama we were to do as well as tell us all the mantras He was going to recite for the puja. As if by magic, I absorbed all of this. He performed the puja (ritual) with such care. I watched every second of it. There were ten of us there, including my dear friend Ramakrishna Sackett the repairman at the IYI.

Several months before when I decided to become a disciple I knew that Sri Gurudev did not approve of smoking, using psychedelics, drinking etc. so at that Moment I gave it all up. Just like that! There was absolutely no problem. It was easy. Even after having smoked cigarettes for some 14 or 15 years, I just did it. Because that is what I was supposed to do. There was absolutely no side effect no difficulty. Now I had already been a vegetarian for some three years, so that was no problem.

Gurudev Story 6A

One by one, we went up to Sri Gurudev's bedroom where He was sitting on the floor at the foot of the bed. In front of Him was a coffee table. I sat down in front of the table—He said my mantra and asked me to repeat it. We did this three times. He then gave me a mala (tulsi bead rosary, I still have a bit of that now just reduced to two little wrist malas). He wrote down the mantra that He put into an envelope for me. Finally, he touched my forehead with His thumb. I was in another state of consciousness. We then went downstairs to the living room. At the end just before I was to leave I went up to Him to give Him a big hug and said to Him, "I want to serve you." He said so softly and gently, "You will, you will." That was it. I knew at that Moment that I was to be His disciple. Which in my mind meant to give everything else up and be like one of the Apostles of Jesus. To me it meant that I was meant to serve Him and to become a swami. Home at last. HOME at last.

A Note on My Holy Gurudev

Gurudev was indeed connected to the universe, to all of nature and its components. He therefore understood what was essential on the deepest level. From that place He understood, and knew what was in people's minds. As such, He had the greatest compassion for the difficulties and troubles that so deeply occupied His disciple's individual minds. That is love.

Interesting Good Karma

Right after the initiation, I had to get back to my place in Berkeley. I had found a place to stay with a buddy in Berkeley where Sharon was also staying. I wasn't sure how to do that so I just walked across the street and put out my thumb. Now, you should know that the street on which the Institute is a four lane heavily trafficked road. Therefore, no one ever hitches there. However, in a short while I got a ride to the freeway entrance. I got to the place I was staying straight away. I attribute this to the grace of Gurudev, and that initiation. MIRACLE.

Gurudev Story 6B

The next day following initiation, I was back in the San Francisco IYI for lunch with Sri Gurudev. I was trying to think of the right thing to say. Actually, I just wanted to say something to impress Him. I came up with this bit of banality, "Sir, would it make you happy if I moved in to the Institute?" I was approaching Him as one would an ordinary teacher, or one's boss. Gurudev's reply, "I am always happy. Nothing you do will make me happy—don't do it for me—do it for yourself."

On His Infinite Greatness

On the deepest level I Knew, not just believed, that Gurudev had attained the highest realization. That He was, in fact, one with the Universal Consciousness and therefore had access to the very energy of the Universe, and thus was one with all that. Being in that state He was able to have access to anyone's innermost thoughts and was also protecting and totally caring for each and every disciple. Having universal, infinite access, when in His presence, meant we were completely safe that He had our best interest in heart. I know this to be true from so many direct experiences with Him. I experienced His infinite love and acceptance. He judged no one, rejected no one. He just embraced us in his loving arms and by doing so He evoked the highest aspect of us. I must also mention His wonderful sense of humor, graciousness and graceful manner as well as His practicality, athletic strength, and mechanical abilities. Such beauty. He was my best friend. He was always there for me. If I had a problem I could just call. That was during the early years. Keep in mind that is coming from a very rational, logical, scientific mind.

From the beginning I never forgot the necessity of meditation practice to clear the mind.

At that Moment I knew my life would no longer be the same.

We were all so young, so naïve.

15. Satsang 1970, near Santa Barbara, CA.   16. Youth San Francisco, CA 1972.

Waves of Gurus Coming to America

This was the decade that the great influx and initial interest in yoga brought so many gurus to America. I met a great many of them, too numerous to name. While a number were sincere and genuine it is worth noting that there are also quite a few who came on that wave knowing that they could take advantage of the many insecure, uncertain young people who were looking for something. Someone to tell them what to do, to give them the idea of security. They would form the many and varied "cults" in this country. A common trait of members in such organizations or groups is that they seem to be hypnotized walking around mouthing the quotations of their "guru" and sometimes even the voice tone of the guru. As well as adopting the posture, smile, and gestures, that they thought were necessary or required to demonstrate this spirituality. Admittedly, many of us were guilty of this. It provided a degree of security and safety. Hopefully, we have advanced out of this. This has been the case for centuries. It is not new. However, during that decade there was a much higher percentage than the normal of that sort.

After about three months I moved to the new Santa Cruz IYI. That was at a mansion complete with gardens and circular driveway, the works. It was run by Palitha Wadley, a surfer dude, very easy going. He has since passed away.

I was very religious about regularity in my practices of meditation and hatha yoga. I got quite good at most of the poses. I carried on my practice for many, many years. Later all that ultra-intense practice was to be the cause of a major damage to my body. One must be grateful for even the little blessings.

Santa Cruz: Part One

As I have indicated this first house in Santa Cruz was like a mansion. It also had a nice plot of land in back wherein we had a little veggie garden. One of the most significant events to take place at that house was the first time I ever heard Sri Gurudev mention anything about LOTUS. No one knew anything about it until then. I remember so clearly. He was sitting on the floor (we did not know the proper protocol to offer a nice seat). He told us that He had this dream to build a temple in the shape of a grand lotus flower and it would dedicated to all religions. Everyone would be included. He went on to explain how in history religions divided us but this would serve to bring people of all paths together. I think at the time we did not fully appreciate the majesty and grandness of this plan.

This area of Santa Cruz was a peaceful, beautiful place. I had the opportunity to do quite a bit of reading then. One of the books that most inspired me was The Way of a Pilgrim. It was by an anonymous writer in old Russia who was a seeker of wisdom and spiritual guidance. It is a recount of his voyages and travels for that purpose. There was one major question in his mind; how to remember God at all times in all places. On his journey he met a wise priest who counseled him to do just two simple things; keep silent and repeat the prayer of Jesus, "Lord Jesus Christ, son of God, have mercy on me." It was the practice of silence in which I was most interested. I thought that would be a powerful tool. Therefore, I proceeded to keep silent for a long time. I had done that practice years before while living at the commune. However, one of my attractions in that little town was a delightful old-fashioned ice cream shop. As I had a massive sweet tooth, I had a yen to go there one day. I had a nice old bicycle so I went to the shop one fine spring day. Of course, I was keeping silent. I wrote a little note for the ice-cream shop man stating my request. "Double chocolate scoop in a cup." Right after serving, he wrote me a note telling me the cost. I thought that was really funny. By the way, this book and the follow-up to it (*The Pilgrim Continues His Way*) are still available and have beautiful spiritual guidance. From the ice cream shop experience, I learned not to make my practices so public.

It was here, I also became a hatha yoga teacher. In those days, there was no such thing as Teacher Training. All one did was take many classes and learn the routine. I had done that. Therefore, I asked Palitha if I could teach and he said, "Sure, just give us a sample class." After my class they told me the only one thing, "Just slow down. You're going too fast." I became a hatha teacher and just loved it.

Santa Cruz: Part Two

A number of years later there would be a second Santa Cruz Integral Yoga Institute. This was a quaint old house located amidst the redwood forest some 2 miles from the center of the city. It was a wood frame house with a beautiful wooden porch around it and about 2—3 acres of property. We were told that it once belonged to some rock group and there was a room lined with soundproofing attesting to that fact. One of the guys, Siva Plocher, had experience at keeping bees so we had a couple of beehives. The center opened in 1974. There were only men living there at that point. Jeeva Abbate was in charge. This was the period in which the San Francisco Institute was occupied by women and Santa Cruz was for the men. Eventually those limitations were removed.

At that time, there was also the third iteration of the Los Angeles Center located near North Hollywood on N. Alta Vista Drive. This was very close to Sunset Boulevard, some of which was not a safe area. However, not far up the street there was also the famous Source restaurant a vegetarian, posh place frequented by many Hollywood types

In Santa Cruz, we opened a natural foods store. We had a nice deli for which we made fresh salads and hummus. It was a lot of hard work but we enjoyed it. The local people loved the store. It did not turn a significant profit. I enjoyed biking from our house to the store from time to time. Of course, we had access to the beach and did a bit of swimming. At one point we made the trek to the university farm that was run by a renowned farmer from England, Alan Chadwick. He was an industrious and energetic man who perfected the system known as the French Intensive—Biodynamic System. He did not use any power machinery just his own muscle power. French intensive method incorporates "double dug beds" to give the highest yield. I incorporated something like this when we did a farm in Santa Barbara.

It was here that I also met that most interesting Zen poet and author, Paul Reps (*Zen Flesh, Zen Bones*).

During my stay in Santa Cruz Institute, I befriended a brilliant chiropractor, Ed Jarvis. He was far more than a simple chiropractor. His deep spiritual practice gave him a special understanding of human nature and healing. There was also alternative practice known as Polarity Therapy. This was so innovative and new I thought I should like to take a class with him. Therefore, when he offered a series of classes I immediately took the opportunity. At that time he had an associate, Pierre Pannetier. The man who inherited the mantle of teaching from the developer of this therapy, Dr. Randolph Stone. Dr. Stone had gone off to India to be with his guru, Baba Sawan Singh. I studied with Pierre. I have used this system for many years and innovated upon it. Polarity is an energy balancing system that derives from the school of osteopathy combined with Ayurveda and Dr. Stone's own understandings and innovations in energy balancing. It works with pressure points throughout the body.

Gurudev Story 7

One day Jeevakan, he was in charge of the Santa Cruz IYI, informed me that Gurudev and one special guest Sant Keshavadas, who was a very close friend of Gurudev, would be our guests for lunch. He asked me if I would do the cooking, as I was the only person there who knew how to cook anything. I foolishly accepted. This was my first meal for Sri Gurudev so I decided to cook a dish from his homeland, Tamil Nadu. I thought that would be a special treat. I decided on idli-sambar. Little did I know that was one of the most difficult of Indian dishes. I assembled my ingredients and carefully and precisely measured everything. I stayed up most of the night watching the idli batter ferment under the pilot light in the oven. Fermentation of the batter is the first step. It just goes along on its own way; I did not have to watch. Sambar is a magnificent soup, very complex in flavor and preparation. Now one of the few Indian foods, besides curried vegetables, that I knew how to cook was chapattis so I prepared a batch of those as well. I just did not want anyone to go hungry. Our guests came and I carefully served everyone and then stood in the back waiting to see what Gurudev's response would be. He said, "This is very good. Well done. But one thing you should note chapattis are a Northern food made from wheat you do not generally serve them with idli."—Lesson learned. Many more lessons to come.

Moving place to place did not make life better. I think this is a very good lesson to know for so many. It took an exceptionally long time for me to learn this lesson.

17. Big hair days, Santa Cruz hills, 1974.

San Francisco: Part One

I soon moved to the SF IYI. It was my intention to become a swami. That was my understanding of being a disciple. This was very much influenced by reading that wonderful book The Aquarian Gospel. As previously mentioned I was also influenced by reading books by and about Thomas Merton who was a great, beautiful Trappist monk later to become a priest. When I saw photos of him, such a peaceful and beautiful person, I knew that is what I wanted. A simple silent life. Many years before the first initiation I even asked Vijay Hassin when Sri Gurudev was going to do that. He said, "Whenever He sees that there are some people who are ready". A wise response. Vijay was always an able leader. His wife Shree was both beautiful and sweet.

San Francisco: Part Two

[Note, I have amalgamated stories from several stays at the San Francisco Institute because a part of it was interrupted by a stay at the Santa Cruz Institute when it was decided that San Francisco was to be female occupants only and Santa Cruz was male. That period was short-lived and I returned to San Francisco. It is all too complicated to sort out. Anyway, I forget most of the order of all those events.]

It is worth backtracking a bit here to tell you something about that wonderful place in San Francisco. The Integral Yoga Institute is a beautiful stone building set upon a hill between the Mission District and Noe Valley. It was built prior to and survived the San Francisco earthquake. Inside the main living room, you can still see the handcrafted plasterwork on the ceiling. There are old brass sconces on the walls, which were once used for gas lighting. The main living room and dining room have fireplaces that once actually worked. They have brass fittings in front of them. The beautiful little Mission Dolores church is just down the street. We obtained the building March 1970. It has beautiful mahogany trim in most of the rooms. However, the prior owner, a rather eccentric woman, had all the walls of all the rooms painted pink. This is true. It was quite a job repainting them in appropriate colors. The basement was a big mess just an ugly, old, dirty basement. I know I cleaned it up. Subsequently Ramakrishna Sackett and Asoka Boyce, both experienced carpenters, converted that ugly basement into a reception area along with two dressing rooms for people who would come for hatha yoga. On one side they built the maintenance room with tools and other equipment. Ramakrishna also personally carried the hot-water heater to the basement and hooked it up.

In the initial years, 22 people lived there along with two dogs and a newborn baby. It was quite a vibrant place. I love that place to this day. An interesting anecdote; in those early years when there was going to be a satsang with Gurudev many people would assemble in the large living room waiting. Because it was a "Yoga" center many people would be in the room sitting in lotus posture "meditating" or more often during headstand and every asana they could do. I thought that was funny.

The San Francisco IYI was a truly divine place, and, at that time, full of tremendous youthful energy. We were all fresh, young and enthusiastic about our new adventure. Teaching classes was always a delight. We had and continue to have a very large upper room, which was once a dusty attic, but soon by dint of great labor it was transformed into a magnificent temple. It had a cupola with a wooden floor into which I put some of our biggest plants. There was "Dave" the giant Dieffenbachia and several philodendra. There was an altar. It had the most magnificent vibration. Teaching there brought one to a new level. It was a meditation. Three tiny rooms on that level were made into bedrooms. The third level had three bedrooms plus Gurudev's room that was set with all His furniture and reserved for His use only. Years later it was converted into a classroom and His bed and altar and chairs are no longer there. It was difficult for me to see that situation when I visited. This was done long before His Mahasamadhi. There is also a large brass gong hanging from the ceiling just above the stairway that continues to be rung signaling the beginning of classes or meditations. I took it upon myself to polish that big thing from time to time. The stairway risers and all parts were made out of mahogany. It was a great time, full of good energy.

Ramakrishna was initially a journeyman carpenter; however, it was not long before he evolved into a master carpenter and builder of homes. He was the man responsible for the building of Sivananda Hall and Gurudev's house in Virginia. I fondly recall when he came to me with such joy and glowing face to inform me of his impending marriage to one young lady who had lived with us when I was in the Santa Cruz Institute. They had been corresponding for a number of months. That marriage lasted for quite some time they had four wonderful children including Jyothi the first child born at the Yogaville, Virginia ashram.

18. IYISF gang. Top shortly after sannyas initiation 1975, bottom reunion 1982.

We became very good friends. We took camping trips together first to the Russian River in a redwood forest. Later on we went to Mount Shasta. One time we camped in the snow and that was in July. I showed him how to pick wild vegetables and Manzanita flowers for tea. It was there we also met Dr. Wherrit and his wife Elevnora, who besides being a gracious host was also the channel for the "higher wisdom". We became long-term friends. She was really a teacher. Dr. Wherrit was a retired old osteopath. One time he gave me a treatment the first part of which was putting his hands under my neck and head. I could immediately feel his healing energy. I thought to myself, "this is what I want to do." That was a critical point in my life because following that I was trained in Polarity Massage Therapy and various other hands-on treatment. I use this important skill to this day.

Sadly, Ramakrishna and Radha's marriage ended after some difficulties. One would think that in the spiritual community such things did not happen. But the truth is that this community is a modified reflection of what happens in the larger world though not to such an extent. There are marriages as well as divorces, births as well as death, not always in the expected manner. In our history we have had passing on by accident whether automobile, drowning or sometimes a bizarre accident and many of the means that one observes in the world. The point is that we are a micro-universe having many of the same events as in the larger world.

I had many jobs in San Francisco. I was receptionist at times and taught classes. I took care of the houseplants, some of which had names. Years later, I installed a beautiful garden in the back with redwood railroad ties as a border. San Francisco had a system whereby they processed sewage sludge sterilized it and combined it with rice hulls from the large California rice industry. That made a product called "Tillo". This combined with the heavy topsoil we had made a perfect planting medium. I found an old Italian lady running a nursery that she took over from her husband when he died. She was an expert gardener. She sold most of the plants at extremely low rates some of them as little as one dollar for a 1 gallon pot. There were bushes, flowers and even the beautiful tree called Princess Pine (unfortunately, many years later most of these were removed). I gave the first "Teacher Training" sessions there. We did not have the official training manual and there was no actual outline for a program. So, I just winged it. Gave the standard class a number of times, broke it down into sections and then said, "Here, now you give it a go." The student would give a practice class while I sat behind the curtain listening to them and gave them corrections. Not the most sophisticated system.

I initiated one of the first seminars in natural or herbal healing in San Francisco. This met once or twice a week for six weeks. It was fun having direct experience with many different herbs and potions. At that time there was an upsurge in the interest in natural healing I became friends with several herbalists. I studied and exchanged notes with many herbalists. There were Robert Menzies, Rosemary Gladstar and Michael Tierra.. It was wonderful. I took seminars with Dr. John Christopher who was one of the most renowned herbalists of his time. Things were much freer then. We would freely exchange information and have open classes. It was a grand wonderful time.

Bhaktan Eberle also lived there, during which time he was a swami (Bhaktananda) he was a skilled carpenter with brilliant ideas. The kitchen then was a shamble, very old and broken down. So he redid the entire kitchen putting in a worktable with built-in cutting board, cabinets etc.. He also installed a bathroom on the ground (basement) level where the dressing rooms were as well as redoing the main bathroom on the second floor, which had a tub and shower. He elected to put in marble facing in lieu of standard tiles around the tub. One day I was just around and helped with those marble slabs, which were quite heavy. He was astonished that I could so easily lift them. I could not do that now.

The Very First San Francisco Retreat

In September 1971, we decided to have a big retreat. We rented a children's campsite near Santa Cruz Camp Kenolin. In retrospect, this entire experience took on a most surrealistic atmosphere. I shall try to summarize.

We were quite surprised at the response we got to our meager advertising campaign. There were some 400 participants. For some reason someone had decided there would be a great need for prune juice and so cases and cases of this was ordered. MANY cases. That same person also, strangely decided that we need massive amounts of Ak Mak crackers (a very plain & popular cracker at the time) and so cases and cases of this were bought. Needless to say we did not use but 5% of those supplies consequently the San Francisco Institute had a many years supply of these two items. However, one very brilliant person—Jagadamba Hensel figured out the best way to have a dining room set up. She thought it would be very clever, cheap and easy to get a big roll of white butcher paper set long rows of this on the floor tape it down at the ends and these would be the dining tables. It was a stroke of brilliance. We have used that idea for many years.

We spent hours doing things such as advanced yoga cleansing practices such as *Sootra neti* (twisted twine saturated with beeswax) Gurudev demonstrated this, also water Neti, stomach cleansing and I demonstrated (but no one did) the technique of swallowing a cloth for stomach cleansing (*vastra dhauti*).

One of the highlights of that first retreat was the birth of Hari, the first son of Vijay and Shree. Most interestingly, it was on Labor Day, announced by Ramakrishna.

19. First California retreat Camp Kennolyn, 1972.

We also had a wonderful, delightful surprise visit by Yogi Bajan. He came marching into the hall announcing in his booming voice, "I love this man, I LOVE this man." Yogiji stood about 6'6" so next to him even Gurudev looked short.

It was during that retreat that I made a request, through Gurudev secretary, Shanthi Norris, to receive a new name. Shortly thereafter Gurudev came by in his little car telling me my new name would be Arumugam (another Tamil name for Muruga). Gurudev then told me, "This was the name of my son in a previous life." I did not know what that meant so I ask someone and she told me that expression means a life before he became a swami. Indeed, many years later, I did meet that man who was Gurudev's son named Arumugam. He was quite young then and had full black beard and long black hair. He looked exactly like Gurudev did in his youth. I have a photo of him and his own son Murugesh. That young son (Gurudev's grandson) would come to America one day and lived at the ashram for a short while where he and his wife had a beautiful young daughter Shree.

Several other retreats happened at that camp, many, many more happened in a number of other locations. Most outstanding of which was in Santa Barbara at the beautiful, Catholic retreat site—Casa de Maria with its gorgeous chapel. Gurudev spoke there frequently.

Throughout my stay there so many other interesting things happened. As there are too many to remember, I will relate just some highlights.

Many Other Gurus

During that time there were many teachers, gurus, and "gurus" and many events involving gurus, teacher and so on. We had an event that we called "Holy Man Jam" (though it also involves women. Perhaps in these politically correct days we would be proper to call them Holy People Jams.) One of these great events took place in a large auditorium in San Francisco Bay. I can only recall meeting two of those people. One was Daya Mata, she was second in line of succession to Sri Yogaananda of the SRF in Encinitas, California. She was, as our all of the leaders of that organization, very formal, and an attempted amalgam of Western Christian and Indian yoga styles of dress and exposition. I must say I was not too impressed. However, then I met with Lama Govinda. He was an elderly man when we met. I had read his books Foundations of Tibetan Buddhism and Way of the White Cloud. He was an elegant man originally from Germany who well before the Chinese takeover (I think in the 1930s) studied Tibetan

Buddhism, then moved there. Deeply involved in the culture he married a native woman and became completely engrossed in Buddhism. He was a dignified, cultured and deeply peaceful and despite his profound knowledge was a very humble man. I loved his books but was even more impressed by his presence. There was also the Yogi Bajan a very charismatic man, he was a strong presence. Founder of 3HO in Los Angeles, now in Albuquerque. As I mentioned he loved of Sri Gurudev and his people were good friends with us.

There was also Rabbi Shlomo Carlbach whom I heard about decades previously but had not personally met. Subsequently I did meet him in a most joyous way. He founded the group in the Haight district of San Francisco called, the House of Love & Prayer I went there frequently he would greet me with great open arms and love. He had also come to a couple of our retreats in California where he was a welcome and joyful presence. His thing was telling beautiful traditional Hasidic stories accompanied by guitar playing with traditional wordless melodies. He never failed to move us deep in the heart.

So many teachers there just to list a few: Chugyam Trungpa Rimpoche, author of *Cutting through Spiritual Materialism*. Known for long bouts of drinking and a very unorthodox brand of Buddhism. The two fellows that started up the Los Angeles Ctr. eventually became his disciples. There was also Stephen Gaskin a brilliant, charismatic man was started up The Farm in Tennessee. It is now a successful community producing tofu and giving courses in midwifery. There was Sri Ramurthy Mishra he had an ashram in New York State called Ananda where he invited Gurudev to have our first retreats. He was thus a friend of Gurudev. So that when he decided to set up a center in San Francisco, he was allowed to stay at our institute for the time being. As he was also a Sanskrit scholar and gave lessons in Sanskrit there. He did found the Sanskrit learning Center on Army Street near Potrero Park. His Lessons in Sanskrit continue with one of his main disciple's Vyasa Houston. Finally, there was Swami Muktananda a powerful Siddha Yoga teacher. He came highly recommended by Ram Dass. For a short while, he gave lectures at the Institute. As he spoke no English he had to be translated by one of his Indian disciples (Prof. Jain) who spoke his language (Marathi). Muktananda attracted many of our people. This caused quite a kerfuffle at the Institute and Sri Gurudev had to intervene informing Vijay not to invite speakers, however well-known or recommended, without direct approval of the Office of Sri Gurudev (OSG).

He later bought an old hotel in Oakland to locate Siddha Yoga Dham of America (SYDA) which is now a successful organization having their ashram in Fallsburg, New York.

Gurudev Story 8

During the years in San Francisco we had several fundraisers for purchasing of the Northern California Yogaville as well as others for LOTUS. I took part in organizing a couple of these. The main mode of such fund-raising was special dinners at nice restaurants one was at a vegetarian restaurant in Chinatown, which also happened to be named Lotus we had a glorious vegetarian feast many people attended. There was also a very posh Indian restaurant known as Gaylord's which is owned by good friends in Hong Kong, the Harileela family. This was actually just one of the large number of restaurants and other holdings they had worldwide. I was somehow tasked to arrange the thing. We had about 100 people for a grand, spectacular meal. It should be noted that I had no clue as how to properly do any of this and I have no idea why the job fell to me except that perhaps I was foolish enough to volunteer. Now here's the interesting part. After the meal we were getting ready to depart, I was to go to the elevator with Gurudev and a few other members as well as the distinguished family from China and California who were close friends of Gurudev, the Chan family. We all crowded into the elevator. There were far more people than was permitted. I pressed the ground floor level, doors close, NOTHING happens. The car does not move I pressed different buttons, nothing happens. I pressed the alarm button, nothing. I think it is my fault. I am thinking furiously of how to get us out I know we're near the floor level. I think I could climb out of the escape hatch in the ceiling, an absurd and foolish idea. Gurudev is meanwhile very calm. He tells us to make room for the elder Mrs. Chan to sit on the floor, as she is unable to stand for long periods. I say, "The repair man will come. I pressed the alarm button." Gurudev was still calm. He then pressed the ground floor button and the car moves gets to the ground floor we get out. ALL things are possible with the guru. A great lesson

Some Anecdotes in San Francisco

Halloween

One year when it was Halloween, we were all invited to join a party at the Santa Cruz Ctr. We all decided to perform a one-act play of the wizard of Oz. Swami Karunananda was to be Dorothy, there was a chap visiting who became the tin man. He even acquired face makeup to make him silver, one of our women became Toto. There was a wicked witch. Bhaktan Eberle was the cowardly lion. He fashioned an entire costume by hand including a beautiful medal out of aluminum which had COURAGE emblazoned on the front. I was elected to be The Wizard. I went to the local Goodwill where I obtained a black tuxedo jacket, white shirt and black trousers as my costume. Wizards, as you all must know, wear tuxedos. Pretty simple. I had a script and we did quite well. It was great fun.

Siva Ratri

Siva Ratri is one of those important Hindu holidays. It is generally celebrated in February for one full night dedicated to the worship of Lord Shiva. There are generally five pujas inter-spaced throughout the night with stories, a yoga class, and maybe howling at the moon, the latter I believe is one of our own American innovations, not part of the official celebration. That night the celebrations were to be held at the Santa Cruz Institute everybody went down except for two of us, Nirmala Heriza and myself. We just relaxed and took it easy. We were up late and around 10 PM when there was a fierce knocking at the front door. I had no clue who it could have been. I went to check and opened the door. There before me stood a wild looking, very disheveled woman with dirty clothes and face she was ranting madly. Asking to be let in claiming to be chased by some "wild beings". She had so much force behind her I couldn't do anything but let her enter. She seemed to know her way around and soon found her way into the main office on the first floor, locking herself in the office. Not knowing where spare key was I tried to push my hand into the wide mail slot at the center of the door to reach the knob and open it from inside. I was not successful at that. She eventually let herself out. We decided to call the police by which time she found her way to the temple on the top floor ran inside nothing I could do could persuade her to come out. Finally the very nice police officer came. Standard police procedure does not allow for removal of one's shoes for any reason. Now, without being told what our protocol was he did not enter the temple instead he called to the lady. She eventually listened to his gentle prodding and came out. He escorted her away. Two extraordinary conclusions: first I believe she was a proxy of Lord Shiva who was delegated to find her way there, secondly I was absolutely astonished at the sensitivity of the policeman who without being told did not enter the temple with his shoes on. Keep in mind this was in the early 70's and all that yoga business was very new even in San Francisco.

Outside Work Stint

When I first got there, I was tasked with getting an outside job. I got one selling newspapers on street corner kiosks. It was somewhat interesting and challenging. At the end, they gave me a permanent spot on the corner of 16th and Valencia which at that time was quite a dangerous place. I mostly had day shifts but sometimes the hazardous night shift. They gave me one of those cloth aprons for carrying change with pockets for nickels dimes and quarters. I carried a lunch box so that I could stuff the full apron into it and safely make my way back to the Institute. 16th St. in Valencia was within walking distance. I would go as quickly as possible from that dangerous corner until I reached Dolores, two long blocks away. Many interesting characters came by. On the back inside wall at the kiosk, I would hang the picture of Gurudev for protection. One time a police officer came by, looked at the photo pointing he said, "Is that a picture of you?" Gave me a laugh. This job lasted for some six months I finally got a permanent full-time position at the Institute.

A Great Surprise Visit

One day the phone rings, I just happen to be in the office at that Moment so I answer. It "happens" to be my Mom, "I'm here at the bus stop. Come pick me up!". "What do you mean Mom you're at the bus stop?" "What do you think I mean? I'm here in your city at the Greyhound come get me." "Mom! Why couldn't you call me ahead of time, let me know you are coming we would be prepared. You could've flown here we would pick you up at the airport." "Airport, airport. I don't care. I'm here." So naturally, I get to someone to drive downtown where the Greyhound station was. In those days it was not a safe district of San Francisco, Lower Mission. Mom was pretty, tough she could take a 10 day bus ride and still be in good shape. As soon as he came into the house she said, "Where is the kitchen?" "Straight ahead." "Now give me your biggest pot." Biggest pot! "But Mom there only four people here" "Don't worry you will eat it." She gets on a little stepstool (she was very short) and prepared a giant pot of vegetable soup. She knew how to do it. She had never used a cookbook. Just knew how to do it. She commandeered the whole kitchen. We did eat the whole thing. It took us four days that's how she did things many times. I don't know how that was possible.

Over the years much as changed in that area of the city. Most has been gentrified, such as 24th Street. The once dirty Valencia is now replete with upscale restaurants, Dolores Park previously the site of roaming gangs and dogs leaving their marks is now beautiful with a wonderful children's section. Even the once very dangerous 16th Street is cleaned up. Most amazingly, Mission Street home to all the real Mexican restaurants and shops now has a vegan Mexican restaurant. Finally, Mark Zuckerberg owns a three-story house directly across the street. He rebuilt it at a reported cost of just 10 million thereby raising the rent for the entire neighborhood.

I spent the short time living at the Berkeley IYI when it first began. They rented some rooms in a house. The owner was Rifka, a much older (maybe mid-50s) woman, ex-Israeli tank commander, who drove "double dumpster" trucks. She assumed that I knew something about maintenance and had me fix her bathtub. I knew bupkis (Yiddish—nothing) about that. She would frequently invite me to sleep in her bed. I very politely declined.

The First Initiation on the Path to Sannyas

In December of 1972 Sri Gurudev sent a letter to the Institutes announcing that He was going to give pre-sannyas (pre-monastic—this is a kin to a novice in the Catholic tradition) and that those who feel ready should submit their request. The grand ceremony took place February 7, 1973 at Yogaville West, Seigler Springs, Clear Lake CA.

Fourteen of us were given this holy initiation. There are now just three people left out of that original lot. It was quite a day, in the middle of winter, in a remote broken down old hot-springs resort where that initiation took place. As it was the very first initiation of that sort in the history of our organization a great deal excitement was in the air. We were told that they would be a "little bit of orange involved". We are also informed a couple of weeks prior to the initiation that the formal attire for all of us all our clothing would be yellow. Consequently, a good number of very large trash bins was obtained as well as several pounds of dye. Everyone was excited about this. We spent numerous hours dying clothing, tossing out clothing that could not be as dyed. We did get that "little bit of orange". It was a tiny scarf that was put around our necks. Subsequently upon seeing minuteness of those scarves, and how difficult they were to tie properly, Gurudev instructed us, as well as for subsequent initiations, to get much larger cloth for a proper sized scarf. We wore those yellow clothes for almost a year when Gurudev was informed that it was the color the Hare Krishna people wore. He then changed the color scheme to simple white. And, that has been the attire for pre-sannyas ever since.

I recall what Gurudev told us that day, "When you go from here, after you meditate on your mantra, you should write in your spiritual diary all the reasons that you have for taking this initiation. Today the sun is shining. Everything is bright and clean. However, know that clouds will come; there is no doubt about that. That is the nature of the mind. So, when those clouds come, and they will, go back to your diary read the reasons that inspired you to take this sacred initiation." I am somewhat paraphrasing but that is the gist of what he said as I recall it.

20. First pre-sannyas initiation, Yogaville West, February 7, 1973.

21. With mom at pre-sannyas celeb. My mom gave me the robe which I assume she made. It has an Om and yantra sewn on front. How did she know that?? A mystery.

And then...

Sannyas Initiation

One of the greatest adventures of this life.

This happened while we were living in the San Francisco Institute I place it below the first part of this process as it seems appropriate. It was in the spring of 1975 when we received notice of the impending sannyas initiation. This was to take place on Guru Poornima July 23 at the Connecticut Ashram the central headquarters of our organization.

There were quite a number of us going to that Guru Poornima. We flew out to New York and then got in vans and cars to Connecticut.

We spent much time preparing for the ceremony. There was the pre-ceremony talk with Gurudev in one of the large rooms. He gave instructions to each one and questioned each person if he or she was absolutely certain that this is what they intended to do. His main point was that we should never take our eyes off the goal of complete and total realization. "Even if you had your head cut off it should roll and not stop till it gets to that goal." Pretty heavy stuff. We then dyed our clothes orange and got our heads shaved. We were to fast on the day before. The large part of the ceremony itself took place in the secluded "Japanese Tea House." It was there the puja and sacred fire ceremony was done. The fire ceremony is an essential part of sannyas initiation. This represents burning all attachments. The other essential aspect is dipping in a river, not having a river we used the circular pond that was in front of the big house. It was filled with fresh water and we dipped in. This represented washing away all attachments and desires. We then went to separate [men, women] places for putting on the orange cloth that Gurudev gave us. The women were instructed on how to assemble a Sari whereas the men had no specific instructions in how to properly put on that very long cloth. However, we managed to look decent. We assembled all in our beautiful new orange cloths in the Satsang Hall waiting for Sri Gurudev to come in. We're quite a group all full of light and joy.

Gurudev entered and got on the stage. I cannot remember all that he said but one of the things he did was to read from Sri Swami Sivananda's book Necessity for sannyas. He selected the talk given to the new initiates for sannyas. Gurudev said he will try to say it in the voice of Sivananda and he did so, "Today is a glorious day...". I believe one of the last things Gurudev said was (paraphrasing) "now you are my initiates and you are here to serve this is your life." We're next presented the immense crowd assembled on the back lawn. It was quite grand and we all were honored by the beautiful reception.

22. Sannyas initiation, CT Ashram, July 23, 1975.

Adventure on the Road

Finally, the day came when we were to return to San Francisco. As I mentioned we all flew out so the decision was made that we would drive back however long it might take. I think we rented cars. The San Francisco group consisted of, Swamis Karuananda, Bhaktan Eberle, Rama Roosevelt, Galen Chadwick and myself. I was navigator. On the first day, we made a visit to Rama Roosevelt's home, which is really a palace. His father traveled the world hunted all sorts of animals and had these animal trophies all about. That was not so great. We had a beautiful meal and gracious, warm welcome. The driving was done in shifts with the guys doing all of the driving. We did not stop for motels but rested in the car. We did stop for food and occasional meals. Now two interesting things happened. As I mentioned I was navigator as I was handy with maps. In the middle of one night somewhere in the Midwest. Rama Roosevelt was the driver. He made a turn somewhere. It was late night, quite late. However, I had my wits about me and I told him, "Rama you made a wrong turn right there, we are going in the wrong direction." "No we're okay don't worry." "No, I'm telling you you're going wrong just look at the map I have it here." The roads are completely deserted, no gas stations, nothing. Finally he looked at the map and agreed we were going in the wrong way, so he turned around went back to the main road. We lost about an hour and a half on that. The next odd thing that happened was when we were in Colorado. Bhaktan and Rama were experienced skiers. So, Bhaktan said let's pull over and do some no-skis skiing. I stayed in the car; I could barely walk in snow. Galen of course went with them he was Rama's buddy, Bhaktan. Soon they came down and Bhaktan had a bit of an accident. He fell and broke a leg. We went to a nearby clinic or hospital where his leg was x-rayed and they put on a temporary splint. Yes, it was quite an adventure.

We have had many adventures in this life.

Yogaville West

In the spring of 1972 Gurudev asked me to move to first Ashram in California—in Lake County at an old hot springs resort, Seigler Springs. He had in mind that I would do a vegetable garden, which I did. It was fenced in, quite small but it provided many beautiful organic vegetables during that growing season for the ashram plus some extra to sell to neighbors.

Gurudev Story 9

The first crop that I had planned was spinach. I thought it would be nice if Gurudev would start the first seedlings. So I prepared a beautiful clean flat of fresh dark earth. I had a packet of spinach seeds a small watering can. I even had a ruler to make straight rows. Everything was set. I invited Gurudev, He came and on a small table in front of him was the flat with soil, seeds and little watering can etc. Very carefully, he made the rows in the flat in with his hand distributed the seeds perfectly in the flat. Tamped the earth back down on the rows neatly, He picked up the watering can, I thought he was just go to sprinkle the water straight on, but instead he held his other hand out to catch the water so that the water would gently fall in the fresh rows. Then someone rushed out of the hall. He asked, "Where are you going?"

"I'm going to get a towel for you, Gurudev."
"No need for that. You see they are dry."

Indeed his hands were perfectly dry never having to use a towel.

We also had a pair of goats that I milked and got a nice supply of goat milk, but not many takers. There were very few who took to the taste of goat milk.

One of my favorite tasks was ringing the meditation Bell every morning at 4:30 AM. This is a big Bell hung up the steps outside the dining hall. I felt as if I was in a Japanese monastery where they have a giant gong (Bonsho) that they bring with a big log

To make an income for the ashram, since we could not have regular programs, retreats etc., we set up a little "food" industry. We obtained bulk olives, drums of olive oil, repackaged them with our own label, and sold that in San Francisco. We also made a strange nut butter combining cashews and carob that was called "cashew carobola". It was absurd. The whole thing was absurd. Oh yes, Ramanan Schultz had a bagel recipe. The nearby town, Angwin, had a large Seventh-day Adventist community. They also had a beautiful grocery store with a very modern bakery we are able to rent the one morning a week (very early in the morning) to make the bagels. We really didn't know what we were doing. We would get up at 2 AM drive 45 minutes to the bakery. We'd put flour and ingredients into a big mixer. Then boil water in a big kettle to boil the bagels, etc. it was a massive amount of labor. The only way a profit was made because the labor was completely free. There was no automation about any of it.

A funny story about that food business. There was a very energetic fellow, Steve Bacon, who did all the deliveries from the ashram to San Francisco. At one time Gurudev was going to give a talk somewhere so a bunch of us went down, a group of us stayed with Ramanan in his little apartment. Steve thought that it wouldn't be safe to leave all the products on the small, unlocked truck so he proceeded to haul everything off the truck and put it under the stairway of Ramanan's apartment building. Next morning while most of us were still in our sleeping bags on the floor Steve came in, he had this very peculiar laugh something like a horse whinnying, he announced to all, "Well, guess what? All the food has been stolen." He laughed a lot. Not much of a joke as that must've been worth several thousand dollars and was our income for the month. But that's how we did things.

There is a very special story about Ramanan. He came to the Berkeley center at the very beginning. However, we had actually met back in 1966. However, I did not find out about that until years later when just two years back we compared notes on our ancient history. It turns out we both were members of the League for Spiritual Discovery on Hudson St in NYC. This was the group founded by Tim Leary, Nina Graboi, & Richard (Ram Dass)

Alpert, with Ralph Metzner as a strong supporter. Richard Alpert & Nina Graboi were especially significant for me personally. Alpert because of his deep, clear communication that came from the heart & Nina for her open and loving heart. Ramanan, then known as Ralph Schultz, was a skinny jittery young chap. I took an immediate liking to him. I clearly recall when he gave me a beautiful photo of Ramana Maharshi and informed me of a meditation/study group they had. I wrote all of this down in my little diary. Such a beautiful experience, enhanced greatly by this recent discovery.

Gurudev Story 10

Dress Up Dress Down

Our little food business made frequent runs to San Francisco and I found various excuses to go there. There was one weekend during a winter storm when Gurudev was invited to speak in San Francisco. I hooked up to go. Now as an inventive character, I thought of something "clever" to keep my trousers dry during the heavy rains. At least I thought it was clever. I had some ankle high boots that would not serve well in the rain. I thought to make some "gaiters". I took sleeves of an old torn up raincoat and fashioned them fit around the ankles to the shins and tie them off with some shoelaces. I thought, "Now this is clever. Gurudev would love this." I wore them with my jeans and work shirt then went on the truck to San Francisco straight to the Institute at the very Moment that Gurudev was walking up the stairway to his room after giving a talk there. Upon seeing me come through the door He said, "Where you coming from?" "The ashram, Gurudev." Looking at me up and down very obviously He said, "Hmm, now that's yoga. Just the way to be." Saying it in the most ironic way possible. I don't know if anyone understood what he was referring to but I did (that my "clever" improvised dress was not very yogic, it was very unkempt.). I was crushed. However, I learned my lesson and that night I threw those gators away. I also threw away the jeans and boots.

Gurudev Story 11

No Job is Below Him

No job is below the level of a Master.

At Yogaville West in the summer of 1973. Gurudev summoned the "guys" to do some heavy work at His house. We all assembled there. Krishnaprem was the man on the job. He was an ex college football player, 6'3" and all the physical attributes that comes with that sport. Gurudev wanted us to remove a big air pump that was used to fill tires, it was bolted to the wall of the garage. It did not look like such a difficult job. Krishna had all the tools assembled but try as he might he could not budge those ancient bolts. Everyone had a different suggestion.

> "Try WD40."
> "No, no use Liquid Wrench, much better."
> "Does anyone have bolt cutters?"
> "Let's all get on it together. That should loosen it."
> "Try two wrenches."

And on and on.

Then Gurudev came out.

> "Hmm, so what have you been doing? Still not moved the thing, huh. All of you together can't do this little job. OK, give me the wrench"

Krishnaprem gave Gurudev this humongous wrench with a 3-foot handle; it must have weighed 20 pounds. He takes it attaches it to the front bolt, presses His foot up to the wall, leans into the thing and without even using all His force, bingo the bolt turns and comes right off.

> "So, I still have to do everything around here, hmm?"

He really was able to do it all and did.

More on Yogaville West

The character of Yogaville West was unique. Technically, it was the very first ashram established in early June 1972. It was a very broken down old hot springs resort. To be frank both ashrams we had in California were broken down ramshackle that I would not recommend anyone moving into, much less establishing a community. The main hotel building had the second floor completely collapsed. However, the hot springs were quite delightful especially in winter. There were several private rooms wherein you could change clothes and step down into a marvelous pool sunk into the floor.

There was also an Olympic size indoor pool, as well as an outdoor pool. If you went to the source of this hot spring, you would find some exceedingly hot water. In fact, one of the major energy companies came to test it for a potential geothermal energy source.

There was a building with a stage where we established the satsang hall in which Gurudev would give talks. Within that building was a well-established community of bats. So we had bats coming to satsang.

There must've been 40 to 50 people living there at first. However, it was no problem with housing. There were several nice cabins for families and children. Individuals could be housed in the many nice individual rooms; all with bathrooms and enough space for a bed and to do yoga.

The problem came during winter. It just so happened that the first year was the coldest winter on record with a major snowfall. It also happened that the sewer system collapsed and failed. It was not meant for winter use at all. So we had to have out-houses. One clever fellow figured out how to get heat for everybody. He collected a large number of 20 gallon used oil drums that were very well cleaned out. He obtained a few truckloads of bricks to set the drums on. Cut out the space for a little door and cut out a space for a chimney, hinged the door and set in the chimney, made a hole in the roof for chimney. It was a great deal of labor. One fine strong fellow would cut wood. He cut a lot of wood. The joke was that for people to get warm they could also walk in to the walk-in refrigerator, which was quite big. In the dining room we created a clever device using two 50 gallon oil drums set horizontally on braces put one on top of the other. With two chimneys going from one to the other and the main chimney going out of the top one through the roof. The idea was to make the fire in the bottom drum and that would heat up the top drum. This warmed the entire dining room nicely.

One of the duties I love was to ring the morning meditation gong. This was a large gong that was hung from the side porch of the dining room. I just loved doing that. I would therefor get up extra early to discharge my duty.

Funny true little story, during that winter the person in charge of cooking was instructed by Gurudev to make very simple meals. He also made a comment to have no more than five items at a meal. Often times she would serve salad. This was in the middle of the coldest winter we ever had and our very able-bodied young woodcutter said in the kindest manner, "I can't work on that." He meant it. He couldn't sustain the energy to cut all that wood on just salad. It also happened that the cook counted tamari as one of the five things in the meal. It was absurd. There were a lot of even more absurd things at that place.

As I mentioned the main "hotel" building was mostly broken down. The second floor was not habitable but it was there that we had an old TV. We watched only one show, but all of us watched it together. It was really a very spiritually minded show—Kung Fu with David Carradine. It was quite enjoyable.

Teaching Yoga to Nuns

Gurudev was a very dear friend of Brother David, a Benedictine monk. A man of high spiritual attainment. He established a retreat house for nuns in Gloucester Mass. One winter I was selected to go teach yoga there. That was very early in my yogic experience, before even becoming a pre-sannyas. It was a beautiful place, a small house right by the ocean. Attached to a large Jesuit retreat house. There were some five or six nuns. Sister Isabel Green, who had a strong commanding presence, was in charge. I'd never been in such a place, I had no idea what this was really all about. They had a priest, Father Bill. He was the most genial farsighted man of the cloth I have ever met. He did not dress in the priestly garb. His main function was conducting the mass every day. However, what he did was so unique and different from the standard model. He would pass around the bread and wine (grape juice) and everybody would offer the host etc. to everyone else. Very unique. It was a wonderful experience. I taught a yoga class every morning they all stood up when I entered the room out of respect even though all of them were quite a bit older than I. There was one young sister, Sister Joan, with whom I made special connection. She was a very delicate soul. Member of the fourth order of Franciscans. We became close friends one day she presented me with a little statue of St. Francis which I still have. They prepared vegetarian meals daily. I had really teeny alcove, with a curtain, for my bedroom. It was just big enough for my little body. We made number of trips to different retreat centers. They were large beautifully built, mostly Jesuit retreat places that looked like old mansions of New England. I observed the Jesuits had tremendous wealth in real estate.

The place I remember most was in Vermont it was called Weston Abbey. Here the monks lived in the woods. For an income they recorded music. Their chapel was a large circular structure, hand constructed of wood. They entered while still in work clothes, then pulled out their cassocks and guitars and did the entire service singing. It was delightful. I learned a great deal about Catholic practices and history while serving there.

Gurudev Story 12

Departure of Vijay & Shree

At one point Vijay and Shree, after so many years of service, decided that they had to go and lead their own lives separate from the ashram. They also had small child to support. This was in the early spring. We all gathered in the Satsang Hall with Gurudev sitting on a couch. We all were paying tribute to this wonderful, beautiful, loving couple. No one could fully express how they felt. Gurudev then invited Vijay to sit on the couch next to Him. At first, he hesitated to do such a thing but Gurudev insisted that he sit with Him. Reluctantly and very humbly Vijay sat on the couch. I'd never seen such a thing where Gurudev would invite anyone to sit with Him. You could see the love and pride Gurudev had for this man.

I must speak more about Vijay. If we were not for the wonderful, thoughtful work that he did in establishing the San Francisco IYI many of the swamis and us old-timers that you see now would not be here. You would not have swamis Hamsananda, Divyananda, Karuananda, and Priyaananda plus the old-timers such as Paraman, Jeevakan and his wife Priya etc. There would not be the beautiful San Francisco Ctr. where thousands of people would have been taking classes, hundreds taking teacher training and so on. Vijay Hassin is a pillar of our community to be held in great esteem.

Meeting an Exceptional Man Who Became a Good Friend

One day a young couple came with a few friends. You could assume that they were special guests as they were all dressed in business attire. The center of it all was a young newlywed couple Mohan & Camilla Harileela. Mohan was from an illustrious, large and successful business family from Hong Kong and close friends of Gurudev. Mohan was the youngest of six brothers all successful, wealthy businessmen. Mohan was a most beautiful, gentle, spiritual man. We traveled once to India together and he became a close friend. He passed on several years ago at a young age.

Selling & Closing Down the Ashram

Eventually we realized that we could not sustain this place. The death knell was that we had to update the sewage system that would cost several hundred thousand dollars. We could not afford that. Therefore, we put the place up for sale and it was purchased by the group that was run by a man known then as, Bubba Free John. He had many other names since. He was once a disciple of Swami Muktananda. Therefore, we shut down the business, sold the equipment, sent the printing press to Connecticut, and most of the folks moved out. At the end there were are about eight or nine people left. It was midwinter and most amazing thing happened Gurudev told us we should all move into his house instead of living in separate bungalows. It would save a lot of energy. We all moved in there I had a nice room in the basement with lots of space to do yoga. I was appointed cook. I made many nice meals. Swami Karunananda did a thorough job of cleaning the kitchen and moving all of Gurudev's things into a safe place. It was delightful being there. We had beautiful little satsangs where I told stories. That was my thing, telling stories. We eventually all moved to our separate places, some to San Francisco, some to Connecticut, while others just went off on their own.

This was yet another learning experience.

I believe that all of those previous ashrams that did not work out had a lesson for us. The two in California were absurd, broken down old places. The one in Connecticut was freezing cold, furthermore one could not really build on it due to zoning laws of that township. It was far too small for any actual expansion. My theory is that all of these places served as training grounds for us to learn how to live together in a community.

Santa Barbara Ashram

In the spring of 1974 we acquired our second California ashram in Santa Barbara on San Marcos Pass Road. It was a broken down old avocado and lemon farm. What did we know about growing and selling avocados and lemons? ABSOLUTELY NOTHING. Nevertheless, like all young people we were enthusiastic and we thought we could do anything. We did have good intentions.

As stated previously this is another broken down place. It had a two-bedroom house designed for one couple. In there we put two more bedrooms. It had a modest kitchen and living room. The men lived in the old barn. We slept on the hard wood floor in the loft. It had one huge coat rack, plus one little cabinet per man for other clothing etc.. We had to use the bathroom in the great outdoors.. I fixed the barn first floor obtaining free sample "books" of carpet squares. I made a nice pattern on the floor. There we put an altar for meditation. Someone constructed a beautiful chair for Gurudev to have satsang right there.

Not long after we all moved in one of our members, Gurudas Haro, arrived and volunteered to take our avocados and lemons to the city and sell them to groceries and restaurants. Thus was begun our first industry. Prana Produce. Later on when I was successful in growing an abundance of celery that was added to the produce.

We were also honored with the visits of a couple of distinguished visitors. Carol King came for one afternoon while Sri Gurudev was there. She was a very plain spoken, home-girl. We will not forget how she got her jeep stuck in our deep, tough mud and how Jai Heard used the winch to free it. We also had the interesting visit of Sivaya Subramuniya Swamigal, who instructed us thrice, "Obey the Guru, obey the Guru, and obey the Guru." That is the only thing I remember about that

The same fellow who acquired this rundown place also got us to purchase a business in the nearby town of Isle Vista close to the campus of the University of Santa Barbara. This was a tiny falafel stand for which we paid a fortune and a much greater fortune for the recipe. What did we know about the restaurant businesses? Nothing. We ran a little contest for naming the place and Suhbadra Jyothi gave it the name, "Friendly Falafel." We all thought that was a fantastic name. I worked there for a while. We made all kinds of unique combinations of falafel with various extras. It was fun doing that. Galen and I would get equipment and supplies. One time we went to Los Angeles to get our beans from this Egyptian fellow in LA. As we were loading the truck he offered us some coffee. "Sure, I love coffee." Little did I know he was brewing up some Middle Eastern, Turkish style coffee, which is the equivalent of taking five espressos at once. The effect, to say the least, was unexpected and intense. I was running for 26 hours. One other funny incident. I was closing up one night when I noticed that one of the outside lights was not working so I thought I would unscrew it and put a new bulb. As I had no ladder I thought I could step on the wooden lid for the barrel of spent cooking oil not knowing it was just a thin piece of wood, which broke. I plunged my leg into that barrel of cooking oil covering the entire trouser leg with rancid smelly old oil. Had to endure that smell for one hour until we get back home. Some lessons are quickly learned. Falafel stand also provided lessons in service, constant lessons in service whatever it was. Also lessons in surrender—a core teaching of my early days.

Over the years we had several health food stores, restaurants, and cafés. There was a store in Santa Cruz San Francisco, the Northern California ashram, New York Ctr. and we now have one in Charlottesville Virginia. We had cafés in the New York IYI, and one at our store in Virginia those also failed. Our store Virginia is doing well. For many years the New York food store and annex vitamin store were very successful until we were beaten out by Trader Joe's and Whole Foods. We finally had to close the New York store, a sad occasion for many. Lessons have been learned and we no longer try to open any restaurants except for a lovely pair of cafés in the Virginia ashram that serve the community and visitors quite well.

What a Motley crew we were back then. How naïve. We had many lessons to learn.

One of the principal things I intended to do there was to install a small vegetable garden. To accomplish this we tore out a grove of dead lemon trees, about 2 acres. We then harrowed and disked the whole area and made contoured double dug beds. I did a lot of rototilling, spread tons of old horse manure compost. I was making compost piles constantly. Then purchased 200 tomato and celery plants for a couple of dollars from a commercial greenhouse which grew plants for the big farms. These plants became too big for the automated machinery to plant so they practically gave them away. We did pretty well with that. We had massive quantities of tomatoes and celery. Enough to sell to restaurants. We grew all kinds of vegetables string beans, corn, squash, beets, spinach, cabbage, etc. It was great fun and a tremendous amount of hard work.

23. Santa Barbara farm. Bountiful tomato field.

The idea came that we would be able to construct LOTUS on this property. How this came to anyone's mind is a great mystery. Long story short we had an architect build a model. As the property was a mere 25 or so acres we selected a small spot where we thought it could go. However, after numerous presentations to the county supervisor's board our proposal was rejected. Thus ended our modest proposal. It would not have worked anyway as the property was so small. In any case the place burned down a decade or so after we sold it. So as the saying goes, "It's all for good."

One of the most important services I ever did was in Santa Barbara working as a nursing assistant. I did this in nursing homes for over a year. It was the most arduous, demanding service I've ever done. Taking care of the daily needs of dying people, elderly men and women with serious strokes was very challenging BUT gave much in the way of great lessons. Washing, feeding, dressing, changing linen, getting food thrown at you by a crazy patient, getting punched, cleaning up after their "accident" in bed, trying to wake up a dead man (This actually happened)—all of this and one must always remember to treat each one with dignity. For although now they are disabled and may not even be able to talk, they all had lives. One was a schoolmaster another was a police chief. Here I learned about the real meaning of service, what it is to die, to be grateful for what we have and to know that all of this is just temporary. I think that every aspirant on the path should do an extended stint of service with the dying or very old people. You will learn a lot.

Gurudev Story 13

Shortly after we acquired the property for the Santa Barbara ashram, a house was purchased for Sri Gurudev. This was located in Montecito, a beautiful enclave of Santa Barbara. Owing to my interest in gardening, I took on the post of gardener for Sri Gurudev's home. Every week we would have karma yoga day there.

Plant In, Plant Out

One bight sunny day Gurudev comes out carrying a beautiful houseplant. It was a "String of Pearls". He wanted me to report the thing. String of Pearls is a very delicate plant. It has very long hair-like stems on which sit many small pearl-like leaves, hence its name.

> "Hmm, Can you please report this plant?"
> "Wow", was my first thought, "He is actually entrusting me with one of His own personal plants—yikes!"
> "Of course Gurudev, do you have a larger pot and some fresh potting soil?"

He then actually RAN into the house and came out with a new pot and a bag of soil [that took my breath away]. I took the whole thing to a quiet corner of the garden sat down and began this project. I went about this very methodically trying to not break any of the stems or lose any of the leaves. I got the thing reported with minimal damage but all the stems were twisted around and the whole thing looked like a horticultural set of dreadlocks. This had to be perfect; it was not. Try as I might I could not get these Medusa's hairdo to unravel and look symmetrical. I thought that if I pushed further I would surely damage the thing and that would be worse. Therefore, with bowed head I came back to Gurudev and gave Him the plant.

> "This is the best that I could do Sir."

Meanwhile the whole crew was there surrounding us.

He just took the pot, held it in the palm of His hand and went about rearranging the affair. While doing it I was sure I could detect Him saying some mantra but I could never make it out. The only thing I heard for sure was this, "Too many entanglements."

The plant was perfectly symmetrical and nothing broke.

Gurudev Story 14

The Right Tool for the Job

Another time He asked me to move a giant agave plant to corner of the front lawn. This was a succulent plant with some 25 broad spiked leaves each about 6' high. OK, this did not look like such a difficult task. I took a spade and very, carefully began to dig around the plant's perimeter. I had many lessons about being conscious and how to treat all things with loving care and not hurt it.

Progress was slow. However, I was not breaking a single root hair.

Then Gurudev, wearing a tee shirt and dhoti, came out and saw what I was doing. Hitching up his dhoti, He asked me, "What are you doing?"

    "Digging up the plant to move it, sir."
    "What are you doing? Are you tickling it? Hmm."

He then goes to the tool shed, which by the way, was always in perfect order every tool hanging in a designated place - all of them clean and polished. He came out with a six foot, massive, heavy wreaking bar (also called a 'persuader'); which is a tool one uses to pry up boulders or bust houses.

    "Now move out of the way, please."

He then jams the pointed end of this thing into the ground right near the plant, bears down on it with all His weight, pushes His foot into it and with two or three more such maneuvers uproots the whole plant.

    "There now you can replant it."

Learned another lesson that day. There were many Moments of learning like that.

Gurudev Story 15

Surprise, Surprise, Surprise

[Hamsananda's favorite story.]

As mentioned above I had studied and was licensed in Polarity Massage Therapy. Therefore, among the many other things I was doing then I also had a little business doing massage in town. This was just another way to earn more money for the ashram. One day I had scheduled giving a massage. On that particular day I was feeling somewhat down. So, what is one of the standard actions we take when feeling that way? Get something to eat—of course. Food being one of God's and man's great mood elevators. Therefore, when I am in that state of mind I want to go stuff my face AND I want to do it alone. You know how when you do something totally self-indulgent you do not want any witnesses around. I am sure many of you can relate to this feeling.

It was mid-day, well past lunch hour. I very carefully selected a small out-of-the-way, family Italian restaurant. It was dark inside. Not a soul to be seen. Perfect! I selected a little booth on the far side. Alone. More perfect! I just wanted a small personal size pizza—something easy. Pizza came and I ate it with relish. Wonderful. I could not finish the whole thing so I asked the server if she would kindly pack it to go and please bring the check. She comes back with the box.

> "Excuse me Miss but where is the check?"
> "Oh, it's on the house."
> "On the house???!" Well OK.

Never one to argue with such serendipitous events I proceed in to put on my coat when all of a sudden I feel someone come up from behind and wrap his arms around encircling my arms. I am pinned.

I think, "Who could this be? Ahh, must be Jeevakan only he could be pulling such a stunt."

Slowly I turn around—there standing way, way above me laughing out loud is Gurudev. All I could say is, "Oh MY GOD! My goodness!!" That is all I could say. Said it three times too. He was just laughing so much. Shanti, His secretary at the time, is also with Him and she was just smiling out loud.

He says, "All taken care of, tip and everything."

As we are leaving the place, I am still dumbfounded, He asks, "What are you doing in town today?"

> "Well, sir I came to give some folks a massage."
> "So when am I going to get a massage?"
> "Oh, anytime you want sir, just tell me when you would like it."
> "Give her (His secretary) a call, she will tell you."

I did call her in a couple of days to schedule an appointment.

It was a double surprise.

The Guru takes care of you in SO many ways. So many ways.

Los Angeles

The Los Angeles institutes had a most unusual history. Firstly, it had three successive locations. Beginning with a stately mansion in the Hollywood Hills, complete with swimming pool. The founders of this Institute were two fellows who came from the New York Ctr. they were fond of such extravagance. That was short lived. We then have center on Melrose Place, which is more of a business district. That also did not last very long. Finally, we had a nice house in North Hollywood on N. Alta Vista Ave. It was not far from Sunset Boulevard close to Hollywood high. The street itself was nice but it was also not far from the lowlife and rather seedy section of Hollywood & Sunset. Not a safe place to walk at night.

I spent a bit of time there conducting a program in natural healing. It even was written up in a small local newspaper from the posh Bel-Air section near Beverly Hills.

As I never actually lived there for an extended period I will just mention a few very interesting points and a couple of anecdotes. It is worth noting that our house was very close to Yogi Bhajan's 3HO center. Yogiji told his disciples to protect Swamiji's children. He loved Gurudev tremendously. Their group was quite efficient, being very well organized. They had a fantastic restaurant, the Golden Temple, as well as many businesses related to healing such as chiropractic.

Being in Hollywood of course Gurudev attracted a number of movie stars among them were Sally Kirkland who used to come by on a regular basis. It was the beginning of her career. The obscure and remarkable guitarist John Fahey also came by frequently as he was enamored with one of our teachers who was at that time a pre-sannyas. They had a very brief marriage. He also engaged me for several Polarity sessions. He was a very strange fellow. But the most remarkable person I met there was Turiyasangitananda (Alice Coltrane wife of the renowned jazz musician John Coltrane). She was a remarkable and very advanced soul who later opened a yoga, Vedanta center in San Francisco for the African-American population. She did great service for the people there. Later on, she opened a small ashram in Alta Vista north of Los Angeles. I had the wonderful opportunity to spend couple of hours with her at our ashram in Virginia.

24. Greeting Sri Swami Chidanandaji at LAX.

A Few Anecdotes About Los Angeles

Sri Gurudev was scheduled to give a talk at a woman's spiritual group (I believe the name of the group was Astarta). This was going to be done at a small community center. Anyway, they asked me to do a yoga demonstration as a warm-up for the group. More likely it was just to fill the time gap for Gurudev to get there. All this happened at the last minute. Typical for those days of organized chaos. However, I had not eaten lunch yet thus I was starving. Therefore, I quickly gobbled down three of the sandwiches they had made for the group lunch. Twenty minutes later, I was transported to the center where they had a small stage with a long folding table on top for me to do the demonstration. I guess they wanted to get me an elevation where everyone could see. Doing extreme yoga right after eating is not recommended nor is doing all that on top of a long rickety folding table. However, I was young and fearless and got through it. Gurudev gave a fine talk afterwards.

Visit of Sri Swami Chidanandaji Maharajah

One of the great disciples of Sri Swami Sivananda Maharajah and brother monk of Gurudev was Sri Swami Chidananda Maharajah, successor to Sri Swami Sivanandaji and president of the Divine Life Society. He was a most humble and perceptive man. One time when He was to give a talk in Los Angeles we all met Him at the airport. When His luggage arrived I went to grab one piece He had but he got to it ahead of me at which point He said, "Too late." I had hesitated just a wee bit, lesson learned. During his stay, we served His meals and tea in his room. At the end of his stay He returned the teapot and cup to swami Divyananda, and very graciously said, "Returned with thanks." I was stunned at such humble graciousness. That was one of the most beautiful lessons of my life. Chidhanandaji attained Mahasamadhi August 28, 2008.

Star Wars & Beyond

One of Sri Gurudev's close friends was Sant Keshavadas, a noted bhakti from Bangalore, South India. He was visiting one weekend during the time that first Star Wars opened. I had seen that movie twice before. The Institute heads decided to buy tickets and invite him. Naturally they picked one of the giant theaters in Hollywood. I happen to be riding with him. He had known me from many previous visits. We parked directly across from the theater. Just before we crossed the street (in the middle of the block) the grabbed my hand and said, "Let's go Murugananda. This is the story about Hanuman (reference to Chewbacca, which told me that he had already seen the movie). Isn't that wonderful?" And we ran across the street to the theater. He had a blast.

Connecticut Ashram

On July 23, 1975 at the ashram in Connecticut, located in Putnam, 28 people took the grand holy initiation of sannyas and received new names and the robes of a swami. It was the most sublime and grand event we ever had. There will be no other like it I received the robes of a monk (orange represents the fire of renunciation) and a new name—Murugananda—Bliss of Muruga—In Tamil Muruga means "eternal youth" Of the original 28 there are now only seven left. Over the years many have come and a great many have gone from sannyas. It's not an easy path. As I often have said—"The easy path is hard enough." [See chapter on Sannyas Initiation].

After we sold our Santa Barbara ashram I was temporarily situated in the San Francisco Institute. Activities there were dwindling so I was transferred to Yogaville East, the Connecticut Ashram. This was the permanent residence of Sri Gurudev and the "Command Center" known as, The Office of Sri Gurudev (OSG) of our organization. All organizational decisions and policy were made there. It was also from there that the first teacher training manual was produced that became the standard for all of our teaching centers. One of the most important events that originated at this ashram was the Yoga Ecumenical Service (YES). This was the original ecumenical service that we now hold every Thanksgiving and Guru Poornima holidays. Here to we are introduced to several persons who were become very close to Gurudev they were, Rabbi Gelberman, Brother David Steindlerast (Benedictine monk of great vision) and Rev. Geshen she was head of a Zen Buddhist order.

The property was originally built as a summer estate for a wealthy cotton thread family. It was on 55 acres in a very posh county of Northeastern Connecticut. The main structure was designed like a British castle. It was a stone structure with marble fireplaces, hardwood flooring etc. There was even a concrete pond in front of the edifice. It was in that pond that the water portion of our sannyas initiation took place. It had a library in the lobby with French doors. In the lobby was a massive oak desk behind which was another marble fireplace. Add to that the sweeping stairway going to the upper floors. It had everything, except good heating. We had two (male & female) large dormitory floors with bunk beds. Some creative individual thought of hanging big sheets to partition the rooms to create "private areas". So much for having "everything". There was large kitchen, a pantry and beautiful dining room with another fireplace. Well, you get the idea. The satsang Hall was large and quite beautiful with an elegant stage. Gurudev gave satsang there every week. The place also had an elegant

Japanese garden in a wooded area with a stream, and a Japanese style tea house etc. in another enclosed area, brick walled, was our vegetable garden.

However, this place was not meant for winter use therefore the mansion got terribly cold. Our solution was to install a massive wood-burning furnace in the basement this was fed with 4 foot logs of word. There was a crew of guys able to shove those logs into the furnace. We had a schoolroom in the former carriage house. There was also a room for the book distribution business. This was run by Swami Priyaananda, then known as Sister Maji. Working there was one of the jobs I had. I obtained a membership to the American Booksellers Association (ABA) and a copy of their massive guidebook of all small and large booksellers in the country. This served as the list of potential buyers for our books. Also did a stint at the reception desk, which was a great honor for me as Mataji was personally assigned by Sri Gurudev to be head receptionist. Our revered Mataji, Swami Gurucharanananda, is our elder swami. She has been with Gurudev for some 50 years now. Previously she was a Catholic nun in Kansas. She is very wise and revered by all.

We had several other businesses then. There was the truly creative Jyothi candle business where they made cut candles. The problem was we had to go out to small country fairs to sell them. Occasionally we would sell to some gift shop but it was not an easy thing. Each candle took many hours to create. Without the all-volunteer help it would never have made a profit. There was also the Babba Burger business, homemade veggie burgers. We even had an automated machine to shape and package them. Once again it was run by all-volunteer help. However, the food business is a very competitive and difficult one consequently it did not make a profit.

We also had an old printing press that served in the official publications center. Initially it was run by Chaitanya Dubidsky who knew all about running it because his father had a printing company. He was a very beautiful man and I don't know what happened to him but I was told that he passed away. We printed all of our magazines and booklets.

Finally we had had a natural healing clinic with three doctors in the town of Putnam where I worked for a short while.

The town of Putnam was quite small they had one little pizza shop and a Greek restaurant. So going out to eat did not offer too many quality options. Some people went to a nearby homemade ice-cream place, Maygold's.

However, we did manage to have some beautiful yoga retreats there which provided an income. The county of Putnam was very upscale so the zoning regulations did not allow us to build the LOTUS Temple. We did, however, have a neighbor who had a beautiful piece of property with a pond and waterfalls. This was a brilliant artist whom Gurudev named Tyagaraja. He was later to become our beloved late Swami Tyagananda. His property was in a separate county. We thought we could build something there. A bit of land was cleared for this. But as you know the climate there was not very conducive to long-term living nor did we have the right size property for what was Sri Gurudev's greater vision. Consequently, plans were made to find the new property, which eventually came to fruition in central Virginia. This is discussed in a later chapter.

25. CT Ashram "Is this beard real?

26. VA Ashram beard pull B [I see a trend].

27. "Ah, "Freedom"—Tyagananda's home in CT, 1980. Frequent fun place. 28. Tyagananda's lake near CT Ashram, 1978.

New York Integral Yoga Institute

[This was an intermediate point in my service before arriving in Virginia.]

I was assigned to New York Integral Yoga Institute in the spring of 1981. This was an extremely busy center. Straight away they gave me the number of classes and put in charge of the reception area. Many things happened there, so this is a scant summary.

This is our center at 227 W. 13th St. in the West village of New York City. It is a five-story building. The first floor had a reception area and very large classroom with other floors having an office, more classrooms, resident bedrooms and kitchen. On one side was a very narrow minimalist health food store. At the very top is a small apartment that we rented to Jim Rado the writer of the musical Hair. He was a very private man. Below that was Sri Gurudev's apartment. This is actually the second center in New York. It was purchased a few years after the West End Ave. apartment was rented. A good portion of the down payment was provided by the generous donation of Alice Coltrane (Swami Turyasangitananda). After a short while, we gave up the West End Ave. apartment that was briefly taken over by one of our members to teach yoga.

This is the most active center we have. Aside from many yoga classes for every sort of body from children to elderly from athletic to limited mobility we have many programs. In addition we had a small food store which was located in what is currently the reception/bookstore. In that tiny space we served hundreds of people. I don't know how we did it. There were perhaps 15 to 18 people living there however, I should like to make special mention of my very dear friend Brother Siva. We had very profound connection and communication. He is passed on a number of years ago I never found out the circumstances of his passing.

The first thing I noted was that the reception area had a very sparse book selling section. I thought I could make it into a proper yoga gift-shop. I got someone to build a strong clothing rack. Then, got a business card printed to give legitimacy. That allowed entry to the massive gift shop representatives' building as well as the wholesalers of yoga clothing etc. With my usual obsessive approach I went to the Indian clothing area, introduced myself showed the manager the card and it got immediate credit for hundreds of dollars' worth of Indian clothing. This proved to be quite successful. I contacted wholesale distributors for New Age music tapes and somehow found amazing deals on very fine alabaster and resin sculpture meant for

Catholic Church gift-shops. Some of those sculptures could sell for $3–$400 but got them for $5 each, as they were the end of the stock.

29. Our gang IYINY, CA 1982.

A Couple of Anecdotes

Driving to Virginia

Despite it being so busy we had occasion to go down to Virginia on selected weekends. That was always a massive undertaking; particularly piling luggage on top of our van. One of our esteemed members always put her belongings in giant black trash bags, which Siva somehow secured at the top along with everything else. There was always somebody who had to give directions as no driver ever bothered memorizing how to get there. One time one of the very young members, Bala Otto, who was just 13 or 14 and an accomplished Bharatanatyam dancer gave directions. Because she was so young, no one believed her. Of course, she was 100% correct.

"Ready for My Close-Up."

I was sitting at the reception desk one afternoon when a fellow comes in and asks me, "Can you do that pose where you put your legs behind your head?" "Yes." I reply. "Well, we'd like to do an advert with you doing that. We'll pay you $400." "Sure, why not." We then set up a date. It happened the studio was within walking distance of the Institute somewhere on E. 10th St. I walked there. It was a large studio. They then gave me a suit white shirt and tie and polished shoes. Thus attired the photographer said, "Why don't you just go ahead and do some things." After a while he said, "Now do the pose with the legs behind the head." I did the Omkarasana and they took the final photos. They gave me some copies. They gave me a check for $400, which I handed to the Institute. Six months later on the way to the ashram in our van Swami Hamsananda, who had a subscription to Sports Illustrated noted on the inside front page an ad for Metropolitan Life with a photo of some fellow doing that pose. She said, "Look at this." I did so and said, "Hey, that's me. They replaced my face with some model. But I did that a while back." So there you go I had my 15 seconds of fame in Sports Illustrated that no one will ever know. Such is life.

Dad Passes Away

Sometime in June 1982 my mother called to tell me that Dad had a stroke. I knew exactly what that meant as I had worked in nursing homes taking care of many men who had that. So I arranged with her to get a taxi to the nursing home where he was staying. I could tell immediately that it was not good he had total paralysis on the left side and total aphasia. He could not speak at all. It looked like a good nursing home so I was happy about that.

It was July 4, 1982 the holy Festival of Guru Poornima. We were doing chanting when I suddenly had a coughing fit. I had to leave so I went upstairs to the kitchen to get a glass of water. At that exact Moment the phone on the wall rang, as there was no one else around I picked it up. Amazingly it was Mom, she informed me that had just died. On Guru Poornima one month after his stroke. I thought this is auspicious he died on a most Holy day and doesn't have to spend years and years suffering from the stroke. I feel this was all due to his good works, kindness and wisdom. This was a deeply felt loss. Mom insisted that if I come to the funeral and must be dressed in a regular suit tie etc. At that time I was extremely diligent about following dress of the swami in no way was I to change that. I then called Gurudev about what I should do and he asked me what is it that has died?

Just the body. That's all there is. Consequently, I did not go. I very deeply regret that decision to this day.

Now here is the amazing follow-up to the above. About a month later Mom comes in to the reception area. I am sitting there on duty and Mom asked me very politely, "May I stay here for a while?" So, I say, "Why would you want to stay here?" "It's so peaceful I love that." "Of course, no problem. Stay as long as you like." She moved in very soon thereafter and of course she pops right into the kitchen. At that time, a very young Parvathi was cook. She was just about 18 then—(she now lives here and is married to our president Siva Moore). Mom took control of the cooking and just adored Parvathi whom, of course, she calls "poverty". Mom had the unique ability to "read" anybody in seconds.

Living in New York was really not my cup of tea. I did not like the city and its vibration. In addition, I had a very stressful conflict with one of the "directors". Therefore, after a couple of years I applied to be relocated to Virginia which was then at its very beginning stage.

Sometimes we do not realize the value or beauty of an experience until viewed through the patina of nostalgia. Which can also transmogrify the most mundane experience into the sublime. We then realize it was sublime all along.

The Virginia Ashram: Final Destination, at Last

Sometimes a great and important quest will take many attempts, many false starts. But we had an opportunity to learn from all of those "false starts". Those were the "training grounds", the opportunity to hone our skills. Thus it was with the quest for this ashram there were other ashram's wherein we learned skills of community living. That is not to say that we have perfected it, rather we have learned skills enough to build a solid foundation. The learning is continual; we are ever honing our skills discarding that which does not work, learning better communication.

So much happened during all these past decades here I will have to limit this chapter to the salient points. One day, perhaps, someone will write a complete and proper history of this ashram.

30. After Satsang (year unknown).

Some Early History

We found the property for the Virginia ashram after many searches and trials. It was the perfect place. The original parcel was 640 acres or one square mile (also known as one section) we subsequently obtained an additional piece of about 60 acres. That original property had just one building on. That brick house known then as "The Main House" now known as The Lotus Conference Center (LCC). It held everything kitchen, dining room, schoolroom, satsang Hall, TV room, receptionist etc.

Across the road individuals purchased plots that they also subdivided. This amounts to some 1000 acres of private land where homes were built by families or individuals. The population of this external acreage varied from small children to retired folk. The population averages 130 individuals. Thus we have now have a real Yogaville community. A little village. In addition to those private homes the ashram set aside an area where families or individuals could build homes and lease the land from the ashram. They would own their homes but not the land. This area is known as YOCOSO, which stands for Yogaville Cooperative Society. This was a great Vision of Sri Gurudev, which is now realized.

Of course, the central focus would be the beautiful LOTUS temple.

Initially we were just a small group of people trying to work things out. In the "Main House" were quartered several people. There was a very small kitchen and the large beautiful room overlooking the river with picture windows. This served as a multipurpose room. In the mornings it was the classroom where Satya Greenstone taught the children of the Vidyaliyam. On Saturday evening it was converted into a Satsang Hall where Gurudev answered questions, backspace. At other times it was a conference center, a place for weddings, and so on. An adjacent room served as a dining room. There was a small living room where we installed the TV. Upstairs, in the attic, was the video department, a small section was set up for a cottage industry that one of the swamis established making greeting cards with dry pressed flowers. They were quite beautiful. There was also a reception area with a small bookstore that I assembled. The level of organization there was very basic. In the mornings, we'd sit on an old dilapidated couch in a small room adjacent to the reception area where we decided who would do what. It was a fairly raggle-taggle group. But somehow we actually got things done mostly through a lot of dedicated service. We worked long hours.

We also installed a new trailer for Gurudev to reside temporarily while his house was being constructed mostly by Ramakrishna. Fairly soon there were a number of dilapidated trailers installed around the grounds that served as residences for the growing population.

However, the primary focus was on the construction of LOTUS and all of the infrastructure required for that. The first thing of course was construction of some crude roadways so that equipment and trucks can be brought in. Siva Moore had much experience with heavy equipment took on that task. He had a bulldozer and built a couple of roadways down to the site. At one point they ran into an obstacle building a roadway. There was a very large stone obstruction. It was synchronicity and good fortune that one of the fellows present at the time, Billy Mitchell later a.k.a. Swami Dharmananda was actually a demolition expert having been trained in Vietnam. When they asked if someone knew how to do a controlled explosive he said, "Sure, I know that." And he was hired for the job on the spot. He was an amazing man having come from difficult military experience to becoming a swami. He eventually left the order to get married. Much later he develop cancer and when I saw him on a couple of occasions during that he was always clearheaded and very peaceful. I was amazed at his equanimity. Even though he had said that cancer was in remission, eventually passed on. He was a remarkable man who will be missed.

31. Clearing land for LOTUS.   32. Yes, chainsaw as well.

So many have passed on in this life, so many wonderful people.

The next project was constructing of the Lotus Lake that was to be the background to LOTUS. The earth dug out from that construction went in building the hill on which LOTUS was to be constructed.

The entire design, planning, construction, and updating of this project was massive. This is a most unique design using something known as "gluelam". These were the main structural beams taking wood beams and by some process making it into a curve that was smooth and laminating large pieces together. I really have no clue as to how this was done. The altars on the second floor were made in India, while all the woodwork cabinets etc. on the first floor were made by a master carpenter who lived here, Sastwatan Quinn, he had many years of experience in finish carpentry, and all the right equipment. Madhuri Honeyman spend hundreds of hours forming and carving the statue arrangement that is in the center of the All Faiths Hall. Many other artisans contributed to all the elements contained therein. The more complete history of LOTUS and its construction are contained in the film made about it. I, therefore, need not go into all the details.

The opening celebration was a grand Festival taking several months to plan. There were numerous special guests that Gurudev had invited. The actual day was a grand magnificent festival attended by some 700 or more people. Back in that day there was no electronic media, no cell phones etc. but we managed. Everyone was fed a nice box lunch that actually came in boxes from a Chinese restaurant in Charlottesville. I do not know how they ever carried that all that off. Amazingly, everything went without a hitch, no one got sick no one was injured. It was so beautiful.

The original plan was to have a multi-religious library on the lower level and I was to design it and figure out what books were to go there. Long ago I had this vision of me running a library. Well the plans for LOTUS changed. Ten years later Sri Gurudev gave me a library (see Appendix I).

Evolution & Development

Following LOTUS many other buildings were constructed the first was Sivananda Hall in which are the dining room, reception area, bookstore, and the original satsang hall. This evolved over time to include the video department (Shakti.com). Soon the meditation Hall (Guru Bhavan) dormitory buildings (Vivekananda Vihar – VV & Ramalinga Nilayam – RN) and the Monastery were all built. We also constructed two private room guesthouses initially called Lotus Inn 1 & 2 but were changed to Lotus Guesthouse One and Two. Eventually a third was constructed as was the Academy building. It was quite amazing considering that all that acreage was originally wild, wooded areas.

Later the Fine Arts Society was established and developed with the Dance Camp headed by our resident Bharatanatyam teacher Padma Rasaya. She also invited her teachers, the Dhananjayans to lead Dance Camp. The Fine Arts Society (FAS) also constructed a building for dance practices and presentations. That lasted for some 26 years but has now ceased operation as the Dhananjayans have retired. Padma is the youngest daughter of Amma Rasaya matriarch of an illustrious family from Sri Lanka. Padma still does performance on special occasions such as Guru Poornima. They have known Sri Gurudev since the 50s when he moved there. Other siblings include Mrs. Raji who along with her husband Mahen were the schoolmasters at the Vidyaliyam. Mr. Mahen has since passed on. He was a great soul with whom I had a special friendship. There is also Jayen now a doctor in Australia but who earlier along with his sister Padma did many dance performances as fundraising for LOTUS. There is also Vasu, brilliant architect, land developer and businessman who had lived in Bali but now has moved back to Sri Lanka. The whole family had to move from Sri Lanka when the war began there.

Later on Distribution business expanded to construct a large warehouse. Much has evolved over these many years.

The programs department, most especially, evolved to develop programs year-round so there isn't a weekend when we're not filled.

Venerable & Renowned Visitors

Many inspiring people came to visit us over the years. To name just a very few: there was His Holiness Sri Swami Chidanandaji president of the Divine Life Society Rishiknesh who was the successor to Sri Swami Sivanandaji. He gave several satsang's and also performed the dedication puja for Sivananda Hall. Sri Swami Marutachalam Swamigal Adigalar head of Perur Mutt, which is the ashram connected to the Perur temple that Gurudev was once in charge of. He is successor to Shantalinga Swamigal and from a great lineage of Tamil Saints. He came to perform the Mahasamadhi rituals. Gave many satsang's and came frequently to perform the Homa which is a very ancient traditional Hindu fire ceremony. There was also Rabbi Gelberman, longtime friend of Gurudev. Zalman Schacter Shalomi founder of the Jewish Renewal movement. Others include: Rabbi Rami Shapiro disciple of Zalman who wrote many profound spiritual books and is a personal friend. There have been many other spiritual leaders, musicians, dancers, as well as a handful of movie stars

Short Story About Peter Max

I had the good fortune of befriending Peter Max many years ago. Many years after our initial meeting I was visiting with a friend in St. Petersburg, Florida and she informed me that she was contemplating a special business notion. She also mentioned that the art museum there was having a special opening of Peter Max's art, and, as I knew him, would I please go with her to introduce him to her so she could see if he was open to that idea. My reply was that it would be a very crowded affair hundreds of important people and I would be just lost in the crowd. Further, as I am rather shy I just wouldn't barge in on him. Anyway we went, got seats in the large auditorium. I was just sitting in the audience as Peter walked down the aisle and "happened to turn" towards me. He recognized me immediately came down to sit by me. I did the introduction and she completely forgot to give him her idea. Without my asking, he introduced me in his speech on stage. Somewhat embarrassing.

Other Remarkable People

Mention should be made of Turiyasangitananda (Alice Coltrane) who was a close friend of Sri Gurudev and helped in the purchase of the New York Institute. In San Francisco she founded the Vedanta Association for the benefit of the people in the African-American neighborhood, Fillmore district. Later on she established an ashram in Alta Vista, California and then thought she might get land in this area where her disciples could move to build homes etc. She came here as well and I had the great honor to meet with her privately for a short while. I found her to be a most gracious soft-spoken and kind person. The large group of the followers came with her bringing truckloads of belongings. For financial reasons it didn't work out.

Though there have been hundreds of wonderful people coming and going from this ashram; I wish to note three people and one family that were exceptional for me. First was my dear, dear friend the late Swami Gangeshwarananda. She was an ex-registered nurse. This was a connection having an interest and experience in the medical field. She was brilliant with many talents. She came from a southern Italian family with a natural love for cooking. Several times we went out to eat, once to a real family-style Italian restaurant. She just loved it. From time to time we'd make an Italian meal for the entire monastery I made the sauce and pasta she the desert. We loved watching Jeopardy together. She got quite sick once and was on life support. At her final days, I went to visit her. Once while she was alert and awake and she said to me, "It's good to be friends."

There is also one of my oldest friends here Atman Fioretti. That was a very long time when I first met Atman; I don't even know what year that was. We have been close friends for many decades now. One of our traditions has been to celebrate our birthdays together as they are just one day apart. Our tradition has been to have a nice Italian meal at his house and watch Godfather parts I & II or the extended saga. He took me to the ER when I had my gallbladder attack. He has been there for me during the tough times. We have also spent many fun times together watching other movies, going to town, having terrific meals and so on. It's good to have a buddy.

I would also like to mention my dearest friend Wandering Turtle. He is from the Choctaw Nation and I was the first person to speak with him when he arrived at the ashram. I imagine that he looked quite intimidating to many people as he is large fellow and wore a heavy leather jacket at the time. But, we connected immediately. He is a most dependable kindhearted and spiritual man. He has had a very difficult time of it but remains positive. He is constantly at work, which he calls "play". Turtle has great wisdom. He understands the highest teaching.

Finally, there is wonderful Tolton family with whom I connected immediately. They had six children two boys and four girls. I was made Godfather to one of the girls before she was born. I know all girls. All are now married, three have children of their own. The youngest boy Eden has become maintenance man, mechanic, plumber, general fix-it man and is now in charge of maintenance. He's a genius with car mechanics. A great deal of his skills came from his late father but there is also another man Nate, who was here in the early days, the mechanic whom Eden followed around like a puppy learning everything he could. Their mother, Lakshmi, has since gotten remarried and moved to the next county. I have not seen her much. They are a beautiful spiritual family.

Over these many years, the ashram has evolved and grown especially since Gurudev's Mahasamadhi. The entire governing structure has been greatly modified. They are now: a Board of Trustees, leadership team, operations manager, program developer and director, programs advertising, spiritual life board, reservations, a maintenance crew, operations manager, farm manager, kitchen manager, and much more. We even have our own Facebook pages, YouTube channels, and podcasts. Quite amazing, especially if you were there from the beginning.

Our Most Special Holidays

For all these many years we have continuously celebrated many holidays. To our especially important to us. These are Jayanthi, Sri Gurudev's birthday, which falls on 22 December. In addition, the holy Hindu holiday of Guru Poornima, celebrated on the full moon of July. We generally observe these holidays on the weekend closest to the actual dates. We observe these holidays with an ecumenical puja to the light, talks by special guests and in the Saturday evening we have performances by many of our talented members. We have a very talented Padma who is the master of South Indian dance, Bharatnatyam, I occasion in the past we had her teachers from Chennai come and dance. We have quite a good number of fine musicians and singers. Once we had Carol King come to sing and play piano. And one special guru Poornima the pop musician of the Rascals (pop rock group of the '60's) Felix Cavaliere, he was spectacular. We even had Jeff Goldblum calm with Laura Dern, very interesting. Also on all those occasions I did my standup comedy. For the first 10 or 12 years I used the name Professor Klapfaddle and dressed in a white linen suit on stage. Basically, what I did then was to read long set of one-liners. Gurudev loved it all. Eventually I gave up that name and went to develop actual sketches and longer bits that I had memorized. The timing and pacing was much better as well as the material. In recent years all of this was live streamed and is still available archives by date online (livestream.com/yogaville).

33. Very early days "stand up"—[sit down] comedy. Prof. Kapsaddle, Virgil R.

The "Great Challenge"—Necessity for Adapting & Innovation

I felt it necessary to include this subchapter as it has had such a great impact on my life now. It may just be attributed to karma.

Going back to the beginning of my days in yoga I had a very supple and flexible body. In fact, with my mind determined to doing so I was able to do pretty much anything and everything related to hatha yoga. Hatha yoga became my life practice. It gave me such joy to accomplish all those asanas. It was a deep part of my daily life.

About twenty years ago I observed a moderate tingling in my hands I didn't think much of it. Over time the tingling became more intense accompanied by severe pain that felt like somebody had plugged my hands into 2000 volts. I was now concerned enough to get some medical advice and as I suspected they attributed this to spinal nerve damage. I had an MRI done of the cervical and lumbar areas. My suspicions were confirmed indicating serious compression of the cervical spine resulting in major damage of the nerves emanating from there. After trying various methods such as traction and osteopath treatments there was no relief. There was serious compression and stenosis of the cervical spine. This was to such a degree that it was life threatening. Very reluctantly I agreed to surgery on the cervical spine (laminectomy C2–C4). It took eight weeks to recuperate. A very long time for me as I had much experience with surgery (9 previous ones) and no such problem.

Many years prior to this surgery I went to chiropractors. One of them took x-rays of the neck and lower back and informed me that I was developing a straight cervical spine and warned me against doing shoulder-stand and headstand. Of course, I did not heed their warnings. I thought I could do it anyway. Turns out that they were correct. For all those many decades, I have been doing both headstand and shoulder stand incorrectly. Doing full extension of the neck in shoulder stand without support, placing full weight at the very center of the head in headstand. Somehow, at the beginning of this career I was informed that was the way so I did it to the extreme. Doing headstand as a young child was also wrong. All this caused compression of inter-vertebral disks that led to compression of the spine. Teaching yoga the proper way is so important. Doing headstand requires strength in the upper back.

Over time, things got worse. My hatha yoga has become extremely limited compounded by advancing arthritis. Consequently, all the strength, dexterity and feeling in arms hands and fingers have greatly diminished due to the nerve damage. Doing all the ordinary hundreds of tasks during the day have become very difficult. Walking, especially climbing the steps, opening jars, zipping zippers, not falling or teetering, even folding a blanket, and so much more, all of these are very challenging Ordinarily one does not even think of these tasks and takes them for granted as part of daily life. That is not in my case.

I have had to make many innovations, inventions and adjustments to overcome these limitations.

By the grace of the Guru I will continue on.

Carry it on.

Gurudev Story 16

Gurudev never failed to surprise me at the most unusual times. As mentioned above I had several surgeries. The first was for the gallbladder that was a serious case. Shortly thereafter I needed a hernia surgery which I self-diagnosed. I did not mention this to Gurudev. I would never even think to do so. The next day, without warning, Gurudev shows up in my room as I'm in bed. Someone had the sense to bring a chair for Him. I was lying there somewhat out of it from the drugs. I had a thought to tell Him about something I did. He just sits there takes my hand in his and is very quiet. I thought I should tell him the secret but he is simply pushes me back and motions to be quiet. He was flooding me with his beautiful healing vibration. Finally, I tell him that I did a trick to get the same doctor doing the surgery as I did the previous one who was the attending for that clinic. I said I impersonated my own Dr. telling them that I was his patient and that they should sign Dr. Shermer to do the surgery. He said, "Don't worry, that was okay, you just needed to do that. There is no harm."

Follow-up story. An event that happened much earlier.

Gurudev Story 17

On the Spot EMT

I was riding my bike one day after a major rainstorm. There were lots of puddles on the road of course. [It was a dirt road then.] For just one Moment I was not paying attention and splash, rode right through a puddle. I was covered in mud. That was upsetting. In trying to avoid the next puddle I swerved the bike, lost control and ended up smashing my leg into the crossbar of the bike. My leg hit with such force that it felt as if it were broken. In any case I could not walk on it so I literally crawled to the nearest phone, which was on the wall outside the Lotus Guest House and called to Sivananda Hall for help. Someone was dispatched and they called for the EMT. All this took happened in the space of about ten minutes. Just as the EMT guys came Sri Gurudev arrived on His little golf-cart—this was not on His normal route, nor was He usually out and about at that hour of the morning. He then checked on what was happening, made sure I was OK and even made sure that EMT guys put my shoe back on which fell off before loading me on to the ambulance.

But, that is not the whole story.

The next day I was in my room flat on my back, in much pain. I could not go anywhere. As I lay in bed I heard a car pull up to the driveway, this being a common occurrence I did not pay it much attention. Within about two minutes, there is a soft knock on my door. I could not get up so I said, "Please come in."

Of course, it is Gurudev. As it was summer, I was just on top of the bed. He just comes and asks how I'm doing, and then very slowly begins to stroke the affected leg. That was the best massage I ever had. Keep in mind I never called Him never told anyone to inform or call.

"You will be alright." As He is leaving the room He looks about, "You have a lot of altars here, hmm. Good." Yep, I had every surface of that room covered with various "holy" objects—statues, photos, tons of crystals etc. (Why take chances?) The leg healed within a week.

So many, many stories. More to be posted.

All the Wonderful Babies

So many beautiful, holy babies. They have been one of my most wonderful experiences here. Those who live here know that. They are to me pure divine beings of light. They do not judge, yet have a very keen sense of vibrations. I have found that there is within me an innate ability to communicate on the highest level with the babies and very small children. Of course our communication is nonverbal, and, of course, baby to baby. They have their own system of communication. They bring so much joy, so much joy. I have been Godfather to two of them. I also babysat for one, who is now married and has her own baby. Babies are in direct contact with the absolute divine. They are all divine beings. They know and can feel the vibrations in adults but most especially are connected with other babies. They seem to have a direct recognition of other small, small children. In most cases, they attempt to make some sort of communication usually on the physical level by touching. They are my teachers as well. Observe how they communicate amongst each other. It is a universal code. Even when I have observed them as strangers in a grocery. Sometimes they put forehead to forehead. I have done that countless times. They first look and see another small child close to their age, and in the very gently stretch their hand to touch the other one usually on the head. They do not carry this out for a long time just a glancing Moment. It is not possible to fully describe or give all the details. It is an inner experience. I have seen so many being born, growing into small children, teenagers, and adults. This is to use that overused word with the right definition—AWESOME.

34. Sweet little Awa.

Sri Gurudev's Mahasamadhi

Abbreviated Version – Diary Entry August 18, 2002

Sri Gurudev attains Mahasamadhi. How can one express what this means. It will take many days to sort out all the feelings. This body is being sent from India tomorrow at a ceremony on Thursday. The whole community is pulling together on this. It is an amazing demonstration of solidarity and maturity.

It was most unusual for Sri Gurudev to make a journey to India during the hottest months of the summer. We gave him a fond farewell before he took off that day. On this trip he also included a visit to UK and his European disciples. This was 2002, August, that He was in India. This was the hottest time of year in the South and normally he would never have gone there. Is our contention that His reason for going both see Europe and India was to allow all his disciples to see him just one more time. Another point is that he went there instead of being here as well as going up in the north so that he wouldn't be in the area where people would make an instant fuss and have Him brought into the top-level hospital to get very special treatments. This was His time to move on.

Naturally, he visited Coimbatore but then took off for a conference in the state of Andra (just north of Tamil Nadu). This is also unusual. Soon thereafter, we were informed of His medical condition and that He was in hospital. It was an aneurysm. [Details of this story are recorded in the video available from Shakti.com, the Mahasamadhi satsang]. It was August 17 while watching a TV documentary that I was personally informed by Swami Sarvananda. I immediately suggested that we delay the ceremony for a week so that disciples from distant points could come. This was done.

Of course never having done anything like this that we had no idea how to do any of this. We had countless meetings and somehow by some great miracle things came together. Naturally hundreds of people came from all over the country and elsewhere. Swami Chidananda was designated to go to the Baltimore airport to pick up the casket as well as special guest Sri Ramaswami of Coimbatore and swami Marutachalam Adigalar of Perur Mutt. This was the ashram connected to Gurudev's temple, Perur, whose head, Shantalingaswami, had officiated at the opening of LOTUS. As he was quite aged, he sent his designated successor. Marutachalam was to officiate the entire ceremony. Ramaswami was Gurudev's nephew and he organized everything.

We were informed ahead of time that all of us they sit in Chidambaram but that was it Swami Marutachalam was going to conduct the entire ceremony. We're also told that will be a point in the ceremony when they would transport the body downstairs at Chidambaram to what would be His tomb. Ramakrishna Sackett and Mitra Metro were up all night preparing the construction. They had to think it out the design it all materials and do it. It is wonderful to note that Ramakrishna was chief builder of Sri Gurudev's house when Gurudev moved here.

The day was here we are all jammed into Chidambaram shoulder to shoulder. Swami Marutachalam began the ceremony. Within a very short time Sri Ramaswami came to all the senior most swamis and told us to come up on the platform to participate in the puja. Since none of us knew anything about what was going on all what to do Sri Marutachalam they patiently instructed us every step of the way. It was glorious; so much was happening we could not keep up with it all. There were loads of came for an instance being burnt at numerous times. It was a very smoky affair.

His holy body was prepared for entombment. Now we were invited to go down with them. The ceremony continued with only Marutachalam conducting. It was quite complex. Cinderblock construction into which they poured bags and bags of holy ash together with rock salt as a preservative. There were also bundles of Bilwa leaves and other sacred Indian herbs. It was broiling hot down there.

Finally the ceremony was completed Ramakrishna and Mitra remained to complete the construction and it was done. The most poignant aspect of the ceremony, however, was really the very next morning when the top of the construction was cemented. During that time, we were allowed to put in any kind of thing in the cement so people brought little precious gems and other sacred objects some people inscribed in an Om with a stick on the wet cement. Then it happened; spontaneously various chants from many different traditions broke out. This was OUR ceremony, a spontaneous rising of love and waves of spiritual energy. Magnificent, Glorious.

35. Last known portrait, Coimbatore 2002.

36. Eternal Light.

37. Blessing malas.

38. Puja to holy feet.

Sidebar note: amazing and "miraculous" events and things. Sri Swami Marutachalam had never traveled to a foreign country thus he had no passport, no visa. Getting such things in India is quite arduous. But, Ramaswami knew how to do things so just 24 hours prior to departure he and Swamiji went to the Indian consulate and within 12 hours obtained all the necessary documents. Absolutely amazing. Included in the checked in baggage were many kilos of holy ash, and countless bags of Indian herbs, camphor, also those things necessary for such an elaborate ceremony. Normally such things would be confiscated by customs. They just let it all through. Amazing. Note—the gate where the flight came in was 108.

What I Did Over the Years

Over these many years, I have had the good fortune and blessing to develop and create several projects. There was, for example, The Library (Vidya Bhavan), and SASTRI. These were very long-term projects stories of which are below in the appendices. Early on I also led services for Passover, Yom Kippur, and Chanukah (see document below). All done with a slant towards the deeper spiritual interpretation.

When Microsoft Windows was introduced, I initiated our Internet connection. A short while after some fellow approached me at the University (UVA) and asked why we have no website. I replied I have no idea how to do that. He said you could find out there's probably some kind of workshop at UVA. I did that and in 1998 took a weekend workshop about how it was done. Then registered yogaville.org as our domain name and we were all set. Having had no experience in this whatsoever and doing all the coding in HTML by myself. The website was not just informative but fun and entertaining. It included many photos as well as all the information about programs and so forth. It included long synopses of every satsang, audios of mantras, as well as a bit of humor. There was also a photo-tour of the ashram. One time there was a special satsang devoted to one of the senior most members who was very close to Gurudev. With everyone getting up paying tribute. I thought, this is a well-known person, that is fine. However, what about the other people who actually keep the ashram running. They are not well known they do not get special tributes. I therefore created a page called, "Meet the People" for those behind the scenes. Took a photo, did an interview on how they met Gurudev, history at the ashram etc. Eventually as the ashram grew, they had to advance to another level and the webpage became a new thing, more commercial, and out of my hands. That was a good thing.

During the time I was doing SASTRI I collected a set of satsang's (72) that were edited for content and created a special CD with the viewer program so people can do searches on their own. With that, I did a slideshow CD on the life of Sri Gurudev.

My Hobby

One of the most fun projects was developing the monastery Koi pond. You could say that this is my hobby.

Some other fellow had built the basic structure that was a big hole in the ground with slate paving stones cemented in place surrounding it and some nice large rocks at the periphery. However, it was left to just sit there. Eventually the hole filled up with rainwater became quite rank. I decided to empty the thing out, put a proper rubber liner in, and get some iris plants then added a couple of Koi. I put in a pump for a fountain and so on. The first few fish died due to wrong solid freezing of the water one rough winter. I put in a deicer water heater and purchased about 15 Koi from the pet store. They spawned several times and there are now about 24. The eldest are about 15 years old and quite large.

Everyone loves the fish. I have a tradition of bringing young toddlers to help feed them. The children just love this as do I. I put in three little gardens around the periphery. Later someone helped create a large waterfall, which took many years to make leak-proof. Now it is beautiful sight having a meditative atmosphere that people love to sit around and watch the fountain and waterfall.

39. Feeding Time.

It does require a tremendous amount of intense maintenance, but is so beautiful. Over the years due to increased disabilities I had to create a number of inventions to make the work easier. One of the best was assistant get the fountain pump box up to ground level where I could clean it.

Previously I was done my work sandals and shorts climb into the pond and retrieve it by hand it wasn't heavy but now doing that bending has become impossible for me. I love inventing little devices to make my work easier. It is something that just evolves over time starting quite clumsy and not very well done. Note that all of this is just a summary of what happened.

Gurudev Stories 18–22

I thought it would be nice to end this chapter with a collection of stories that all took place at the Ashram, some of which relate to the portion above. A compilation of experiences indicating the generosity, kindness and Supreme awareness of our Gurudev.

Beginning the Website, Announcement, & Cameras

Over the years, Gurudev has not been averse to admonishing me in public. Not a pleasant experience, I assure you. The opposite has been equally true. So when I began the webpage, He was informed, of course. So at the very end of the next satsang He says, "Look what he is doing putting us on the Web, WWW, why didn't anyone else think of that?" A short while later I saw the need for a camera to do a proper photo spread and so I put the word out to Prem Anjali. She went directly to the source something I would never even think of doing. Soon thereafter, I was gifted the very first digital camera Gurudev ever had. This was an elaborate affair capable of taking thousands of photos, video with sound. It was quite bulky and heavy akin to the first cell phone. It also required proprietary software and some hardware ("SCSI card", young folks will have to look this up). It worked quite well and I took hundreds of photos. However, a few weeks later I was sitting in Sivananda Hall, the receptionist informed me that I had a phone call. I took the call in the booth and it was Gurudev. He asked, "Where are you?" I tell him I'm in Sivananda Hall. He says, "Stay there, don't go out, I am sending you a better camera." Shortly thereafter Swami Nirmalananda, arrived and hands me a much more compact camera. It still required special software and a different SCSI card. It worked wonderfully.

Gurudev was extremely generous, always gave one tools needed to serve better.

Computer Assistance & Much More

One time I was at His house showing Him how to use various features on His computer. We came to a point where it was necessary to write down a few instructions. Instead of pulling out a fresh piece of paper from the stack on His desk, He pulls out a very neatly folded piece from the trash-bin. It had only a little bit of typing on it. He carefully unfolded it, smoothed out the creases and wrote down the instructions.

Gurudev – The Consummate Recycler

One day while at my desk I got a call from Sri Gurudev. This almost never happened. Immediately a chain of reactions is set off: "What did I do now?" "My God He personally is going to boot me out. OK Face the music man."

It's all delusion.

What He said was, "Are you busy now?"

> "No, Sir."
> "Can you come up?"
> "Of course, I'll be there right away." I quickly walked the distance.

There He was waiting for me in his spacious bedroom/office. He needed to know a few technical matters about His computer. They were very simple things and I was all set to sit there and just whiz right through it all. But, that is not how things were done. He just wanted me to tell Him what to do and He would do it. This took about twenty times longer than if I did it all myself. He wanted to learn the solutions by doing all the steps.

It was a major test in patience.

On another occasion, I had sent Gurudev a floppy with some scans of our yantra. I was walking down the road from the office building one day when He passed by in His Jeep. He stopped and said He received the disc but could not open it. At that time He had a Mac, a system of which I know next to nothing. He asked me if I could help Him view the images.

> "Sure, when would you like me to do that?"
> "Are you free now?"

Nothing like striking the iron when hot, "Sure."

"Get in."

He opens the door and I hop in and we go.

"Oy, a Mac, I think, "Now I am sunk."

Well He did not have any imaging software and I try to find something on the net for a free download. But, it takes too long, and anyway I have no idea how or where to install such a download. I have to be humble and admit that I know nothing about the Mac.

It was OK.

On another day, when He had a PC system he asked me to show Him something about which I did know a lot. This was fun. We did all sorts of things. Then He asked me to show Him how to work a new piece of hardware. It was one of those multi-function things—the sort of machine that scans, copies, faxes, prints, does everything but make your coffee.

I had never used this piece of equipment so I asked Gurudev if He had the manual. He did of course, neatly filed away in the desk. Everything there was, as always, perfectly organized so that all documents and manuals were in one file. He pulled out the manual and handed it to me.

Now, understand that when one is asked to do something by Gurudev one may not dawdle or space out. So, I had to read the manual in about 25 seconds and figure it all out. That being done He asked me if we could scan a page and then e-mail it. I requested a page of printed material to scan.

"Anything will do Gurudev."

He goes into his trusty trash bin-retrieves another very neatly folded sheet with some printed material on one side. "We'll this do?" "Yes, Gurudev that will be fine." And we scanned it. Now most scanning programs allow you to edit the result in any word processing program. Not this one. Try as I might the resultant text would not convert to any standard format. This was a proprietary format.

"Gurudev, this text cannot be converted to standard format and therefore cannot be sent as e-mail."
"So what good is this?"
"Not much, I'm afraid."
"OK, let's move on."

We then did a bunch of fun stuff with the programs. I had such a good time when it was time for me to go I just bounded out.

Then Gurudev came to the door as I was leaving.

> "Murugananda, you forgot something."

He was holding my jacket, which in my excitement I had forgotten, and left hanging on the back of the chair. I felt such a wave of kindness when He handed me that jacket. I find, as time goes on forgetfulness has become a common trait.

But, that was not the end of His kindness. Since I had walked up there I expected to walk back, but He had called ahead to Swami Nirmalananda and instructed her to drive me back. This happened every time I came there. It should be noted that during the short time I was there he received perhaps five or six phone calls from people in need. And, He was always ready to serve on whatever level was needed

A Perfect CD

While working on the SASTRI project I had decided to make a CD with the selection of the satsang's to be included with a special software so anyone can do a search and view the entire satsang. I was going to sell this as a fundraiser for LOTUS and/or the library. I thought it would be nice to include some photos and after a bit it came to me why not make complete slideshow of all these photos. There were over 150 photos. As I did not know the locations where some of these were taken I thought it would be nice when I showed Gurudev SASTRI He could also see the slideshow and could therefore fill in the gaps in information that I had on that. We ran through it quickly and he identified most of the photos. Sometime later Gurudev came to me with a CD saying, "Maybe you can use some of these for your show." It was a CD of photos Gurudev took. It was of the lotus flowers that were in the pond near the farm. Every photo was perfectly done. Of course, I did include several of them in the slideshow. So much generosity, so much consummate love. I am forever grateful.

Be Careful What You Wish For

Before we had the monastery, we all lived in trailers near what is now called the Lotus Conference Center (LCC) but was then referred to as the "Main House". One day as I was walking from my trailer on Rt 604 (the county road on which the ashram is located), headed to Sivananda Hall, I saw Sri Gurudev driving in to visit Amma at her trailer. "Wow," I thought, "It would be so cool if He would visit me some day or at least if I rode with Him in that big old car."

I proceed down the road towards the hall. About half way down His car comes by slowly and stops about 30 feet ahead. "Oh my God, what have I done now? Is He going to really bust me??!!"

I run to the car. Bend down to His window and say, "Yes, Sir how may I serve you?" He says something quietly but I can't hear a word.

> "Excuse me, Sir."
> Now I hear, "Get in."
> "Oh My God! This is it, I'm a dead man." I'm saying my mantra as fast as I can.
> Gurudev is just driving VERY slowly. He pulls up in front of His driveway, and that was it.
> He was just giving me a ride.
> *"Just a ride?"*

From His Own Hand

There is a story included in the appendix on The Story of the Library wherein I describe how Gurudev gave me hundreds and hundreds of books with His own hand from His personal library. Every time he gave me a book from Master Sivananda He would say, "From Gurudev." One time he gave me an old 78 RPM recording of Gandhiji speaking in Hindi to the assembly in New Delhi. After some time I had someone translate it for me, as it was also printed out in Hindi.

Here endeth the chapter on the Virginia Ashram.

Over the years, thousands of people have come and gone from here. Some have stayed for longer periods; some have done great work others were just passing through forming a chapter in their life. Some remained some have passed on. There have been marriages, divorces, births, and death. I have seen so many babies. Seeing them grow become teenagers, go to college and then have beautiful children of their own. So many, many stories. Too many. Long forgotten stories. Each of us has our stories. Each one is precious.

Carry It On

I believe that all that is all that has happened, however it may appear to be, is a gift coming from the grace of Sri Gurudev. His great vision of Yogaville as it is now came through the evolution of all those other places that on first appearances being wrecks ramshackle disasters. Including all our absurd non-workable ideas came through his vision for us. They were just places of training and learning. Learning how to live together in community, learning what enterprises we should really be doing. Learning that what we are really good at.

40. My first photo, 1966.

Pilgrimages, Adventurers & Miracles in India & Nepal

Over the years, I have traveled to India a number of times. I had wanted to go there, for a long time, to see the great ancient temples and absorb the intense holy vibrations as well as to visit the holy places where Sri Gurudev had been. During those trips there have been many amazing and wonderful experiences it would be impossible to put them all down here so I present some of the highlights. There have been so many places, so many temples, so many people and experiences that I could not possibly remember them all. Putting all of them down would take an entire book.

Moreover, truth be told there have also been some difficult and unpleasant experiences. Not everything was a "miracle". I won't necessarily go in the order of events within each trip.

I refer to some events as "miracles" because that's what they seemed to be at the time. One may also refer to them as serendipitous events or synchronicity or, I might say that these were further examples of the numerous situations in my life where I was taken care of, protected by the grace and infinite love of Gurudev.

On all the trips where Gurudev accompanied us I had unique experience to be in His presence in his hometown. Those were always the highlight of our trips. Everywhere we went I could see the absolute reverence, love and honor that everyone gave Him. He loved them so much you could see why He wanted to be there, why He spoke of that place with such reverence. I have not the words to adequately relate that experience. Another thing about the culture worth mentioning. Tamil Nadu is an ancient culture. The language is ancient as well. There are aspects of the culture, the mode of communication that I could not understand. It was as if they had a secret language. However, there is highly evolved definite class factor despite what they might tell you, the caste system still exists.

My First Trip to India – October 1984

There was a group of about 38 people. Most of us met together at Kennedy Airport. Swami Dayananda (before she was a swami she was sister's Sharanya) was the leader. She had prior experience in the tour industry so she was a natural. She always took care of others. It was quite exciting many of us meeting for the first time. We all had our passports, visas and quite amazingly—Travelers Checks. That is something one no longer uses these days. But, there were no cell phones, no laptops, and no iPads. Imagine traveling 8000 miles with none of those things that we take for granted these days. So, instead of checking iPhones every 40 seconds we have to have actual conversations. Not only that, we all had cameras with 35mm film—some of you younger folk will have to look that up. One of the people fashioned very nice pouches that we could hang around the neck to hold our passports securely. One of the members actually forgot her passport at home. Fortunately, she had her son there with her. She quickly dispatched him home in a cab to fetch her passport; amazingly, he came back in time.

We arrived in New Delhi October 31, 1984, mid afternoon. Which "happened" to coincide with the very day that Indira Gandhi was assassinated. On the flight, we were informed that our hotel had to be changed because there was some sort of "strike" our assigned hotel. By great fortune, we were placed in the Akbar hotel where Gurudev was staying. That was a five-star hotel whereas our original hotel was probably a "one star" somewhere in downtown New Delhi. As soon as we got to the city the place was in a frenzy. The hotel was buzzing with emotion. Everyone glued to the TV's which at that time were very crude. The term news-cycle had not been invented but that is what was going on. We gathered in the lobby where Gurudev was sitting and he told us, "Take this time as a retreat. Don't go anywhere. Okay. Everything will be all right, don't worry."

Did I listen? No, of course not, I "needed" to get out. I was quite naïve thinking I could just go anywhere in the city. Here I was in one of the great capitals of the world I could not miss my opportunity to go on a little shopping trip. I inquired at the front desk what public bus would go to the Connaught Circle area. That was my first mistake was asking about public transportation, a difficult endeavor in the middle of one of the most complex cities in the world. I thought I heard the man's directions correctly, but of course, I was totally confused. Consequently, I got on the wrong bus, which cost only a rupee or two. I ended up at the other end of town having no idea whatsoever where I was or how to get back. Out of desperation, I walked up to some strange young fellow who had a motorbike and asked if he was available. He knew the directions to the hotel. I gave him a good tip.

Saved Again

As mentioned the city was in chaos people were burning tires, it was havoc. It "happened" that this hotel was also THE hotel for airline pilots as it was very close to the airport and quite comfortable. We had among us a very audacious swami, having immense chutzpah, actually walked up to a few pilots asking them if they happen to have an empty plane going to

Chennai, which was our next stop.. Amazingly, he found one fellow with a small empty plane going back to Chennai. He had a few other customers coming along but it was mostly us filling the plane. Gurudev got a first-class seat.

We were all saved. All protected.

Gurudev Story 23

We were all visiting the ashram of Sri Gurudev's first guru, Sri Swami Chidbhavanandaji of the Ramakrishna order in Tamil Nadu. At that point, Chiddhavanandaji was in his early 90s. Quite elderly and frail. At first Gurudev was sitting on the floor next to where Chiddhavanandaji was sitting on a chair. Gurudev bowed in full prostration at his feet with such humility in total respect. It was awe-inspiring. Gurudev had His photo album of Yogaville and with such great pride and joy He was showing His first Guru all of what was happening with the building of LOTUS. He was like a proud child showing his Dad all that He had accomplished. There was a glow and a beauty about the whole thing.

Gurudev next told the story that we had heard so many times, about when he was sweeping the ashram grounds and with the dustpan picked up a bit dust and tossed it over the fence to the other side. Gurudev smiled. After a few Moments, Chidbhavanandaji said in very a hushed tone, which almost no one else heard, "You keep telling that same old story." Gurudev laughed so much.

The next day two chairs were set up in front. Gurudev's chair was on the left Chidbhavanandaji's on the right. The person who set it this up put a nice orange cloth on the Gurudev's chair. Both of them walked in simultaneously Gurudev then looking at his chair with extreme delicacy, unobtrusively quickly removed the cloth that was on his seat. He did not want to have anything extra that his Guru did not have. Anyone else probably would not have even noticed the cloth or done anything about it. Almost no one else in the group noticed this, I did.

41. Sri Swami Chidbhavanandaji His Ashram Tamil Nadu, Sri Gurudev showing LOTUS photos.

Saved Again

We were in Bangalore for a special conference of teachers, including Sri Gurudev and His Holiness the Dalai Lama. It was quite late at night; we had done a lot of traveling that day. There were several speakers before the specially invited guests then after Sri Gurudev spoke, His Holiness spoke. Then some secondary speakers who were, to say the least, quite boring. It was now very late and I was exhausted I needed to get back to the hotel and sleep. HOWEVER, I had no clue how to get back or even where the hotel was. In my senseless audacity I walked out onto the street saw some guys hanging out, their mopeds close by and just at random I asked one guy, "Are you available." He understood my meaning he said, "Yes, of course". I didn't even know if any of those fellows spoke English. He said, "Where do you want to go?" "Holiday Inn." I got on back of the moped not knowing if this guy was going to take me to where I was going or some alleyway take all my money and passport. I had everything on me, passport, money etc. I had no clue where the heck this guy was going. He asked me where I was coming from all the usual questions when I told him I lived in Virginia, USA he told me he had a brother in Washington and asked if I knew him. As if I knew all the Indian people in America. Sure, all Americans must know every random native Asian Indian in America. Well, he took me right to the hotel and he wanted to talk so I obliged. We on the steps and he asked me all sorts of questions mostly the usual questions that people ask of a swami. Even in that late hour, totally exhausted, somehow, answers came, they were just there inside of me, I didn't have to think about it. It was getting late so you asked him how much I should pay. He told me, "No problem you have given me more than any money."

A Few Coimbatore Events

On another day we went to Sri Gurudev's birth home in Chettypalayam. A Mr. Tanguvelan, who lives near there, took us in his car. It is now a meditation place and has a library for children. All beautifully kept. Sri Ramaswami has been buying up land adjacent to it so that it may one day be a school or study center. (Now home of the new LOTUS in India) There were many beautiful trees on the grounds. The house had been repaired and had a great vibration. I am so sorry that I did not bring my camera. Prem Anjali kept asking Gurudev to tell her the exact spot that he was birthed. Of course, there was no exact spot that Gurudev could point out so He just gave a general idea.

42. Chettypalayam described above, the required group photo me in 2nd row.

Visit to the "Mystic"

After our visit at Gurudev's home we went to see the gent that Hersha Harileela had recommended, she said he was a "mystic". OK, so the whole group went to his home. A rather dumpy, funky little place with a few tattered couches and amazingly it had a TV. We of course had something to drink first—YAY—fresh coconut. The man—Murugan Iyer—was about 70 or so, very chubby, wearing only a dirty dhoti and spoke no English. There was a fellow there who acted as translator. He looked at each person and gave some comment. To Mataji he said "someone is jealous of you—you need to bury ("I don't remember what?") something and you will build something. (Difficult to understand). To me he said, "No evil will touch you. "You are protected (well I know that) and then he asked why I am in India or if I had a question. I vaguely mentioned that I have a medical situation but said nothing about it. He said—and this was amazing—you have a nerve pain in your arms and hands, also in your feet (exactly CORRECT and how did he know? I never told him.). To correct this take 2 cloves of garlic every morning. I did buy a few bulbs of garlic (Ponda in Tamil) the next day and managed to have some for about a week but it did not do anything.

More of Coimbatore

Next day I met Arun Gokulal—he is a Gujarati businessman (there are MANY Gujaratis in Coimbatore. Gujaratis are a business community from the north near Bombay.). A short very energetic middle-aged fellow who spends his whole time investing in the stock market and is very obsessed with donating blood to the Red Cross. But, he is also a very generous fellow, he allowed me to use his computer to get e-mail and go on the net. There was an extra computer in his bedroom that he no longer used. Well, that was quite nice. Right after my visit with Arun I went to the main market area on DB road to go purchase some of the garlic. On the way to the vegetable stall whom do I run into but Mutalakshmi's son, Vikram, who just happened to be in the hood. So, he accompanied me to the stall pays for the garlic then asks if there was anything else I needed. "Well not really, but maybe some snack items to take with us on the tour." OK sure we go to a place nearby. We next go to a shop that sells dry fruits and nuts—perfect for travel snack. Shop is called Hema's and I pick up some cashews and figs—very nice little shop with a most charming fellow who runs the place—he spoke perfect English. Now the REAL AMAZING thing is that this man is the father of Kumud who is the young wife of one of our close members David Vanderveer (a juggler who lives near Charlottesville.) Synchronicity!!

"Interesting" Aspects of India

The following is just an assortment or perhaps a listing of observations and oddities of India. In no particular order.

Among of the most peculiar things you notice when you first land in India are the overwhelming odors. It can't be pinned down exactly but no doubt, it is a combination of the incense, a multitude of "exotic" spices, with a touch of diesel fuel. You eventually get quite used to it in fact after you have departed the country you miss all of that. The next thing you notice are the immense crowds constantly everywhere no matter where you go. It is unlike any other city I have ever been.

When you get to the airport and you are alone in a big city, the thing to do is to go to the taxi service window at the airport and get a cab to your hotel. It is quite amazing how efficient they are at doing this. Tell him where you want to go he gives you a ticket. Go to the payment window, pay, they give you a ticket with a number which is the license number of the taxi. Then as always there another bureaucrat who stamps your ticket, take it outside another bureaucrat checks your ticket and within a minute or two, the taxi comes. You look at the license confirm it tell them the hotel and off you go.

The same efficiency with a similar multilayered bureaucrat system is noted when you shop the government run markets. They all come under the name Gandhi Khadigram Bhavan, or something like that. Anyway, there are dozens and dozens of men all around you go to the section where you want something pick it out and a man at the counter gives you a ticket, it has the price but he doesn't give you the merchandise. Instead, it goes to a packer who carefully packs your merchandise in a paper package. We then go to another window give the ticket to the man, pay for your purchase, then another window where you collect your purchase. It is all very efficient and gets to employ many people.

Within all of this experience, one should not think India in an over romanticized vision. Along with all the beautiful temples, and so forth, and it is beautiful, there is that tendency to think in some much romanticized way. However, there is also overwhelming and pounding poverty. Despite what they claim, there is a depressing prejudice, racism, and the caste system still prevails. Especially these days, with Mr. Modi as Prime Minister, there is terrible Hindu nationalism and extreme racism. That is the reality despite what some people who promote tourism will tell you.

There is also the horrendous pollution in every big city there are millions and millions of diesel-powered transport whether it be mopeds, buses, lorries as well as very slow bullock carts and bicycles. The almost impossibility of crossing streets safely with massive traffic and very few traffic lights. The best way I found to cross the street was to find to a small group of native folk and when they went, I went, one does not hesitate, ever. I call this, "the Tamil Two-Step". I find that when in most cities crossing a street takes special skill, insanity, a positive attitude, coupled with a rather blasé detachment from physical life.

There also is constant noise in any big city 24/7. This is because they have a rule which states that when you turn a corner or want to pass another vehicle "Honk Horn". They even have signs with that instruction. Speaking of transportation every city and town has what are known as "auto-rickshaws". These are actually a kind of three-wheeled motorized thing (a sort of motorcycle) with a little carriage on back. It is always open on both sides, generally has two benches where about five or six people sit, though it actually is comfortable for just four. There are millions of these all over India running on diesel fuel. More common are the hundreds of millions of "two- wheelers" or small mopeds you frequently see a family of five riding altogether on one. No one wears helmets. Strange. Bicycles, they are 50 or 60 pound heavy steel things with a built-in lock, very clever design. Finally, you see lorries and buses all painted in garish colors. Frequently you see an image of a deity somewhere and just as frequently one may see such a vehicle being blessed by a priest outside a temple. Religion occupies almost all acts and activities. It is an essential aspect of India.

More Things

You can purchase any prescription drug without a prescription at thousands of little shops.

You can get a terrific full course lunch for $.50 or less. Almost all restaurants have 100% male employees; the exceptions are special women-run restaurants and ashram-run restaurants.

You can get a fully customized set of clothing for amazingly low price. The tailor will measure you exactly and copy the style of trouser you have exactly. It will generally take one to two days to make the outfit—amazing.

India has the most delicious coffee, served with steamed milk, BUT served only at breakfast with massive amounts of sugar. If you ask for coffee at lunch, they'll think you're crazy. If you ask for coffee or tea without sugar, they look at you as if you are loony. Tea always means black. Chai is the universal name across the country. In USA people think, wrongly, that chai means that spicy stuff with clove and cinnamon, etc. so people wrongly say "chai tea" which in fact they are saying "tea, tea". All such hot beverages are served super-hot. That is why they give you a little round saucer with high walls with the coffee or tea this enables you to pour it back and forth from the saucer to the cup thereby cooling it. Why they do not serve it in a proper temperature in the first place is another one of those mysteries of India.

Most of India has delicious local foods especially in the South. However, do not ever try their "Western style bread" or "Western cheese" they're an abomination. You have been warned.

Pretty, young girls stringing and selling jasmine flowers.

Lots of beggars—but only in front of temples. Some of them are disguised as swamis or sadhus. It is not looked upon favorably by most natives.

They all eat dinner at absurd late hours like nine or ten PM. They usually have something very "light" like iddlis or dosa. That is like calling bar-b-q "light". You can never get rice at night. Evening meal is usually very greasy—real heart-attack diet.

No one is ever on time for anything. Sometimes they don't show up at all.

Things they DO NOT have in India

* Gay bars
* Joggers
* Skateboards
* Inline skates
* Speedos
* Racing bikes
* Houses with front lawns
* Women who work in restaurants
* Women in shorts

What they do have

* Mobile phones
* Holy Temples
* People
* Two wheelers (hundreds of millions)
* Pollution
* NOISE
* Pollution
* Women who work on construction crews
* Pollution
* Internet "cafes"
* Trains that go ON TIME
* Every kind of specialty shop

* Very cool women who wield machetes to open fresh coconuts
* Very cool guys who drive 3 wheeled auto rickshaws

Cotton and cotton products are one of the main industries of Tamil Nadu. I found several items that are exceptional quality. Years ago I purchased some T-shirts and underwear, they were all fine very soft cotton, comfortable and perfectly fit, and they lasted for a number of years. One of the more interesting products in this line is the towels. They're all with a very fine nodules, the amazing thing about them is they dry one so efficiently after a shower.

In the early days, getting bottled water was always a major undertaking. On our first trip we got it by the case. There was only one brand then, Bisrilli. It was essential to have bottled water for any kind of drinking and even brushing teeth. These days they have every kind of bottled water. Our very first trip the gracious host in our hotel offered us something called "Limca". It sounded like a nice lime-juice beverage. Not so, it was a horrid sugar saturated soda. For some bizarre reason we kept drinking it.

A sure way together a crowd's by pulling out a camera. Everyone there loves having a photo taken especially the young people. They all grew up around you saying, "Photo, photo, photo." They're not shy.

Hotels have TVs and one of the constants is fashion shows. Only these are done with exalted bad style. They also have loads of old American TV shows.

There are absolutely no road signs, no street signs and no stoplights (well maybe 11 stop lights in the whole country all of them in big cities). As a consequence we would frequently get lost. Most especially the last trip when we were in a small van. The driver was clever and knew how to ask directions.

Am very impressed by the skills of the Dobi, the washer-men, they managed to keep perfect track of hundreds of customers while at the same time impeccably washing and perfectly ironing every item.

Shower stalls by the way are interesting. There is no separation on the floor between it and the rest of the bathroom. It is all on one level. Drain is in the floor—and BTW all floors are made of marble. Marble is cheap, plentiful, and easy to clean and lasts forever. Also, I learned that it is proper to always close the bathroom door—the reason for this is so that the vibrations are kept contained and do not spread out to the rest of the apartment or to your bedroom. It shows how this culture is sensitive to energies. Just one further example how much further this culture is advanced compared to ours.

The most amazing shop I was in there was a Tiny Ayurvedic shop—or more accurately a stall. This was across the Kapileshwari temple in Chennai. However, the fellow there had EVERYTHING I asked for. Now, you need to know there are literally 1000's of different meds in Ayurveda. He would have them. The place also looked like an absolute cluttered mess, dozens of shelves and 1000's and 1000's of bottles all over the place. How he was able to know where anything was, a miracle, and he was able to find it all in a flash.

India has some very strange contrasts. They have the ancient 5000-year-old hand-hewn stone temples and in the sanctum sanctorum, where they keep the sacred Deity you find it illuminated by giant fluorescent lights and adorning the deities therein are hundreds and hundreds of Christmas lights. They love those things even in their most sacred temples.

So many interesting things.

Temples

Temples in India are a central aspect of life. They can be little roadside shrines with just an icon and a light and a place for offerings. It may be a modest building of 3–500 sq. ft. or a massive complex up to 40 acres with 100's of priests and factotums. These compounds are a wonder to behold. With courtyards and many sub-temples and the main temple which may be 500' by 300'. Usually made of granite. The S. Indian temples have a very specific design setup. There are always little shrines for supporting deities. The central sanctorum is to one deity and it is deep within a cavernous structure. There is a very specific mathematical relationship to all the aspects, as you would find in any cathedral. At the center point in front of the main hall is a pillar called the *Vimanam*. It would have what is called a "foot" (pedestal)—in Sanskrit it is the peedam and at the top is a tapered structure. It may be of gold or plated with gold. It is like an antenna to attract positive forces. There is always a long passageway to the inner sanctum. There may be guardian deities at the entry to the sanctum all made of granite. In the South Siva and Muruga are the main Gods. I was always invited into the sanctum. There is an advantage to being a male swami who also looks Indian. It also helps if you know someone or a bit of the language and the customs. There are a LOT of elaborate rituals involved. Every place has ticket vendors from whom you buy what blessings or rituals you want the priest to do. One more aspect of South Indian temples they usually surrounded by a wall of concrete or wood. The main feature of these walls is that they have wide vertical painted stripes of alternating white and red.

The "Big Temple" in Tanjore is especially impressive—we went there twice. It is massive—it also has 108 Siva Linga around the perimeter, each in its own little alcove.

All South Indian temples have the architectural structure known as a Gopuram. These are stone carvings that rise up on all sides above the building and usually begin about the roofline or just below. It has the shape of a trapezoid and many layers each with dozens or 100's of carvings depicting gods and the stories of Gods. Many are gaudily painted. Some temples such as *Tritani* and *Perur* also have painting on the ceilings in squares depicting the stories of the main deity. *Perur* also has the unusual flourish of having many granite statues of Siva. Also what you may call "artistic additions" of granite chains that hang about 3 feet from the ceiling. No one knows what these are for or what they mean. My friend Sai Ram said they are just things the artisans did for fun in their spare time. Spare time indeed! These are made of solid granite and are like expert wood whittling things you see except that these are made of stone not wood. There are always some special ceremony, music, and rites going on. It is always an amazing experience. Meditation in most temples is always sublime.

India is replete with thousands of temples. Every village has one or more. Up north, there are a number of mosques and in New Delhi there is the Baha'i Temple structured also in the shape of a lotus. Most memorable is the *Sri Raja Rajeshwari* temple with its solid gold cupola and tiled roof. There is also the magnificent massive *Chidambaram* with an equally massive granite *Nandi* (bull) the vehicle of Lord Shiva, He is principle deity of the temple.

Beautiful Experiences

Bede Griffiths

While in Tamil Nadu we enjoyed the opportunity to go to the ashram of Father Bede Griffiths. He was a very saintly British, Catholic priest who came to India after meeting founders of this ashram in France. They were two Catholic priests who founded an ashram called Shantivanam Ashram, which was also known as Satchidananda Ashram. He beautifully combined Hinduism and Catholicism showing that the essence of mystical experience is the same throughout. He is essentially an enlightened Vedantan. He has written several very fine books, there are also numerous beautiful YouTube videos of him. I had the opportunity and blessing to meet him in person at his ashram. Here was a very soft-spoken, kind and gentle man. There was a temple there in the design of the typical South Indian temple with Gopuram but instead carvings of Hindu gods he had Catholic Saints. There they would teach both Hindu Scriptures such as Thirukkural, Bhagavad-Gita along with the Bible. In India he is also known as Swami Dayananda. He also had Indian citizenship. It is well worth reading his biography (The Golden String) or any of his books.

Perhaps the most beautiful and interesting thing was a little gazebo with a large life-size granite carving of Jesus sitting in lotus posture. The unique thing about this statue was that it faced in four directions so they were four carvings. We decided to sit there in meditation. As we're sitting there began to rain. That meditation was one of the most powerful beautiful experiences I've ever had. I was so very fortunate to have met him.

Prior to that meditation Father Griffiths told us that Jesus had come to India during the interim years after He taught in the temple and His return to Jerusalem. There he was known as "Isa." This is documented in the book Jesus the Lost Years by Richard Bach.

43. With Father Bede Griffith at his ashram, Tamil Nadu.

Palani

Palani is a very sacred temple in Tamil Nadu dedicated to Lord Muruga (*Dandayudhapani*). Sri Gurudev spent several years living there. He also received the sacred initiation of the *Siddha Bhogar* who created the image of Muruga out of nine poisonous metals. Those nine poisonous metals (*navapashanam*) after being consecrated by Bhogar became a healing agent.

Gurudev Story 24

On the first trip to India with Gurudev Palani was one of the highlights. Palani is actually on a small mountain—you can climb up about 300 steps or take a little tramcar winch. Naturally, most of us took to the steps, while Sri Gurudev and his hosts took the winch car. Gurudev first led us to the Bhogar Samadhi where the great Saint is interred. We sat there in meditation for about half an hour. When Sri Gurudev came out, he was in an altered state, Samadhi. It was magnificent. I have a photo of Him at that point sitting on my altar.

44. Palani Temple, Bhogar Samadhi after meditation, 1982.

We next went to the temple where they were doing a special puja for us. Sri Gurudev's host was Dr. Mahalingam. He is the very wealthy industrialist of Tamil Nadu who was a major sponsor of LOTUS. One of the things included in this special *puja* was the *abishekham* where they pour various liquid offerings (yogurt, water, ghee etc.) over the Idol. Remember, this was created with nine poisonous metals (some sources say herbs but Gurudev always said it was metals). It happened that on this occasion one of the members of the tour was painfully ill with some stomach thing. He drank a little of that and in within an hour he was perfectly fine. Truth.

The second Palani story was on the last trip that I made to India. I was in Coimbatore and wanted to go to Palani so asked one of our prominent members if there was a way I could get there. She said, "No problem. I will arrange it." Now that is something one hears frequently and normally one would pay it no mind. But, the next day she called and said it is all arranged for you Swamiji to go tomorrow. A car was to come at a prearranged time. However, word got out and there were a couple of young women taking teacher training there they wanted to come and the two other people on our tour also wanted to come so we had a very, very full car. No problem, we're going. That was fun.

There are 3000 people waiting to get on the tram winch—but our guide knows people and knows whom to pay so we get right on. No problem. See, when you go to a place like India it pays to know someone who knows the right people, it really does. This guy also gets us through the line of people who are all waiting for darshan when the priest does puja. I get right there. It is JAMMED. Priest comes out loads me up with garlands, big bags of holy ash, and a quart of abishekam. Don't know what I did to deserve all that. That it was a great blessing.

Well, I did not know it but that day also happened to be THE MAJOR Holiday of the year for Muruga, Thai PusamThere must have been 15,000 people at this place (NOT exaggerating). There are all these guys with drums FANTASTIC drumming—I mean they could move a stone pillar they were so wild and GOOD. And there are these guys carrying things that are called Kaavadis—they are large wooden half-circles about 5 feet in diameter with flowers all over. They are balancing them on their shoulders. This is done as an offering and part of the pilgrimage. They walk for many miles with these things (which must weigh some 40 pounds). They also have a bucket of water on each end.

Amazing Memory Skill

Coimbatore, Tamil Nadu,—interesting experience at the Annapoorna hotel in my second or third trip there. It was the original hotel we where we stayed on the very first trip with Gurudev. It must've been eight years later that I came back to the restaurant, which is well known fantastic Dosa. I entered the restaurant wanting a Dosa and the coffee the manager came up to me all cheerful and bright welcoming me, "Welcome back Swami Murugananda. It is so nice to see you again. Please have something." He actually remembered my name I had no clue who he was. Can you imagine, the place had thousands of customers and after all those years, he remembered me. He sat down with me. I asked for coffee without sugar. He looked at me as if I came from another planet but complied telling the waiter in Tamil what I wanted. It was a delight.

Continuation on to Kerala: Katakali Dance & Other Things

This segment of events occurred in the last trip, led by Swami Divyananda (2003)

Visit to the Advaita Vedanta Ashram

The swami, Bhoomananda, was actually leaving shortly for another engagement but he took the time to meet with our little group of three swamis and four tourists. Three of our group knew nothing about Integral Yoga or Sri Gurudev. Anyway he spent almost the entire time extolling the wonders of the mind and that we should spend more time in the mind. And at the same time he was saying that our Gurudev was teaching ONLY the physical yoga and that was really not the right path. For the first time ever Mataji wanted to correct a speaker but she held back out of politeness. She really did not care for the Swami's whole attitude and that he was saying that our teachings were limited to Hatha Yoga. We all got back in the van took our preferred seats had some water and went off for the four hour ride to Kerala.

Kerala is on the Western cost of India. There are some mountains separating Tamil Nadu from Kerala called the Western Ghats. Not so much mountains as hills actually. The language there is Malayalam—the only language I know whose name is also a palindrome—it is in did Dravidian class of languages a close relative to Tamil. [Other Dravidian languages are Telugu, Kannada.]

We arrive at our hotel in Kerala. It's rather decent actually. Naturally, the first thing I check out, of course, is the eating-place. They have two restaurants—AC and for the natives non-AC. Of course, I head to the non-AC with our translator Satish we are roomies and buddies too. Kerala food is a little different. The breakfasts have well-cooked plantains, which cannot be eaten raw. Satish shows me how to eat them. They are saturated with oil and really heavy so he takes a bunch of napkins to soak up the oil. They also have a kind of Utapam it is not like Tamil Utapam. Main difference is the rice (sadam in Tamil) in Kerala they have red rice which is denser and more nutritious—quite good. I get a thali, of course, and vacuum up the whole thing. I was HUNGRY.

Later I room with a young lad named Thirumalrajan I suggested, as a joke, that we should write up some guide-books, "Top Thali & Dosa Places I Have Known."

We are then scheduled for the standard tourist stuff ALL of which here is SUPER, UNSPEAKABLY boring. First the harbor. Boat ride—boring. Then to an old Church and Synagogue—neither of which are in use now. Guide has no idea what he is talking about when it comes to Catholic or Jewish traditions—he got everything confused, but follows his script even when Mataji corrects him about idols in a church he just is on automatic. Near the place where the church and synagogue are located, are also dozens of tourists shops and the special breed of Tenacious Tourist Touts who are ready to trounce upon us tourists. They actually follow you around like lost puppies at your heels trying to get you into their trinket shops. However, there was also an interesting spice section in one of the shops with big bags of cinnamon sticks, ginger root, tamarind pods, turmeric roots and all sorts of other items—all beautifully arranged. Naturally they were all over-priced.

That evening Divyananda takes us to a traditional Katha Kali dance. It is in a rather funky, not very clean place, with hard uncomfortable wooden chairs, crowded and poorly lit. We are of course late. This is a form of dance with a lot of heavy make-up and elaborate costuming. They do folk-dance telling stories from the Hindu epics and there is a narrator. In this case he was just explaining the form of the dance and giving examples but not actually doing a whole dance. The narrator was way over the top in explaining things in an exaggerated tone. Later that day I did a parody of this dude in my room, which cracked up my roommate. It was pretty absurd. Actually, it was so uncomfortable sitting there that one of the other members, Kirsten, and I got up and took an auto-rickshaw back to the hotel.

The next day Divyananda decides we should all go to the capital city Trivanduram—about two hours away. They have another "palace-museum". They also have an ice-cream shop which Mataji LOVES to the max. Ice cream is actually pretty good. Mataji always has pistachio and chocolate. She loves ice-cream, but insists that it not come from any pre-packaged thing but from scooped out of a big tub. In some places, after hearing her requirements, they will simply take it out of the little cup and shape it into a scoop. That is enough for her.

Travel with the next translator, Sai Ram, was excellent. He is more educated and older than the previous two fellows. He and I manage to find some good eateries in Kanya Kumari and Kovalum. The next day, we go on the "backwater barge trip". This proves to be the only good aspect about the Cochin part of Kerala. It is a slow boat, very relaxing—with thatched palm roof and wooden prow. They served a nice meal on board. It is an easy trip. When we get out we go to a so-called "palace" which may have been palatial at one time but is now a funky, ill-kept museum that looks like it was put together by a third grade civics project.

The last day at Kovalum—we are packing to go on to Kanya Kumari. Since the hotel breakfasts are so horrid coupled with even worse service Sai Ram & I decide to venture out. We see a place called Fast Eddies—sounds like an old hippie place. It actually had good Upama, coffee and dosa. Cheap and actually living up to its name by being "Fast". It was nice. Speaking of breakfast. Mataji would always order the same stuff. Here we are in a country with so much fine local cuisine but she gets toasted white bread with jam. Imitation Western foods pervades middle-class India it is basically dreadful. Worse than the worst white bread you've ever eaten. I always avoided that as one would Velveta so-called "cheese".. If you took the really worst white bread you can find age it for 3 weeks and take out any flavor it may have had - that would be better than Indian bread. She requests two cups of coffee. It was always an ordeal to get TWO cups, which no local ever had. I would have to agree that one cup was never sufficient.

Mataji is the Shopping Queen. Every place we went to, every temple, museum anything she would take every opportunity to shop. Not for herself, most was for getting gifts. She always was interested in some special mala, or altarpiece. She was good at it, not accepting second best.

Hardwar

Hardwar d this is in northern India on the way to Rishikesh on the banks of the Ganges. Here is the resting place of the Holy Ananda Maya Ma, Her Samadhi. There was just a small group of us. The building was unimposing, very modest. It was immaculate inside with marble floors and central altar that was Her resting place. It was so quiet. I sat in meditation and had the most peaceful wonderful meditation I had in years.

Shankaracharya

This happened on the trip with Sri Gurudev in Tamil Nadu. By ancient tradition there are four Shankaracharyas established in India. They are equivalent to the Cardinals in the Catholic Church; that is to say, they are the administrative director of the swami orders in that area. There are four "Muths" or centers, one for each area east, west, north, and south. The southern one is in Tamil Nadu. That place is known as "Kanchi Kamakodi Peetham" or simply Kanchi. In this instance there were actually three individuals, the eldest who was retired, his successor who was also elderly and about to retire, and finally the young successor. Gurudev was with us and explained all this. We had brief darshan of the two elder swamis and an audience with the young successor. Of course everything said was in Tamil, Gurudev translated. Naturally, Gurudev had his little photo album and showed the young swami all about Yogaville and LOTUS and so on. Much earlier in our trip we learned a traditional Tamil devotional song, Kalarkum, which we would sing any time we had any audience in Tamil

Nadu. They all seemed to enjoy it and were always surprised that we knew something in Tamil.

Just a short note illustrating the interesting contrasts you see all over India. The hall were we met the Swami was very austere, no furniture at all. He sat on a wooden platform atop a light blanket nothing else the floors and walls were bare wood. HOWEVER, hanging from the ceiling in the center back of the hall was an enormous analog clock with a very large ad for Bank of India. Interesting.

Rishikesh

45. Sri Swami Sivanandaji Maharaj Samadhi Shrine.

On the first trip, despite all the chaos that had occurred in the beginning, I somehow managed to convince the group leader to get us to Rishkesh, Sri Swami Sivananda's most holy center, The Divine Life Society. There I had opportunity to have met so many of his great swamis chief among which was Sri Swami Chidanandaji Maharaj, president of the DLS and successor to Swami Sivananda. There were also Swamis Dayananda guest master, Premananda the sweetest and most loving one, Vidyananda—the devoted musician Veena player, Krishnananda, and Madhavananda who was a very strict teacher. This ashram is at the banks of the Ganges River so that you can walk right down to it and dip in. The entire atmosphere is permeated with holiness. I was never one to go around chanting anything but while walking around there I found myself spontaneously chanting. Having meals there is quite an experience. The kitchen is adjacent to the dining room. The kitchen has enormous cauldrons sitting over fires right on the stone floor. One cannot attest to the sanitation of those conditions but somehow none of us got sick. We'd all sit on the floor in front of long bamboo mats with banana leaf plates, as is the tradition in most of India. Men would come with big buckets of food quickly serving all the different parts of the meal. It was always delicious. One other experience that stands out is the dear old roti man. His sole purpose was to give out hot roti's and no doubt, he also made them. He was so loving and efficient flipping out two folded rotis onto your leaf. He was keenly aware if you wanted more without any hesitation or loss of his rhythm he went down the lines dispensing his product.

Swami Vidyananda was the music master. A master of the veena. He was always up at 4 AM to play and sing holy bajans. His tiny kutir was always crowded with visitors. I had the great blessing of being there one morning.

Swami Chidanandaji was an erudite and fully enlightened man. He was also a humble man, for example, he would not allow anyone to touch his feet, as is common practice when meeting a great Saint. When we were there, he remembered everyone's name however long ago he had met him or her.

I will never forget on one visit when I was there and he was going to do a dedication of a little shrine that someone donated. I was the only member of our group in the audience at that time. He was going to perform the puja in that tiny shrine. So naturally, he had the donor in there with him along with the donor's business associate. Then He pointed to me to join Him. I was astonished and much honored. As an interesting aside, when he sat down at the table containing puja items he immediately noted quite a number of missing things, "Where are the bilva leaves, where are the matches?" Similar omissions have happened at our own ashram wherein we have been similarly admonished by Sri Gurudev. Interesting how some things are the same no matter where you go.

I also will not forget my visit to the Ayurvedic pharmacy. I walked in there alone; curious as to how they did things. I happened to come to one of the preparation areas and they showed me how they made the Amla oil (Made from the fruit grown in South India used for many Ayurvedic healing preparations as well as air oil.). They had dozens of large burlap bags filled with raw herbs lying about the floor. The giant cauldron with the base sesame oil into which they poured the various and sundry herbs. They also showed me how they dried the special shilajit on the rooftop in giant cookie pans. Shilajit is mineral pitch. On another occasion during the evening satsang, which began the recitation from the Baghavad Gita, the fellow handing out booklets gave all the other tour members the English copy and he gave me the Sanskrit copy without transliteration. Interesting.

Climbing the stairways in Rishiknesh really keeps you in shape. Then I note the pilgrims walking the very long road to the holy shrines of Badrinath & Kedrinath, actually a couple of hundred miles, frequently without shoes. Now, THAT is real dedication.

Saved Again

On my very first trip to Rishikesh we were given nice guest rooms. The room had a lock on the doorknob for security. Sometimes the key would be stuck and it was an ordeal to open the door. I did not realize that the doorknob was very sharp so when I was struggling to turn it, it made a deep cut in my hand. My hand was red and very painful. Bad news! Rishikesh is very isolated, there's absolutely no medical facility within 300 miles. That would be an all-day trip. What was I to do? Get infected? Well, the idea came that I'm here by the holy Ganges I could just walk down there, dip my hand, pray, and hope for the best. Well by the next day there was no redness, no swelling no pain, the hand was completely healed. MIRACLE.

The Ganges is a most sacred river. It is said that the Ganga descended to earth to save humankind, to cleanse the ashes of the departed, and to irrigate the fields. Every bit of it is considered sacred. That is why one often sees the cremated remains of the loved ones poured into the river and for many great Saints who refuse cremation have their body dropped into the river to be carried away. This is how His Holiness Swami Chidananda chose His departure.

Vaishishta Guha

Vaishishta Guha, is the cave where Gurudev had his first enlightenment experience. It is right beside the Ganges up a few kilometers from the Sivananda Ashram. It is a beautiful serene place. There is no sidewalk, no pavement just a rocky place. The cave is quite small, with a low ceiling so that it requires you to bend down while entering. We had a nice meditation and then changed into swimming attire in the little dressing rooms that are built right there. Then we walked straight into the river. They didn't tell me that water was so bitterly cold. Anyway, I was quite young, I had my old, **really old** swimming shorts, took my three quick dips, **really quick**, came out, got dry, changed into my Indian "Street" attire. Immediately one of the caretakers hands me a cup of tea. Now in India you do not get porcelain cup instead you get one made of brass. As with all Indian tea, it is burning hot and loaded with sugar. So hot that I could not hold the cup. I do not know how those folks do that. It was a beautiful experience.

We took this old rickety bus from the cave to the ashram. On one side of this one lane road was the hills on the right side was drop off to the river that could be as much as 100 feet. The road was quite curvy and on occasion, another vehicle or a rickshaw would be coming in the opposite direction there was no fence between the road and the cliff so the driver would have to be extra cautious. I noted that he had massive upper arms and forearms, like Popeye. He was amazingly skillful. We had the very same experience on the road from Kathmandu to the starting point of the Nepal, Annapurna trek.

Magnificent, crazy and divine things are expected to happen at any time.

Ramana Ashram

Ramana Ashram in Tiruvanamalai, Tamil Nadu was the residence of Ramana Maharshi, one of the greatest realized men of India in modern times. Many decades ago someone showed me a photo of Ramana and I immediately saw a beautiful kind and great soul. The first time we came to the ashram there were not that many people there and so we sat in His darshan room and had a terrific meditation. The final time that I came it was quite crowded, they had built the Temple for puja. There is now a great dining hall. The darshan room is now packed, body to body. Most pronounced was the ticking of the pendulum clock that hung on the wall. I did climb Arunachala Hill and sat in his cave for meditation. They served lunch to hundreds of people at a time, separating the Eastern and Western folks. They shunted me to the Indian section. Lunch is served in double-quick time featuring a fellow with a 2-gallon teakettle serving water I lifted my glass up to receive it he said to me, "No, leave it." He poured directly from the 2-gallon kettle without spilling a drop.

Tea Time

Every day they have tea at 4 PM. This was served in a separate building from the main dining hall. Everyone would line up and pick up two steel cups (one for the tea and one to pour into to cool the boiling hot stuff). They were able to serve everyone in five minutes and once served we would sit at some place on the floor, pour the tea back and forth in the cups and have our drink. I saw that as well as tea they also served hot milk. Now, my entire life I absolutely detested milk. I would actually get sick from drinking even a little of milk. I never drank milk. But, on one day, I was really hungry and the crazy notion came to me that I will give this stuff a try—once. I had tea first and got on line for milk. *AMAZINGLY*, it was very delicious. It was hot, sweet, and very fresh. They have their own cows there so the milk was no more than a couple of hours from the cow. After that, I would get two cups a day, something that most of the people would never do. I think this was a sort of miracle—for me to actually like milk. It was right from the cow to the serving and not processed.

Small Miracles

After that wonderful meal everyone proceeded outside to the washbasins to wash our hands. There were hundreds of people there.. An elderly, kind gentleman approached, he says to me, "Swamiji—you left something by your plate. Kindly go get it." I am thinking that "Oh darn I left some food and he is rebuking me for not eating everything." I ignore him. But, he repeats himself, "Swamiji you left something by your plate." I figure, OK let's see what this fellow is talking about. Sure enough, when I run back in there is the wristband that I have to wear EVERY DAY lying on the floor. I took it off so that I could eat more freely. Now I really had to have that band or my hand would be in so much pain I could not even open a door. That was great.

Gurudev is always watching over me. ALWAYS.

Final Little Miracle

Later that day when I bent over to pick up my shoes the precious yantra fell off. The loop that attached it to the chain had worn off and it just dropped right then. But, had it fallen any other time I would have NEVER known it. It would be lost forever. I had a jeweler repair it soon thereafter.

Kanya Kumari

Kanya Kumari is at the very tip of India. In the colonial days they called it Cape Comorin (which is a rather bizarre misspelling). It is famous for having three oceans meeting together, The Arabian Sea, the Bay of Bengal, and the Indian Ocean. It is also known for its *Meenakshi* temple, as well as the famous Vivekananda Rock. There also is a very new massive statue of *Thiruvalluvar*, author of the *Thirukkural*, one of Tamil Nadu's great spiritual guides. The J before departing to that destination I told our tour leader, Swami Divyananda, that I would skip the morning activity because I was too tired so she should be sure to not wake me up. Well of course that's not what happened I get a phone call at 4 AM and she informs me that the van driver is there to get me so I should definitely come. This was par for the course. Well, as long as I was up I said, "Okay, I'll take a shower and move on."

I get into the van and the driver takes me to a place wherein I have no clue where I am. I, do not even know name of our hotel, nada, I could have been stuck there for eternity. I asked the driver, "Should I leave my *chapels* (sandals) on the van?" He nods yes and that's what I do. My first stupid move. There could be anything on the streets broken glass, human excrement, who knows? I should have thought ahead and taken one of my simple shoulder-bags and then put the sandals in the bag as I entered the temple, but I wasn't thinking well at that hour. I thought I would avoid the bustle of leaving the *chapels* outside. I have no clue how far the temple is, and so on. But, once again a little "miracle" happened. The temple priest was standing outside waiting for me, immediately instructing me take my shirt off (standard procedure for men entering temples). Entering this temple was like going into the labyrinth with endless rooms, doors, passageways and sections. I would never have found our group without the guide of the temple agent. A finally takes me to where the group is, alone in a small chamber.

After our meditation, we go out to greet the dawn. There is a vast crowd at the very edge overlooking the three oceans so they can get a view of the sunrise. From this vantage you can easily see the massive *Thiruvalluvar* statue and close by is the Vivekananda Rock. Legend has it that Swami Vivekananda swam from this point to that island to meditate. When viewing the violent currents there it is almost impossible to believe that. We next take a ferryboat to the rock. A turbulent, wild ride on that small ferry.

The temple on the Vivekananda rock is beautifully done in white marble and quite small. I start to meditate in the beautifully done main hall when one of the attendants informed me that the meditation place was down below. So, I complied and went outside down a very narrow stairway to a large chamber below ground. People were sitting in comfortable chairs all quiet. It was very peaceful. The only illumination was an 8-foot neon lit

OM on the wall in front of us. Once again the juxtaposition of the luridly modern with the traditional. I had a most wonderful meditation.

It was all good.

Curious Experience

In that same hotel in Kanya Kumari I was out of toilet paper at night so I called room service for a roll of paper and a young fellow came up with it. He was obliged to fold the first sheet to make a point at the end just like the way they hang every new roll in the rooms. I was going to put it to immediate use. What was the point of that point??

Perur (Mutt) Ashram & Temple

The Perur Mutt or Ashram is associated with the temple of the same name. At that time the head of the ashram was Sri Shantalinga Swamigal (who has since passed on) he was also at the opening of LOTUS.. They follow very a strict path in the Tamil tradition. The Perur ashram is especially devoted to that tradition and language. Their main work is to carry on in the Tamil devotional literature (Thevaram, Thiruvachagam Thirumantram etc.) They have a beautiful school where they teach computer science, among other things. The man running the ashram now is Sri Marutachalam Swamigal Addigalar. He has come to the ashram many times first performing the rituals for Sri Gurudev's Mahasamadhi and then every few years to perform a special Homa.. They were so welcoming and gracious. In one visit the lady running the kitchen immediately sat me down and made a big plate of Dosa for me. It was perfect timing was I was quite hungry. Sri Shantalinga was there at that time. I sat on the lawn with him and he immediately told me I was welcome to stay, no need for the usual introductory letter (which is their mandatory requirement for a visit to stay). I had to decline his kind invitation as our trip did not allow for that. Besides that, the ashram was really quite austere, beyond my capacity.

On a separate occasion, I had the blessing of going to the Perur Temple, which is a marvelous place. It is on the outskirts of Coimbatore. This was Gurudev's family temple where he served as executive director. It is small compared to the most temples. Consequently, one is able to have a nice meditation. They also have an elephant which is unusual for such a small temple. What I like best is that it is so quiet; there are no throngs of people pushing you around. There also no hawkers of souvenirs. Another unique thing of this temple are the 63 brass statues of the Nayanar Saints. The Nayanar Saints are the special group of revered saints of Tamil Nadu.

46. Group tour, Perur Temple, 1982.

47. Perur [year unknown].

Orphanage

Following the temple, we went to a little orphanage not far away. Called Families for Children. They are, in part, sponsored by some group in Finland of all places. I have no idea how there is a connection between Finland and this obscure place in Southern India. Anyway, there are about 200 little kids here—mostly girls—mostly abandoned by either unwed mothers or because they already have a girl and can't afford a second one (this is because of the ENORMOUS debt any family gets into when they marry off a daughter—see below on the wedding.). There are also babies with severe birth defects and diseases some with HIV. But most are quite healthy. With so many toddlers I had a total love blast. I just loved it all those really CUTE girls in little pink and yellow dresses. So I went and hugged them all and asked them what their names were in Tamil—by now I learned a little Tamil—something I intend to get into more.

The orphanage also has a few older "children" some up to 18 years old. They have little cottage industries there such as the handcrafted cards that have embroidered flowers on them also small zippered pouches for the passports or money. I bought a few of these items.. There was one young woman (I'd guess her age to be about 24—but it's hard to say) she was very tiny and deaf. Somehow we connected I signed "I love you" and she came right up to me with a big hug. There is a woman who runs the whole operation. Lives and sleeps with the kids 24/7. She must be about 25 or so—she is like a Mother Teresa—a real saint.

Kovalam Beach

One of the most fun places on my visit in 2004 was to revisit the Kovalam beach in Kerala. There are plenty of coconuts, lots of sun and a beautiful clean white-sand beach. After we got to our modest hotel my first task was to locate a decent restaurant separate from the hotel. (Of course). I found the place where the workers went. This good food and service a lot cheaper than the hotel. Kerala is also home to many Ayurvedic treatment places. One thing that happened on this trip was that I was placed in a room with no AC so I had to keep the windows open. I discovered later that right outside the window was a stagnant pond, which is a potential breeding ground for malarial mosquitoes. I woke up the next day with hundreds of little bumps on my arms and body. Very concerned about this I hastened to the nearest Ayurvedic shop where I saw a most congenial doctor. I showed them what it was and he said not to worry it's merely a heat rash we have the proper medicines for it. Then he proceeded to ask me what I was doing here who I was etc. I told him I was a swami visiting from America etc. He then asked many questions about yoga, practices and so on I did my best to respond. I then asked him what his fee was, "We do not charge for this consultation you pay only for the medicines." That amounted to about Rs.100 or two dollars. I learned that this is the common practice for Ayurvedic physicians, no charge for consultation just for medicines, which is always reasonable.

After breakfast of coffee, iddly/sambar I would get right to the beach. I was fascinated with the fishermen who had these huge wooden boats with 6 to 8 men rowing (no engines) in a boat. They get into the ocean early in the morning to spread their nets out. Then at about 1 or 2 PM they would come in with their catch, pull the boats up to the shore, then form a long line to haul the nets back in. Those nets looked to be very heavy but they were always arranged into perfectly neat piles. They were short men, and amazingly strong.

One beautiful day the sun directly overhead, I decided to have a lie down on the white sands. A policeman, fully clothed in his heavy uniform came by. He said nothing but I saw that he just stood about 150 feet away. My tour friends told me he was just guarding over me and making sure that nothing bad happened. Interesting. I also went for an Ayurvedic "massage". It was the most hasty, superficial, nothing massage I've ever had. The man there was actually the doctor in charge of the place. Well it was only Rs.100 so it was not that bad. I also discovered the Kerala has the largest Catholic population in India. Kerala was the place where St. Thomas came to found a church. Interesting.

Short Takes

The Restaurant Finder

One of the first things I would do when I got to any city after checking in the hotel was to scout out the area for good places to eat that were not the tourist type restaurants. Inevitably, I would serendipitously find something excellent. I would then inform any of the interested members of our group to come along and try something more genuine and a little different. It soon became known that I would know the good places to eat. This was a very fun thing to do. There were always a few brave souls that came with us. Dharma Benicasa would always come. Dharma was an old friend who lived in the Connecticut ashram. Here is always a jovial happy fellow. Very fun to be with an adventurous and searching for different restaurants with me. Here is a great asset on our trip.

India is 8 ½ hours ahead of New York time. What's with a half-hour?

Gurudev Story 25

On one of our side trips after our meal Gurudev was served traditional Pan, and item frequently was served after lunch. It consists of betel leaf, smeared with lime paste and filled with chopped betel nut (Areca) red katha paste (made from the khair tree) and rolled up into little wad. This is then chewed well until saliva comes, which is quick. Gurudev did this and in a few Moments. He said, you spit out the saliva, don't swallow then he showed us His tongue all bright red. I tried that and it was quite tasty and invigorating. This substance is actually addictive and you see globs of red stuff on the sidewalks. The men who choose this frequently lose their teeth. It is addictive because it is slightly narcotic.

Kaumara Maadam

On one of the trips with Sri Gurudev we visited this ashram. It was run by Sri Sundaramororthi Swamigal. He was one of the honored guests at the LOTUS opening. Their specialty is granite sculpture. All the granite sculpture at LOTUS (the elephants, the central Yantra, the Angels with garlands, etc.) was made there. It is quite magnificent to see all those men squatting on the wooden floor with hammer and chisel sculpting away. All this takes place on a very large open-air deck with roof. While we were walking I attempted to ask the swami if they had a Moorti of Arumugam (another name for Muruga and the first name I received from Sri Gurudev). I'd never seen one and thought it would be interesting if I could purchase one. He quickly instructed something to one of his aides in Tamil. The man ran off and came back with an extremely large solid brass Muruga. There was even a space for the "spear" (Vel symbolic of one-pointed concentration by which Muruga attains his power). I thought that this might have come from Swamiji's own altar. It was so large that I had to purchase a separate piece of luggage to carry it on the plane. I still have that Moorti on a little altar near my bed.

Skipping the Taj Mahal

While in Delhi one of the planned excursions was a trip to the Taj Mahal. For some reason I decided not to go. Most likely because I just wanted to avoid the giant tourist crowds. So I hung out, went to a different restaurant, met some people etc. Hours later when they came back everyone told me I had made the right choice because the bus broke down somewhere on the road. There is no one nearby who could fix it and the driver had to go many miles to find help. It took an entire day for them come back. They had no food, nothing to do but wait—BORING. Sometimes you make the right choice.

That Certain Member of the Tour

On my very last tour we had just three or four other members all of them women. One of them was there for just a week or so her name was Lizzie. I noted that she was constantly writing in her diary book. She was a quite an energetic high-powered and a rather self-absorbed person. She didn't say much to me except that she was a writer. Much later on I discovered she was Elizabeth Gilbert, author of *Eat, Pray, Love*, etc..

Fresh Coconut Joys

One of the most enjoyable things I did in South India was getting fresh coconut every day it is called "Illaneer" in Tamil (sp?). You will find someone selling it everywhere they pick one up make a small slice off the top with a super-sharp curved blade, called a Kathir Aruval. This looks like it takes great skill not to slice one's hand. They give you a straw or you can drink directly from the little hole that they put in the top. It is quite delicious and refreshing and according to Gurudev most healing for upset stomach. After finishing that beautiful liquid you can make a slicing motion with your hand indicating you'd like the coconut opened which they do, then fashions a little scoop with a piece of the husk for you to scoop out the very soft jelly kernel. It is very filling.

Find the Train

Small Miracle – Serendipity

On my last (2004) pilgrimage I started out in Chennai as the guest of Mr. Senthilnathin, a most gracious and gentle host who knew Sri Gurudev since childhood in Sri Lanka. After three days there, I had to get to the train to Coimbatore. Senthilnatin's able assistant took me. Chennai's train station is enormous. There must be 10 to 12 platforms each with its own pair of trains. You not only have to find the correct platform and train but the car where your assigned seat would be. It is the most crowded place you can imagine, furthermore no one there spoke English, and so it was most fortunate that I had the help of that man to find the proper train and the right car. This was the first serendipitous event on my last tour. I had what you might call a business class car with a reserved seat. Most of the passengers there were businessmen, most of whom spoke good English.

After several hours of riding alone a gentleman sits near me, well dressed and young. He asks the usual question, "Coming from?" Most Indians think I am also Indian but from the north—like Gujarat. That is what I look like. I say I am from an ashram, a swami etc. I always have a pocket photo of Sri Gurudev to show people. He asks me "What is your philosophy?" So we have a two hour discussion. It gets boring for me because he has not much to say. Actually, he is a doctor, and the guy behind me is an electrical engineer. Then he gets off and the next gentleman coming in is also going to Coimbatore, he is a visiting professor of some sort (Culture I think) anyway he offers me a ride in case the person who is supposed to meet me is not there. It is fortunate that he was there to show me my station. There was no way I could have seen the sign for the station.

It is worth noting that the Indian railway is a very efficient system trains always leave on time. It is also, by far, the largest employer in all of India.

There is an interesting array of employees on the train. Train ticket dude is a very officious sort—collecting tickets checking everything. That's his life. He lives to collect tickets and check on everything.

There are fellows (kids actually—no more than 16 years old) constantly coming by selling tea—coffee. They Sing out "Chaiya, Kapi, Chaiya, Kapi" These guys all have their own uniforms. (Dirty brown shirt and trousers and a military type of cap, same color.) I am so happy that I had some food packed before going because what they sell on trains is dreadful.

Chennai Beach

While on the subject of beaches. Chennai is on the coast. The beach there is HUMUNGOUS. It's about 900 feet wide from the start of the sand to the ocean's edge. There was not a soul there. It was a vast empty space and very clean, pure white sand. There was one lone guy pushing his little ice-cream cart. Did he really think that anyone was actually going to buy anything at all??? There are also lots of homemade boats with neatly piled up fishing nets.

The following bits occurred on my final trip, which was led by Divyananda.

The Local Ice-Cream Place

Not far from the IYI on DB road right next to the little Ganesh temple is a soft ice-cream shop. Chidananda told me about it. I went one day. Very nice, clean and no customers. They have good ice cream. About 20 RS for a big serving with chocolate sauce. Run by a couple of Nepali fellows. I recognized that they were Nepali straight away. They also have a deal, which Mataji did a few times but I could never do, "eat all you want in 45 minutes for 50 RS." I can't eat that fast and besides the one serving was more than enough for me anytime. They also had a neat game where you can get various discounts. They had a big velvet bag with various colored tokens, each with different values of discount from zero to 50%. I would pick one (not looking into the bag) I usually got the 10% off. They had a giant TV set that was perpetually tuned to cricket matches. You remember Indians are total cricket nuts.

The Roots Factory Complex

I forgot to mention that Ramaswami, the owner—or as they call him the Chairman, of Roots is a cousin of Sri Gurudev. His father, Krishnaswami, was Gurudev's uncle; he died early this year at age 94. On one day, Satyanarayana called and asked if I would like a tour of the Roots place. Yeah, sure, I thought anything to break the boredom. This gent is in charge of human resources at the Roots Company. He is very polite, always saying, "Yes, Swamiji, Yes, Swamiji." In fact, that is how many of the people are. Now a bit of background. Roots is a multi-level manufacturing company. It began in the manufacturing of automobile horns. It then branched out to other automobile parts such as filters and even further out to precision testing of scientific equipment. When Ramaswami was young, he had some training in engineering. When he got married he spent seven years thinking up a design for a car horn. He then started to make that horn. Soon he had ten or fifteen designs and all sorts of orders. They do the entire process from blacksmithing to winding the wire. All with individual machines. Slow work. He has contracts from Ford Motor to do 100,000's of horns. It was quite impressive. Besides horns, he also makes other car parts: such as brake fittings, ignition parts, all sorts of stuff most of which I know nothing about. They also have contracts to do precision measurements of some kind. For this, they have built a special super clean building with controlled atmosphere. I saw all of that. We then went to the brand new office building. Very modern. Ramaswami was as they say,"out of station." Meaning he was traveling out of the country so I did not see him. He is a very dynamic young man. They have all sorts of computer systems and some even in the temperature-controlled rooms. Yes, it was impressive. All of it the work of one man.

Gandhi Kadhi Shops

In every major city, there is a Gandhi Shop—known officially as the Gandhi Kadhi Gram Yoga Bhavan. They are government run shops that specialize in the handloom (kadhi) industry. Therefore, they sell mostly dhotis and ready-made men's clothing: shirts, kurtas, vests (which they call jackets) pajamas, and even hats. In addition, there are shoes and Ayurvedic products, incense, malas and some jewelry like the nine gem stone rings (Navaratna). The quality of late has greatly improved. I got four shirts from the shop in Chennai and they are all a perfect fit. Moreover, after washing keep the size and stay well. I also got a hat there, which is pretty cool. In previous years, I got vests and kurtas. However, the kurtas all wore out rapidly. The price is always "fixed" by government and is always fair. No bargaining or haggling. However, they often run "discounts" which amount to just 10%. They are always well run, very orderly and the workers are all competent and respectful and, as always, they don't care how many times you come back or how many items you try on. In fact, they remember you when you come again, even though they saw you just once seven weeks ago.

Power Outages

This happens a lot. They even schedule it for different sections of the city on a weekly basis. Reason—there simply is not enough power to go around for such a large population. Almost EVERY business and shop has a diesel generator. When the power is out and I walk down the main street, there is a constant roar of the generators. Makes any normal conversation impossible.

Nature Cure Camp

In the Coimbatore area about 20 minutes from the IYI is the Satchidananda Nature Cure camp. Started by Ramaswami's father, Krishnaswami, in 1989. It is a small complex right next to Ramaswami's house and the Roots factory. The camp gets about 10 to 15 people at a time. Most are overweight women. Some gents come too. The main program is weight loss. Ramaswami invited me to come stay at any time. Therefore I called his office and spoke with the man who met me when I arrived, Satyanarayanan. He said I could come at any time and he will get me a ride there as well. I signed up for 4 days.

I came on a Thursday and they set me up in one of the nice private apartments, with two rooms and a bathroom. Very clean and quiet. They have four residential buildings, some with private apartments plus the main building with little rooms, dining room, and treatment facilities. There was a young lad named, Lakshmikant, he could not have been more than 15, who was to get me what I needed. All I wanted was a yoga mat and a bottle of water. I got the mat soon but it took him six hours and three reminders to get some water. I then went to see one of the doctors. They have two women docs. Both speak excellent English, they come from Kerala where they have 100% literacy. The younger one whom I saw asked about my problems etc., and what I would like to do. I opted for massage one day and mud bath the next day. They have all sorts of treatments including, mud bath, what they call "vibro" massage, sauna, hot-tub. Diet is most important. They have three good meals a day. Some of the best food I've ever had, no oil, nicely prepared. Plenty of fresh fruits for breakfast, I could ask for as much as I want, including fresh coconut, papaya—my favorite. The food is all lovingly served and prepared. When you get to the meal they know who you are and check that your individual menu is that was set by you and the doctor. Also in the morning, you get this amazing drink of "grass juice". I did not know exactly what it was but it felt powerful and tasted good.

The first thing they do in the morning is give you a mudpack. This is a towel wrapped around cool mud about 2 inches thick by 6 inch long that you put on your abdomen. It did not do much for me. I then went for hatha class and the Agni Hotra (fire ceremony) in a section up on the roof of the main building. The setup for this is in an enclosed area where they have a little stage. On the stage is a TV and they do this sacred ceremony with a TV behind. They have a brass square container about 7" high in which they burn cow-dung chips. They then do a lot of chanting in Tamil, none of which I understood. They claim that the smoke is supposed to be healing. I did not experience anything except discomfort. The hatha class is also there. On the hard concrete floor which is covered only with a sort of cotton rug. Not at all comfortable. I had a mat. How they expect all those old guys to do any hatha on that hard surface is beyond me. A curtain divides the room lengthwise. Men on left women on right. Class is in Tamil so I did not understand a word. I ended up doing the hatha in my room.

That afternoon I signed up for a massage. They direct me to the area where all treatments take place (except mud bath, which is outside.) They have a number of rooms that are sort of curtained off and a waiting area with benches. There are three or four guys there waiting. I go in and there are actually two tables in this room. There is a client on one and I get on the other. It is very plain, no head rest, very little padding. I mention that I must have a pillow for my neck. This takes 10 minutes of repeating and translating until they got it. This scenario is to repeat itself each time. (Treatments are twice a day) so after getting all set the guy comes in. Massage in India means oil bath. A sort of Ayurvedic thing. However, this was quite different. For one there is a crowd of about five fellows in the room, clients and staff, all watching me and ALL jabbering away in Tamil, including the fellow who was doing the massage. His technique was really the worst I have ever experienced. It felt like he was fixing a car.

The best treatment was the mud bath. I went outside to a walled off area. There is a concrete bench and a wall with a sort of well in which is the wet clay. The guy puts this clay all over my body. I stand there. The sun is wonderful and strong. He instructs me to stand facing the sun until all the clay dries. I just love this. I stand with arms outstretched back and front. After about 10 minutes, it is all dry and I take a terrific bucket shower.

The other thing they do is so-called exercise. Actually, it is just slow walking around the compound. BORING. They also have a badminton court. It is pretty weird to see two young women hitting the bird while wearing their saris. While sitting on a bench outside one woman asks me the usual opener, "Coming from?" "Ashram in the U.S." Standard answer. "What do you do?" "I am a swami." I show her the photo of Gurudev. No response. "Do you have a family?" "No I am a swami." What is your salary?" Indians do that; they see nothing wrong with directly asking the most personal questions. "No salary, I am a swami." Seeing that this was going nowhere I end the conversation. They did have a little garden for veggies and I saw a man hoeing the field with one of those short handled hoes with a wide, thick blade. He had to be always bent over to do this. **Backbreaking work.**

The final observation in this place happened on the last morning. I am about to go when two ladies arrive. "Clean room." "No, that's fine—room is clean." "Clean room." "No it's fine, thank you." It was a statement not a question. I let them in and they are like a dance team. Perfect coordination, they are so efficient. They completely clean the room, change all the linen in about 3-4 minutes flat. It is really clean. It was amazing.

Women's Work & Construction

There are NO women rickshaw drivers, no women bus drivers or workers on the trains BUT there ARE woman who work at construction sites carrying big bags of cement mix, bricks etc. on their **heads**. You can see them on the roof of a construction site walking ever so slowly and so straight and elegant with a bag of cement mix and the drop the contents right where there is a guy mixing it with water. You also see women working on road crews—digging ditches by hand—really back-breaking HARD work in very hot conditions. Moreover, all these women are doing that work wearing saris—very amazing. One day I saw them digging a ditch for an electric or Internet cable standing there was an older woman with one of those farming hoes, which is a short handled very thick steelhead hoe made for scooping and breaking the earth. She was quite adept at scooping up. It is curious that they would use such ancient methods for something so modern as an Internet cable.

The other feature is how they build scaffolding. They have no steel scaffolding (too expensive) instead they use bamboo poles lashed together with strips of palm. They will often have an awning for shade made of whole palm leaves. It's all handwork. No power tools.

Tanjavore Artisan Shop

Next day we all trek to the man artisan shop run by a chap named Jai Prakash Singh. This was perhaps the most interesting place I have been to in India. It is in a small village outside of Tanjavore. What he does is to fashion traditional brass statue made by the "lost wax" method. They have some guys making clay molds. Very intricate work. Then there is a fire pit into which some fellow sticks a long-handled ladle with the metal mix. It's really hot there. He carefully melts the metals and then pours it into the molds. Amazingly, he never spills any of the stuff. After cooling, they take the statue out and another guy files down the imperfections. I purchased a very intricate Nandi. He also has some men who make "Tanjavore art". Which is painting on glass. Quite beautiful. Very delicate, much too fragile to transport. Alas.

At the end of our visit, the workers gathered in the display shop to get a blessing. Each one came one by one bowed to Divyananda and my feet for a blessing. It was quite moving. This also happened several times on my trip. Once at the Big Temple in Tanjavore a gentleman came to me and bowed. Fortunately, I always had a supply of Holy Ash to give as prasad. It is all Gurudev's blessing.

The area in which this little shop is located is mostly Moslem. Lots of small huts, goats, barefoot kids and all the usual stuff. When we were walking back to the van, I saw a most interesting thing. Outside of one hut, sitting on an overturned box was a lady --- talking on a mobile phone. So even in a shantytown village they have mobile phones. Amazing

Note on Hatha Class at the Institute

I gave a few classes at the IYI there and observed a few. All the women who come, some older, always wear full dress. Salwar Kamiz or even Sari. It is amazing that they could do any asana that way. In addition, when they do inverted poses like shoulder stand they have this piece of cloth belt that they tie up their kurta with so it does not flop down. Wild.

When I gave a class in the IYI it was on the rooftop. I had to almost shout because the traffic noise is so loud. In addition, one guy had a cell phone that he answered in the middle of the class. There was also a guy who actually came in 25 minutes late. They do not think anything is wrong with that.

The Institute had very thick, bulky mats we provide for the students. We also carried them on our tour. Every stop we would roll them up, tie them with some heavy twine and stow the whole thing atop the van. It took up quite a lot of space. But, they did serve the purpose of protecting the body when doing hatha on a hard surface like concrete or marble.

South Indian Wedding

One afternoon Divyananda offered to take me to a wedding that evening. As I've never been to such an affair, I thought it might be interesting. I did not know that Divyananda's idea of "evening" meant 10:30 PM. I later learned that was standard for her. Even at that hour, the place was jam-packed. It was a very formal, structured set up. One of the requirements being that every guest, this can be hundreds of people, have their photo taken with the couple. They are all dressed up in elaborate costumes with silk clothing and all sorts of jewelry standing on the stage. They must have been standing there for many hours in those very hot getups. We then asked if we wish to eat, one does not refuse that invitation it would be very discourteous. So we sit down, we are almost alone; waiters immediately serve us a batch of deep-fried foods. We're then offered ice-cream which we cannot refuse as it is considered a great delicacy. I later learned that this kind of gala event could go on for three days. Since the bride's family pays for it, as you might expect, many families go bankrupt marrying off their daughters.

The Glory of South Indian Food & a Special Surprise

There is a special beauty, style of service, and etiquette regarding South Indian food. In the old tradition, the meal is served on a big banana leaf. Sometimes the opening course is three or four types of rice. There can be a sweet rice, lemon rice coconut and pungent rice. More often, you get a variety of items. However, it also can be on a thalli with rice in a big mound in the center surrounding which are a number of katori, little bowls, filled with many things including different vegetables, sambar, rasam, and some kind of sweet. There is a prescribed order in which one consumes all this usually going clockwise starting with rice sambar, vegetable sometimes is a bit of pickle in the middle. Going to rasam and then the final part is taking another big pile of rice mixing with yogurt (tair, In Tamil). However, they are very forgiving if you do not know the order.

One time I went with one of the tour guides he took me to a simple workingman's lunch place on the thali was what looked like a potent single, dry, long chili pepper. I thought, "I dare not even touch it". It looked like as if it would explode in my mouth if I tried to eat it. But, my friend said, "Try it Swamiji you will like it." So, with a bit of rice and yogurt I very carefully and with much hesitation bit a tip of that pepper. It was absolutely delicious I consumed the whole thing. This is my introduction to mor mulugai. The yogurt and salt-cured, fried chili pepper is surprisingly not at all spicy it is, however, delicious with a delightful texture.

Most often, when we were guests anywhere in India hosts will most gracious and generous. I recall one time in someone's home we started a nice juice followed by a terrific mushroom soup. This was followed by the best of all North Indian dishes my favorite among which was sag paneer—spinach with fresh made cheese. This meal was in Jaipur the hosts were Sindhi people. The husband was a high-court judge. This was common anywhere Gurudev went the people he spent time were well-positioned, physicians, judges, filmmakers and so on Gurudev moved with people with connections. Good to move in high places.

Pondicherry, Aurobindo Ashram

Pondicherry is on the West coast of India. Very modern. It was once a French colony and the European influence is still there. The main influence and industry now is the Aurobindo Ashram and the very independent Auroville. These two bodies do not get along very well. Auroville is enormous, really, really big—maybe 2000 acres, more than twice the size of Yogaville. The ashram is small. The ashram has the Samadhi of Sri Aurobindo his successor The Mother (a French Woman who became his disciple). It is quite beautiful and peaceful. It has a bookshop and the house that they lived in. Many years ago I had the privilege of actually meditating in the bedroom of Sri Aurobindo. They do not allow that now.

We then proceeded to the center of the ashram, the Samadhi of the Mother. We had a wonderful meditation around the Samadhi of the Mother. They keep it all very clean, with heaps of flowers. However, they are really very super controlling. That is how they are at Auroville as well. They tell you where to sit, when to come, when to go. It is very tight.

They have a bookshop. I did not go but naturally, Mataji was right there in line getting all sorts of stuff. It was too, crowded there so I meandered off to the street. I was quite tired and my feet really hurt so I did not get very far. Directly across the street was this guy squatting behind a blanket on which lay bowls of Rudraksha beads. I was in the market for some special beads, ones with one, two, three "faces" etc. This guy looked like something out of a scary movies. His few teeth were all yellow and crooked. His face was a map of wrinkles. I thought, "Cool, this is my man.", I say in Hindi and Tamil Ek Muk, Do Muk Teen Muk (one face, two face, three face) well he has them. And, he understands my broken Hindi—cool. I look, we bargain and I come away with a set of 3 rare beads that I got mounted on a silver chain which I now wear. He also gave me a little rosewood mala and a single small bead that I gave away as gifts to friends here. In the midst of the who should show up but Mataji. She gets what she thinks is a set of beads that have Siva's Trisula (trident) on them (Well not really, but I won't ever tell) and the real prize a seven face bead that is quite rare. Good price too.

Next day we head off to Auroville. That is an international community. It has all sorts of industries, incense, notepapers, publishing (lots of books by Aurobindo & the Mother), all sorts of local craft. There is a lot of friction, political and otherwise between the Ashram, Auroville and the town of Pondicherry. Anyway Auroville is SUPER organized. The big thing they promote is the Mandir. This is a building sort of like LOTUS dedicated to all the world religions, but not necessarily to unity of all religions rather to be a place for meditation and the mastery of the mind. It is immense 4 or 5 times bigger than LOTUS and round. Made of ferro-cement. There is a REALLY long line you need to get on, but first you have to check your bags and they do not even allow any bottles of water, no cameras, nothing. They have security all over. They insist that I check my bag and everything that I am carrying, and they keep reminding you not to talk as if the 139 signs posted all over the place were not sufficient. However, the line moves fast.

The distance we have to walk is about one quarter mile or about 25 times the distance of the LOTUS path. It is all very neat and lined with 1000's of potted plants. A rope separates the incoming and outgoing lines. At last we get to this massive structure, everyone is silent; we are all sweating and nearly fainting (remember they took our water) and guess what—this is still under construction, yes, they let us in but there is scaffolding all over the place. They have been doing it for over 45 years.

Jaipur

Speaking of Jaipur (okay, I just started doing that now) we were there once with Gurudev to visit the marble statue making place. This was for the marble deities to go at Kailash. I recall the place was in the back of a very narrow alleyway. It was filled with statuary. I took a beautiful photo of Gurudev sitting amongst several of them. I keep it on my altar. Jaipur is a most unusual city in the state of Rajasthan. Men wear these enormous turbans. It is a colorful place. The Jaipur marble factory was a special surprise for us. This is down a long narrow alleyway a small unpretentious building. It is here this all the marble statues that are now at Kailash were made. It is astonishing to see all those men [and they are all men] sitting on the floor with little hammers and chisels carving away in his hard substance. How they do it is astonishing.

48. At Jaipur marble factory, photo [by SM].

49. Mahabalipuram. Rock carving of Mahabharata.

There have been dozens and dozens of temples, hundreds of experiences, many delightful, some wretched, many forgotten in the shifting sands. We have to skip Vadallur, Venkateswara mountain, temple, Madu Malai, the streets of New Delhi, so many restaurants, special meals, lost things—I have to stop someplace. Ah, maybe another book. One never knows.

Carry it on.

The "Great" Departure Experience – Last Trip to India

On my final trip to India I thought I'd add a couple of days at the end in Coimbatore just for fun. This turned out to be a most dreary endurance test. The Institute did not offer any food so I had to hunt down places to eat which is especially daunting for an evening meal as restaurants didn't open till quite late. The nonstop noise of irritating car horns, the pollution, and the heat all added to the burden. Thus for the last few days I counted the hours, the minutes to the Moment of departure. It was brutal. Since I arrived by way of Chennai that was my departure point. I took a short flight there and was met by my host. I stayed overnight. Finally the day came. My kind and generous host got me to the airport but he could not enter as he did not have a ticket. Thus began the great bureaucratic Olympic hurdles.

Only ticketed passengers may go through the entrance door therefore you had to show proof that you had a ticket just before your entered and right there were conveyor belts to carry your luggage to x-ray even before you even entered. I went to the check-in counter; where again they checked my ticket and luggage. When exiting India there is a special, green customs ticket to demonstrate you have nothing to declare coming or going and you must present that tiny green slip along with your passport at the second check-in point. This was a very long line. The official to check those documents first checks the green ticket (foreigners declaration of goods being taken out which also serves as the exit pass) that he stamped that and the boarding pass which he stamped. You are to hold onto the little green slip. When nearing the end of that very long queue I thought I had the green slip in my passport but it was not there. Therefore, I thought to go back to the first check-in fellow. It was not far, so I ran back and asked the man if he had my green slip he said, "Sir, you put it in your pocket on the left side." Of course, he was right. Those fellows are very, very observant and they remember. Astonishing. They would make great witnesses for a crime.

Well, it was getting late so I jumped the line running pell-mell to the head. No one stopped me. I then gave the fellow at the second checkpoint my green ticket, which he took again, checked my boarding pass which he stamped for the third time. Once again they check the passport we then go to the x-ray lines, one for carry-on luggage, and our bodies go in another. Not just one line but TWO. More opportunity for employment.

Retrieve carry-on luggage go to a desk where men open them and physically check contents.

At last head for the gate thinking, "Well, I'm home free." BUT, there is yet one more check-in fellow who will stamp your boarding pass one more time. How do they have room for so many stamps?

The great Indian governmental bureaucratic employment service. Thus ended the most annoying bureaucratic experience of all time as well as this chapter.

Nepal & Many Great "Miracles"

This is the longest sub-chapter as it was where the most significant "miracles" happened. I use the term "miracle" in a very general sense. These are fortunate events, one can also call it serendipity, but "miracle" will do as well.

It was 1998 with Swami Chidananda of the New York IYI. He is an experienced and wonderful tour guide. I had always wanted to trek in the Himalayas. Nepal turned out to be one of the most beautiful places I've ever been to. The people there are kind, generous, and gentle. More than any other journey, this had the most of what one might call "miraculous events".

I had decided to travel on the first leg with Swami Chidananda as he was the most knowledgeable traveler I know. For some reason he decided to travel with Kuwait airline with a three-hour stop in Kuwait then to the capital of Kerala, Trivandrum [Thiruvananthapuram]. As we were traveling from the ashram we took a shuttle from Dulles to Kennedy. This required a six-hour layover at Kennedy, plus a one-hour delay. That seemed okay but little did I know how it extended our journey. Following that was a 15-hour flight to Kuwait then 4 hours to Kerala. Despite the delay at Kennedy, we got to Trivandrum on time At this point Chidananda decided to go directly to Coimbatore by train. He knew his way around town so we went to the train station got tickets. And then he took me to his favorite little breakfast restaurant where we had a modest breakfast There was an additional three hour wait for the train. I decided to do my hatha yoga right there on the train platform. This is India; people are used to things like that. Some people stared anyway. We had 11 hours to Coimbatore, this was the final leg of a 47 hour journey.

First Minor Miracle

Luckily, in our train car was a friendly local man who shared some of his snacks. More importantly, he informed us beforehand that were nearing our stop otherwise we would never have known it because we could not read the signs from train. The train the stops for 95 seconds. Imagine my surprise when Chidananda asked me to negotiate the taxi. He, the master traveler is asking me a relative beginner. Well after 47 hours of travel, we were not in great shape so I did the best I could. Gave the driver the precise location and district of the city. Coimbatore is a very large city. The taxi driver did not know where it was so had to stop three or four times to ask for directions. Naturally, every time we stopped to ask for directions seven or eight people came to advise him each with different ideas of how to get there.

We get there happy and exhausted. Could not sleep at all despite total exhaustion. The jet lag plus the extreme heat and noise were just too much for me..

First Major Miracle

Next day I'm all bright and sparkly and decide to go for a nice lunch at a restaurant I knew that was in an alleyway off the main street (DB Road). It is the only restaurant I've ever seen run by women. Lunch is "set" meaning there is no menu. It's all at a very low price; they serve you as much as you want. I then return to the Institute where I ask Swami Divyananda is she wouldn't mind making a visit to Gurudev's birth home in Chettypaliam. She said, "Certainly, if you could just wait for me to get the things set up for satsang." At that Moment I hear a very loud bang, to me it was the sound of a bomb but Divyananda questioned my assertion and wanted to just look out onto the street. Sure enough hundreds of people were running. It turned out that bomb was exactly on the corner where I had just turned not five minutes before. It was just down the street where the Institute is. It happened that this bomb was meant for the right wing Hindu leader (Adwani) who was supposed to give a speech at that corner that day. The bomb was set by the Muslim fanatics against this man. I avoided that bomb by mere minutes.

Saved

The following day we were informed there was a massive car-bomb around the corner. I forgot to mention that there was a large group of us at the Institute. Everyone else was there for a special India tour. We were told to evacuate the building and a few of us were sent to stay with Gurudev's grandson, Murugesh. He and his wife lived in a nice apartment at the far end of town. They were extremely gracious and kind hosts. Swami Atmanananda (now Sundaram) was with me the whole time. Previously he took me to a couple of temples showed me all the deities there etc.; he is a true Hindu. During that time he got quite sick so I took care of him with Ayurvedic herbs and tender coconut water which was very helpful. Murugesh told me that he was sleeping on the very same cot Gurudev had used long ago in Sri Lanka.

Chidananda had to move ahead during that crisis so for security he gave me half of his travelers checks that amounted to $10,000. I said, "Sure I can do that." In a few days I went ahead to New Delhi. I got a taxi the next morning to the international airport.. This taxi driver spoke no English so I chatted up with broken Hindi referring to the photos of his guru. We got to the airport in plenty of time and I proceeded to the gate.. In those days New Delhi airport, even the international terminal, was a very drab affair. The gate was mostly deserted except for one Nepali couple.

Beginning of Next Major Miracle

It is interesting to note how synchronicity plays an amazing role in the experiences I had on this trip. I was alone; opposite me was a Nepali couple. One can always recognized the Nepali man as they have a typical kind of hat (Nepali Topi) which they always wear. There I am all decked out in bright orange, with holy ash on my forehead, "The whole 9 yards". The husband motions to me gently to approach him, which I do. "Coming from?" (Standard SE Asian conversational style) "America." "Going to?" "Kathmandu."

"Are you a Sadhu?"
"Yes Sir". "What do you do?" "I teach yoga." "Oh, please tell me is yoga good for insomnia." "It most certainly is. I teach very nice deep relaxation and pranayama. I would be happy to show you."
"Oh then, where are you staying in Kathmandu?" "Kathmandu Guest House." "Well, you must come and join me for supper at my house. My wife will come and pick you up take you wherever you wish to go. Is there some special thing you would like to get in Nepal?" "A woolen shawl would be very nice. Please give me your good name (proper formal Indian conversational style in asking for someone's name) and contact information. What time will your wife come?"
"She'll come at five, she will show you around the city and special places. If you like she will take you to a shop where you can do some shopping."

The gentleman gives me his card, it says, "Dr. Pandi , Royal Physician." "Sir, does this mean that you are the physician to the King?" "Yes, that is why I am here in India. Where the King travels I go with him. My wife comes with me as well. So there it was, meeting the King's personal physician.

50. Path to Muktinath Nepal.   51. With my dear friend Arjuna & village kids.

52. Guest house kitchen, one flame wood stove.   53. Walking though typical village on trek.

Kathmandu Beginning

Chidananda was there to meet us at the airport. There were about 14 of us on that tour. I was happy to unload the $10,000 back to Chidananda. We checked into the guesthouse, which was quite nicely done. We had three days in Kathmandu before departing for our trek. One night they showed the Martin Scorsese film Kundun, a beautiful film about the Dalai Lama. The little theater they had was decked out with old car and van seats. Tickets were a dollar, popcorn about a dime. Pretty good deal, I thought. I nodded off half the time.

Next day I tried to fax the doctor to make sure of the time that his wife would come, (my standard OCD in operation) but the fax was not working. I spoke with the receptionist at the hotel. However, first he asked if yoga could cure eye diseases. I offered what advice I knew. It is amazing how many questions I would get while traveling there. The receptionist makes the call for me, they verify the pickup time of the doctor's wife. I asked the receptionist what I owed him for the call he said, "No charge."

The doctor's wife came to pick me up at the appointed time and gave me a beautiful Tibetan prayer wheel, which I still have. She took me to a local shop, not the tourist kind, and I pick up a shawl and purchased a very thick Tibetan type woolen cardigan. This would prove to be of great importance later on. [TBC]. She took me on an automobile tour of Kathmandu and outlying areas. I was able to see the Himalayas the day that happened to be Siva Ratri, I learned later that it is quite auspicious to see the Himalayas on that day. She pointed out mountains *Gauri Shankar* and *Ganesh Himal*.

Kathmandu is an international stopping place a vibrant, energetic city. There is a magnificent Buddhist temple at its center. This is the starting point for all the tourists and trekkers. You see many Israelis, so many that restaurant signs are in Hebrew as well as English. The next most common groups are the Germans and Japanese. I found the main trekker restaurants known as "Pumpernickel". They serve every kind of food aimed at Westerners. I went there for breakfast ate a very big bowl of porridge, a brown roll and yak cheese, and coffee all for about $.30 probably three times that which the locals pay at their own places. Kathmandu is much quieter and cleaner than any city in India.

In the nearby town there is a Tibetan refugee camp and monastery. They are perfectly clean and beautiful. In that little town I purchased handwoven fine woolen scarf. I got this is the most reasonable price after a very gentle bargaining with the proprietor of the shop. When bargaining with these wonderful people the process is so gentle and sweet very unlike the experience in Northern India. The prevailing experience throughout was one of great love and peace. I also obtained two hats one a traditional Nepali topi and the other a unique two-sided handcrafted hat with the Tibetan mantra embroidered. I still have those hats and that scarf they are in perfect condition. I love them. One day while walking through the city of Kathmandu I heard this beautiful chanting of the sacred Om Mane Padme Hum. It pervaded the atmosphere it was so lovely I immediately purchased the cassette (that's what they had in those days). The flip side had what I perceive to be the Chinese mantra *Namo Quan Shir Yin Poo Saa*. This is the tribute to *Quan Yin* she is the Chinese version of *Avalokateshwara* (deep kindness, compassion and sympathy and grants blessings to children).

One day I was walking to the airline office to reconfirm my flight home, this is on the major boulevard in the city. It was beautifully laid out with little parks along the way. On my way, a gentleman with white shirt and tie stopped me and very politely asked, "Swamiji, I please ask you a question?" "Certainly." He then asks me some personal question about his marriage. The answer just came to me; I did not even have to think about it. This sort of thing was a frequent occurrence on this trip. The Nepali people are the most gentle, kind and soft-spoken people I have met in Asia. It is also worth pointing out that that the Tibetan temples and the Tibetan refugee camp are the cleanest places I've seen in Nepal.

After many visits to areas around Kathmandu most notably the beautiful Tibetan temple, that is the center of the city, we got ready for our journey to the jump-off place for the Annapurna trek. The first segment of this journey was a five-hour bus ride from Kathmandu to Pokhara. There are parts of this bus ride that are treacherous. As pointed out previously on the bus ride to the Vanishista Guha the road often turns into a one-lane road with two-way traffic. One side being a 400 foot drop-off cliff, with mountains on the other side so that when there was a vehicle coming from the opposite direction the driver had to very carefully adjust his position.

Pokhara is a lovely town with one massive tree in the center of the main street (don't know what kind of tree it was). Amazingly even in this remote village and early days of Internet they had Internet cafés. One of the members of the tour was what you might call a dedicated nerd was constantly trying the wi-fi. Our stay there was but two days after which we got on a tiny single engine plane with just enough room for this group. We were headed to Jumsun, a village that has but one guesthouse and an old Tibetan temple. In this region of Nepal 99% of the people are Tibetan Buddhist. The little plane went past the massive Annapurna mountain. I could see why people up there worship the mountains. This was truly a massive, snow-covered mountain. I could feel the power of this mountain spreading out and I could feel how tiny we were compared to it. The thought came to me, "You do not mess with this mountain. THIS is the Mother of mountains. In comparison to this what we have in the US I just little hills."

Jumsun is such a peaceful beautiful village. Nearby was a beautiful small Tibetan monastery with wooden floors and doors. Wood is a rare find in northern Nepal having so few trees. In all temples were many hand-carved adornments and, of course, prayer wheels and flags.

Nepal was the most beautiful place I've ever been to. We did a two-week trek around Annapurna. Many years before I had a dream about going to the great mountains. I was determined to do that, I am so glad that I did.

Throughout this trek there was one narrow path upon which we trod, with many small branches leading off in different directions. The important point here is to know that there are no vehicles with wheels at all on any of these paths, that is to say all transport is done on human backs or on small ponies. There are no mopeds, no bicycles, not even a cart. You see men carrying big loads of rice on their back supported with a long thick band around the forehead. They walk all those kilometers in flip-flops, I could not imagine how they were able to do it but they did. Also note that all heating and cooking is done on small wood burning stoves. One has to walk many miles to find wood. Wood is therefore a very precious item and no one would ever steal it. You see the wood stored perfectly in neat rows atop the roofs. The other consequence of this shortage of wood is that all houses, walls etc. are constructed with stone and furthermore you do not see mortar just sand and stone. As mentioned almost the entire population there is Tibetan Buddhist so that before the entry to any little village are a series Tibetan prayer wheels inscribed with the sacred mantra Om Mane Padme Hum. You can feel the vibration of this mantra as it is there to protect the village. One always walks with the wheels to the right and may spin them clockwise as you walk. This was a wonderful experience.

All along the path we ran into one of the major means of transporting large amounts of goods which were the pony trains. Little ponies with lots of bells strapped to their necks adorning the tops of their heads with tall "trees" of beautiful red fabrics. You can always hear the ponies coming far away. Once or twice they were actually two trains of ponies coming from opposite directions somehow they managed to get by we, on the other hand, had to scramble up the sides of the hills to get out of the way. Traffic jam in the Himalayas. The beauty of it all.

Early breakfast is the standard sliced apples, porridge, black coffee chapatis, Bob Marley on eight track. Most every day we had the same lunch—"dhal bat" that is plain dhal with rice perhaps some vegetable turnip greens, or turnips, or potato, and a bit of spicy chutney, no coffee. Our guide throughout is Rajendra, affectionately known as Raju. He is amazingly fit after 25 years of trekking. We had quite a motley crew. There was a Swiss lady who could walk miles, a German lady was quite strong, very nice fellow who played guitar and always made friends with everyone, swami Jyothi's sister Karen and her husband Don—so I called them "Donna-Karan". Others whose names I forget. There is one wonderful lady who thought to bring bunches of balloons to give to the children. It was grand to see such happiness coming from such a simple gift.

One of the most important people for me was Arjavan, an African-American fellow from New York. He started out with us in India. This man was unique. Firstly, he was about 6'7" with fantastic dreds that went all the way down his back. So, that while traveling pretty much every woman in every town would stop to touch his hair. Apparently they had never seen anything like it were quite taken, it didn't hurt that he was quite good-looking and 6'7". When we were in Coimbatore and there was the bomb, and the additional bomb scares, he was taken into police custody while simply walking the streets. I guess you may say, he stood out in the crowd there. You would wonder why. It should be noted he was a very calm, easy-going man. Police questioned him. He stated that he was an American Yogi. They asked him what that was about and he demonstrated some yoga postures. They let him go. The important part for me was aside from him being so easy-going and good to be with was that on the first part of the trek he was my roommate. All the previous times I've been to India I never got sick. However, one day shortly after Jumsun, in the town of Mukthinat, I got horribly sick, terrible pain in my stomach. Now I am quite used to pain, however, that was more than I could take. It was ceaseless and there was no way for me with all my skills to make it go away.. Chidananda came to offer some remedies none of which is worked. Finally, the middle of the night I just threw up in the bathroom it was quite exhausting and I was too tired to do anything so I thought to let it go until morning. When I awoke, I found that it was all cleaned up. Arjavan, my wonderful, roommate had done a great service for which I am ever grateful. I wonder where he is now.

Mostly it was a delightful, easy-going, fun-loving group.

One of the people on the trek, Daya, from Connecticut got quite sick. I suggested that she meet simple meals such as porridge. We tried to find some peppermint or fennel tea to ease her stomach. She had no problem with the porridge that is a common dish. But, when we ordered peppermint tea at this café Pokara they gave her a glass of hot water with two or three very tiny leaves of peppermint. I know this was never enough so I always had to ask for more leaves. The guy looked at me as if I had just escaped a lunatic bin.

Common Findings on the Trek

Most guesthouses had no hot water and hard beds. There were many beautiful terraced gardens with rice, mustard, turnips, or potatoes. Every 4 to 5 days we would be at a place where they had hot water, always in a very limited quantity. As it was, of necessity, solar heated we had very brief hot showers. Toilets were often Indian style one or two for 18 people with one tiny water basin for all the people. Much to adapt and adjust. At one wonderful guesthouse the owner gave me his room it was "princely" as it had an actual bed. I slept all night and was warm.

One village, Marpha, had all the streets going off at various angles. It appeared at first glance to be a jumble but there was a purpose to all this in that there were very fierce winds in that area and putting the buildings off at all those angles effectively blocked the winds from intruding. Brilliant. As we progressed south we could see beautiful green rice paddies with the farmer walking behind the plow pulled by a small buffalo. This was always a magnificent sight. They were female buffaloes; they also supplied beautiful milk from which a most wonderful cheese was made. We often saw signs, "German Bakery" I wondered why not "Danish bakery" with some other nationality? It must have entered someone's mind that the appellation of "German" would mean to most Europeans something special. No doubt it took but one local individual to come up with this notion for everyone else to imitate. There were signs that also said, "Life is short, eat sweets first." Invariably nearby was a little shop selling Snickers, Milky Way bars etc.

There were many of those narrow swinging rope bridges to cross the river. They had slats of wood set far apart. It was quite slippery when wet. I often felt like Indiana Jones.

There were many, many beautiful little children. In one town I saw a group of them playing with a rolled up bit of dirty old string using it as a football (soccer). Even in the poorest of conditions, children will find something to use as a toy. They do not need all those disposable electronic things, no Legos, etc.; they just did with what there was.

Of course, no laundry facilities at all. The people were so beautiful, the whole atmosphere had beauty in it. We learned to adjust. Along the way I had to get some new socks and shampoo as my shampoo bottle spilled all over the place in my knapsack, I did not plan well. Should have wrapped the shampoo and all liquid things in plastic bags sealed twice. Ruined my camera as well. Bummer.

At the very beginning of the trek our guide, Raju, found some slender bamboo poles which he offered to cut for walking sticks for whomever wanted one. I got one. That was a smart move. That stick really helped me tremendously over very steep slopes and such.

Our next to last station was a wonderful town called Tato Pani, which means, "Hot Water". They had a hot water spring and large pond. This area's climate is subtropical. They had tangerine trees. The fruit was marvelous. It was here that I saw the children playing with the twine "soccer ball". There were ragged, dirty but very happy children. I got into that pool went directly to the source of the hot water and sat right down. It pure pleasure to say the least. They also had a town "Dobi", laundryman. I bundled up all my dirty clothes, which was pretty much all of it and brought it down to the man who had piles and piles of clothing to clean. I don't know how he actually managed to do all that in a search short period of time. Nevertheless, within a couple of hours thereafter it began to slightly rain as he was using these long clothes lines to dry the wash. I ran quickly get my stuff and amazingly it was already packed everything up into a clean, dry bundle. He just gave it to me. How does he remember what goes to whom? What skill.

It was here, too, that had my first and only taste of Tibetan butter tea. Contrary to what others might say, I found it delicious.

Next Big Miracle Part Two – All Things Linked

Long before we started, Chidananda informed me about the weather. He stated that it is very rare for there to be any kind of precipitation during that time of year. Consequently I did not prepare for any rain, snow etc. However, midway during the trip it started to rain quite hard. I had my very fine down jacket that kept me warm. We were exposed and my jacket got soaking wet, as did my knapsack with the camera. In the next guesthouse under the long dining table, they had an oil drum with the sunken lid that had the coals from the wood fires used for cooking. It kept the place warm. I tried somehow to dry the down jacket near that fire. All I got were burns in the shell of the jacket. Well the jacket was another goner, so I wrapped that in plastic, stuck it in my backpack. HOWEVER, I had that heavy wool cardigan. That is what kept me warm for the rest of the trek (great serendipity). You see had I not met the doctor at the New Delhi airport and befriended him, had I not had that afternoon gone with his wife who took me shopping, had I not selected that cardigan on a whim because it was the right color, all those things linked in synchronicity. Had all that not happened I would've surely frozen during the rest of the trip.

I still have that sweater. It is in perfect shape, no holes (amazing for a wool sweater), with all the original buttons, and it is still beautifully warm. It hangs in my closet now.

One More Really Big Miracle

On the last leg of our trek, Chidananda picked up the pace. I was losing track of them. Chidananda made the fatal error of not having a back-man, which is the man after the last person in line to make sure that the last person went in the right direction. This is a basic tenet of group trekking. We were crossing a very large dry riverbed at one point. I had given my water bottle to Raju for safekeeping but he left that behind at one rest stop. I was without water and extremely thirsty. While crossing the riverbed I lost complete sight of the company ahead of me. I was totally alone in this vast dry area having no clue where the group went. I did have one bit of information stored in my head, the name of the guesthouse in which we were going to stay. The Yak & Yeti. I came to the end of the crossing of the riverbed and saw two pathways one going at a right angle at the level of the riverbed the second going up a steep hill in the same direction. As my motto goes, "The easy path is hard enough" I chose the lower path. However, just before turning I "happened" to look to my right and at a great distance I was able to see this man standing outside of his hut laughing, with arm outstretched pointing upwards. Now two points, first at that time, I was greatly visually impaired and being able to see him was quite amazing, secondly there was no real reason for me to turn to the right but having done so I followed his direction and went up the hill. Fortunately, I had the thin bamboo walking stick that helped a lot. I was walking along knowing I didn't speak the language AND I had no idea where the hotel actually was. I was extremely dry and thirsty and very tired. I assumed that the hotel was on the main road. A valid assumption. My plan was to stop by some shop stall, so prevalent there, and would ask by just pointing, "Yak and Yeti?" I did so at the first shop I found on the street. The lady nodded. But, as is often the case in this region people nod "Yes" even though they do not understand a word you're saying. That was a case there. However, standing right next to me (SERENDIPITY) was a young man who understood English and said to me, "Come I will take you." He took me by the hand and led me to where the hotel was. He pointed to a miniature sign on the side of one of the buildings that I passed which said the name of the hotel with an arrow pointing to where it was. That sign was on the side of the building that I would not be able to see as it was at a right angle to the direction I was walking and was so tiny I would not have seen it even if I had looked straight at it.

Everyone was out on the lawn drinking water, relaxing. I collapsed happily on the lawn grabbing a bottle of water from the center and was very happy. This guesthouse was quite different from the others. The manager was extremely rude, the food was horrible but it had a nice bed and hot water. "One should be grateful for small things".

Saved Again Big Time
We hopped the bus to our next stop.

Final Days
After the Annapurna trek we visited the Chitwan Jungle Nature Preserve for two days. We rode on the backs of elephants and viewed the native rhinoceros. It was a very interesting portion of our travels. When we returned to Kathmandu we were given a little native music dance and review, which you might say was more like a junior high school show. Nevertheless, it was cute and delightful. Before our departure, we had one big festive meal with many native vegetarian foods such as Mo-Mo, Tibetan style dumplings.

The Final Chapter

Two More Wondrous Events, Saved

Coming back to New Delhi I went back to the Nerula hotel where I stayed prior to departing for Nepal. I requested the desk clerk to make sure there was a taxi ready for me at 4 AM to go to the international airport. "No problem." Standard Indian response. Next morning a taxi was there and, surprise, the very same driver who took me when I left for Nepal. Not really such a surprise since it was the same hotel and basically the same time. When I got to his cab I saw another man sitting in the front seat next to the driver's. I just concluded that he was an assistant and that seemed fine with me. However, as it turns out he was not an assistant but a competitor who strongly contended that I was his passenger. They were having a loud angry argument. I had already loaded my luggage into the cab but it didn't matter to me. The door on my side was ajar so I was very willing to get out and get into the other cab I was reaching to open the door and my fingers got to within edge when my driver slammed the door forcibly. My hand was within a 16th of an inch of that door. Had I moved my hand forward 20th of a second faster all my fingers would have been broken. That would definitely not be a good thing to happen anywhere in India. That was VERY scary. Here again there was some Divine Protection at work. WHEW! Another miracle.

Flight Home – The Indian Airport Experience

We got to the airport in plenty of time for an easy check-in on Kuwait airline. I even checked my trusty bamboo walking stick. Wonderful. Travel to and from India is always an "interesting" experience. Meaning it is often fraught with obstacles and difficulties. [See chapter just prior to Nepal]. Not much to do before the flight so I just rested. Observing how people deal with their big luggage. Some people have giant suitcases. I observed one family unpack and repack the entire case. I was happy I did not have to deal with such things. There was supposed to be a two-hour time difference between arrival at Kennedy and departure of shuttle to Dulles, however, there was a stopover in London that caused a snag.

Following my normally obsessive thinking, I had arranged for a number of contingencies. First, I obtained a set of keys for the New York IYI in case I totally missed the shuttle. Even though it would be very late at night, it didn't matter. Then I arranged with one of our members who lived 10 minutes from Dulles in case my friends did not get to the airport it wouldn't be too difficult for them to come pick me up and get me back the next morning. This was in place. As I expected there was a delay in London. The line to re-board was jammed mostly with Kuwaiti women who had no compunction to shove their way to the front. I had a nice seat, some good meals and a couple of good movies. As I was watching the clock. I became quite concerned. I noted that the two-hour span was slowly being reduced. As we approached Kennedy it was down to 35 or 40 minutes. I requested the cabin attendant to let me sit up front with my carry-on luggage so that I could get off quickly and zip through all the protocols get my luggage and get to the shuttle. They let me do so. I did zip through immigration quickly having no one in line there may have helped. As I was exiting I asked the fellow where the TWA building was he said it's three buildings down, no problem. There was now drizzling rain, very cold for me as all I had was a little wool jacket that I purchased in New Delhi, FREEZING. 10 minutes to go. Walking as fast as I can. Pulling extra luggage. Happy to be in excellent physical condition. Got to the TWA there must have been 200 people on the line, so, I just jumped the line. However, the lady at the counter saw this and said, "You have to get in the back!" I explained that I have but 10 minutes to catch my shuttle. She motioned me to come to her spot, looked at my boarding pass, she checked the flight data and informed me the flight was delayed by 40 minutes due to inclement weather. You call a drizzle inclement weather. Ha! Anyway, I got through very quickly went down to the shuttle area and waited, and waited, and waited. The exit door led directly to the tarmac with a bit of a walk to this tiny plane getting more wet and cold. There were just three people on that little plane at 1 AM. I was quite surprised when the flight attendant requested that I moved to the other side to balance the plane. "You want ME to balance the plane? Ha!

Finally arrived Dulles about an hour and a half late. Remember in those days your friends could meet you right at the gate, but there was no one there. My buddies were not there. So I went to baggage-claim, which was totally empty. Looked around still no one there. Yikes! I proceeded to my next backup plan. Remember those were days without cell phones. I had some coins for the payphone and proceeded to call my friends in Herndon. Just as I was completing the dial I felt a tap on my shoulder, turned around and what are you know it was big Ben my buddy from Buckingham and his then wife Mangala. I was overjoyed. Ben was a local fellow who worked for Sprint. He took my luggage, we got into his car. I was just so happy. I was freezing so I asked him for his coat which is about seven sizes bigger than me. Didn't matter.

Finally, HOME AT LAST. My Room, My Bed – AHHH. So Fine.

We each have a journey, each is unique.

In this life have been on many roller-coasters, have had many close calls, made numerous foolhardy choices, great & greater challenges, joys and great sorrows, many dear and loving friends, all the most precious loving babies. Most of all the unconditional love and supreme wisdom of my dear Gurudev.

The original title for this was, "My Story". On further reflection, I thought "Journey" to be more appropriate.

Epilogue – Postscript

One can never really put the whole shebang in just words let alone in a single book. There is just too much. It would be like making a map of The USA on a scale of one to one. Each of us has our stories. Most think that they have a story that would be interesting for others to hear because it is interesting to them. These are some of my stories. They were interesting to me and I hope that they were the same for you.

Can't remember even 10% of the totally foolhardy things I did. Which is just as well, this mind is filled with enough stuff already.

Sometimes I wonder what happened to all those many, many people I've been fortunate to have known in this great journey. How many have passed on, how many are still around and what are they doing now?

Carry on. Carry it on.

Herewith are the "extras", additional writings, a bit of dessert as well.

Appendix I: Spiritual Essays & Brief Ruminations

The mystical experience. It is the great mystery. Science is not the field wherein this can be understood here not the tools within this frame of reference to address this question. I use the word "understood" rather than "solved". For a mystical experience there is not a single answer as in mathematics, it is the experience that transcends all other experiences. As Shakespeare put it "There are more things in heaven and earth than attempt of in your philosophy...". Or as one of the great 19 century naturalists J. B. Haldane put it, "... The Universe is not only queerer than we suppose, it is queerer than we CAN suppose."

It is generally difficult, may in fact be impossible to put The Truth into words. Words are symbols. Symbols which we understand in one way by the interpretation and filters of our mind and which any other person would understand in a slightly different way through the filters of his or her mind. Or, as was put by neuroscientist Alfred Korzbysky, "The map is not the territory." The map is a symbolic representation in a reduced form but it's not the actual territory. As he also said, "If you scribble on the map that does not change the territory. Our words of symbolic representations of The Truth however many words we might add it does not change the fundamental Truth. Each of us will understand it in a somewhat different way according to the mindset with which we came. The mindset may change according to our experience and understanding.

Herewith is a collection of short pieces I have written over many years collected in my spiritual notebook. I've chosen only small pieces rather than long essays which would be more suitable in a separate book. There have been many influences in the formation of my outlook. Of course there was Gurudev in the most subtle of ways. Throughout the has been my rational, logical, scientific way of observation of how things work in the universe. Of late my interest has been in how the universe operates under quantum mechanics and cosmology. But that is a vast and different subject.

Starters

- ॐ Meditation practice must be the center of one's spiritual life. Whatever style or method you prefer that is not matter as long as it clears and focuses the mind towards the aim of understanding and realizing that True Self.

- ॐ If you find a writer constantly quoting or paraphrasing other teachers then know they have not found their own truth. We must find that truth which comes from our own experience and hopefully be able to express it in an intelligent way.

- ॐ Look past the noise to see the Truth.

- ॐ The knowledge of our way of doing things is only a model. Knowing when to use and when to discard such a model is the key to cultural and scientific literacy.

- ॐ Being able to examine the pertinence or value to our life of a current system is far more valuable than to regurgitate statements gleaned from popular book or seminars on the subject of management.

- ॐ Sometimes we should just drop the ball just to see what will happen.

- ॐ Clarity comes when you can express your needs in a language that is unambiguous and free of emotional subtext, free from subtle manipulative games. In terms that can be understood by all who are listening.

- ॐ It is very important to know that all that we see all that is comes from the single source which one can call, The Divine Consciousness or in Kabbalistic terms the Ayin Sof. Everything that we know does not "come from" that source but is an expression of that source. The subtle difference. Every rock every atom, the time space continuum itself in fact IS That. There is nothing but That. It is a grave error to think of God as some being who is male with big white hair and beard, residing on a golden throne of fire. That is to say, the notion expressed in the Old Testament of a jealous, despotic old man whom, shall we say, is in need of serious anger management. Yet there are millions upon millions of believe in that concept. God is not a concept like that. Not a judgmental being, not someone who distributes rewards for good behavior and orders punishment for even the slightest disobedience like a vindictive parent. I am convinced of that.

- ॐ As I get older the river of time seems to be moving faster and faster, the last ten years are just a blur—pretty soon there will be nothing - who knows maybe it will be so fast that it will go in reverse.

- ॐ There have also been countless lessons, lessons almost every day. One that comes to mind today is this; all the anxieties, worries, upsets, emotional wrangling etc., none of them are worth the expenditure of so much good energy. They do not attain healthy, useful, peaceful results.

ॐ Some platitudes are also true.

ॐ If you just allow the mind be quiet, be still, all the turbulence will settle. It does not require nay it should not require any effort. The mind will be calm on its own. Therefore you will be calm.

ॐ When in the presence of the Holy Master He makes you see, feel, and understand what is possible. Not only do you feel this but you also begin to comprehend of how you CAN do this. You see the unlimited is real in you. He not only loves you unconditionally but makes you realize that you fully deserve this. Not only that but you see that such an expression of love is possible in you.

ॐ Consciousness is not a static thing. It is constant motion in stillness.

ॐ If you could stop thinking completely, how could you start again? You'd need some type of thought or conscious cognitive act to command your mind to resume its normal activity. Wouldn't the mere fact of being able to summon up such a command indicate that you hadn't really succeeded in going totally blank?

ॐ "When there is no longer hide and seek" "I & me", "good & bad I" trying to change—it's like a naked man trying to lose his shirt.

ॐ I have been frequently astonished and dismayed at the limited belief systems that were given to me by my father and his father to him. It tells me that I must believe only in this and not that. Since dad was Orthodox Jewish and did not accept the possibility of other beliefs as in Buddha, Christ, Allah and so on.

ॐ The question of consciousness what neuroscience says. We do know that it involves the brain, but not all of it - mostly the cortex, amygdala, & hippocampus and it is not the number of neurons but how they are connected and how they communicate. This is one way, it's clear but very complex, and there is a lot we do not know. Here is where all sorts of possibilities can creep in. Speculation, conjecture and what not. Where is the truth? Just what is it that we call consciousness? AND does it exist w/o the mind i.e. the brain? Not so simple.

ॐ The question is what happens in deep sleep - you can measure brain activity. At that point, brain activity is very localized and limited - so there is energy but a measurably lower level. Next Q. is what happens in a coma, in so called vegetative state and so on - it is not an on/off thing but rather a continuum - this is a most interesting subject

ॐ THE SELF - that is what connects us - the universe- all things - all beings - it IS the matrix of which we are a wave when in this body and to which we return when no longer in the body OR which we fully know when we are EN-lightened. Tat Twam Asi

ॐ "I've always felt that existence is very odd. Other people apparently feel that existence is quite even. That is to say they think it is ordinary. My problem is that I view the whole of existence; all of nature is very strange. Indeed that the fact that I am is the strangest subplot."- Alan Watts

ॐ Emotions are energized thought patterns. Because of its powerful energy, it is not easy to watch in an unattached way. It wants to take you over unless you have practiced well the presence of mind. You will be free of the pain when you are free from the identification with the pain. It is the mind that gives emotions its power. AND if you insist on repeating within the mind over and over that reaction, that emotion becomes a reality—it gains solidity. In our society, all the common forms of communication: news, TV shows, movies, all of it insists that we are those emotions. All of that gives full belief in investing in the reactive mind. This is especially true for the negative emotions such as fear, anger, jealousy and even righteous indignation- a most insidious trap. That, however, keeps us from living within our true Self. NONE of that is who we are. They keep us from knowing "what's what". Our knowledge of the Self is obstructed by reactions, our emotional responses. When an emotion comes we should see it as a feeling that can come and go—"this too will pass". Emotions are subject to the laws of opposites pain/pleasure cycle. Pleasure comes from things outside and when you lose it, it's pain. What we call love (relationships) has an opposite. However, real love has no opposite there is no clinging or attachment. Normal addictive relationships can also have their Moments but the mind comes back and it's gone, obscured but not destroyed.

ॐ As I dive into the great depth of Kabbalah I discover the same truth is found in all mystical paths, but expressed in different ways. As I see it there is one great vast consciousness which is beyond all words, in fact it is so great no one mind has ever or can ever grasp it all, since the mind itself is just a small part of the Great Whole.

ॐ To know he Self with the mind is like biting your own teeth. You get it? There is just the Now - but you can never get a hold of it - you can never get out of it either. It is in itself a paradox on one hands it is there in stillness and on the other it is in constant streaming ticking along. Ahhhh.

ॐ It is very often the case that the anticipation of some pleasure or event gives one more enjoyment than the actual thing in itself. This is basically due to our very active imagination.

ॐ There are some who carry pain inside and you may never know this because they see to go about their business quite well. There is no visible sign, no wheel chair or such thing. So you cannot really know the extent of the difficulty. For each individual it is a unique experience, although there may be some commonalities with a certain group, say cancer for example, the individual experience is different. And too, the way of dealing with such pain is different from person to person. For some acceptance is the way - but that is needed in any case, then others can move ahead from acceptance to transcendence and pushing ahead. But what you can do is to understand as best you can and to - even though you can't fully get it unless you too have a similar circumstance, and to surround that one with love light and service.

ॐ I think, therefor I Think I am.

ॐ Just because you know what you are talking about doesn't mean what you're talking about is worth knowing.

ॐ THE SELF - that is what connects us - the universe- all things - all beings - it IS the matrix of which we are a wave when in this body and to which we return when no longer in the body OR which we fully know when we are EN-lightened. OM TAT SAT - Tat Twam Asi

ॐ We know that we do not know all there is to know- so consciousness can be seen as actions in the brain BUT is not the brain - there is a Consciousness that exists beyond the brain - there are all the forces of electromagnetism, gravity and consciousness it's just that we don't know how the unification of it all works.

ॐ Upon reading my journals done in the early days I noticed how much turmoil and worry mind I had. Certainly a great wastage of good energy.

From My Diaries

1. I started a set of diaries many years ago. The Yoga Life Diaries begun around 1972.

2. I've recently reviewed and reread them as best I could. I found myself constantly criticizing and evaluating myself. In rereading these after so many decades, I found this to be quite foolish and tiresome in many ways. I did not find much value in constant self-criticism. However, I did find a few valuable entries, which I note here.

3. April 20, 1977—The guru is my best friend. I surrender to Him. What does that mean? Surrender is total and complete openness. You must cut out all our preconceived notions and concepts about yoga, guru, and preconceived notions about spiritual life. They're all limiting. We are unlimited. You may stumble 1000 times but 1000 times you will keep going on.

4. It is said we are what we eat. In the kitchen is a nice pot of soup, potatoes, carrots, zucchini, etc. We are all served from this pot. The vegetables etc. all in one pot all friendly happy together. We eat this. In a few days, the essence of the food becomes our blood, and brain, etc.. Now, what were only potatoes, zucchini etc. as all sorts of arguments ensue. Balance and confusion. Very difficult to understand.

5. September 4, 1977 the reason I'm working at the falafel stand is to learn service. Serve all without any ego at all. Complete non-attachment. With all of them to pay attention. If I can pay attention here, I can pay attention to the more subtle things in the mind and more subtle realm of the superconscious. If I cannot get together on this ordinary plane how can I ever expect to get it together on the more subtle plain?

6. Physics is the interaction of what we call subtle particles, which come into being by their very interactions.

7. September 30, 1979. If you really want to remove cloud from your life, you do not make a big production out of it. You just relax and remove it from the thinking. You are never given a wish that the power to make it come true. However, you may have to work for it.

8. If when you give there is still the idea of you being a giver, you are still not free from ego involvement.

9. Love everyone as if Christ Himself were there, because, in fact He is.

10. You cannot be happy if you work from fear or a feeling of obligation.

11. No One NOT even your guru can give you happiness. NO ONE can give it to. We already have it. If you don't see it that is because your eyes are clouded. You are looking in the wrong place. Learn from the great teacher of experience. It is all a good lesson; so, don't be sorry for whatever happens. Even experience must be dropped for as long as you are "trying" to do what is right it won't happen.

12. Sectarianism is a binder. It keeps one imprisoned.

13. Whatever you do just do without the idea of "doing." Not with the idea of personal benefit. Because then you're not "Here"; the mind is on some futuristic goal (maybe fantasy) and you cannot be happy because you'll never get that.

14. Just as soon as you get what you think you need to be happy you discover you no longer really needed it in the first place. Then another one instantly comes up.

15. Written on Facebook April 9, 2020 during the Covid19 pandemic. It does not further to mull over the past nor to speculate on "it might have been". It might be a tiresome cliché but—Be present in the present knowing that nature is always around you—you are in perfect harmony. Be in harmony. Not being trapped by fear for that is also a prison as much as selfish ego. Take care. Be safe. Enjoy.

16. Why were Saints, Saints? Because they were cheerful when it was difficult to be cheerful. Patient when it was difficult to be patient. Because they push on when they wanted to stand still; were silent when they wanted to speak; and they were agreeable they wanted to be disagreeable. That is all it is quite simple and it always will be. [Found on a card on the bulletin board of New York IYI.]

17. You cannot light the incense unless it is directly in the flame, coming close will not do. You get it only by direct contact. Therefore, the heart can only be lit up by entering the flame of surrender. Burning away attachments.

18. March 3, 1983. We often emphasized in our philosophy you need to reduce the ego. There is no question that giving up selfish ego is

beneficial. However, we seem to misinterpret this is giving up our own uniqueness; our own God-given qualities. There seems to be an expectation that we be blind, obedient beings this is not It.

19. It is a priority all of this layers up (it's a setup) in this false battle of what is yogic and not yogic. There is an evolution of spiritual growth. That is an error to set this battle up. It is a trap of dualism good/evil. It has many subtle ramifications. It also creates a tremendous source of anxiety. This is not useful for spiritual growth.

20. At the pre-sannyas Diksha Gurudev said, "I do not follow any 'ism'. So if anyone asks you from what did the orange scarf come, what Scripture? You tell them that came from The Swami (referring to Himself). My word is Scripture" he also said, "One who loves is grateful. Gratitude is the sign of the real yogis.

21. June 2, 1984 New York City. Note from diary. Gurudev is here. I dialed Premananda on 34 but got Sri Gurudev on the phone. It was quite something.

22. "We know very little, and yet it is astonishing that we know so much, and still more astonishing that so little knowledge can give us so much power." Bertrand Russell

23. There are two ways to live your life. One is as though nothing is a miracle. The other is as though everything is a miracle." - Albert Einstein

24. "The secret of health for both mind and body is not to mourn for the past, not to worry about the future, nor to anticipate troubles, but to live the present Moment wisely and earnestly."—The Buddha

25. "Now, the trouble is trying to make yourself stupider than you really are, is that you very often succeed." C. S. Lewis

End to of diary entries

In Addition

- ॐ Our life is but a blink of a snip of a snip of one eyelash in cosmic time... how we use it is what counts.

- ॐ For all these years how the ashram has grown in unimaginable ways yet we remain true to our core beliefs. The foundation remains strong.

- ॐ Facebook Post April 10, 2020 during Covid19 Pandemic. Do you not know that you come from the infinite source? In Kabalah it is known as Ayin Sof. The great Kabbalist Isaac Luria added the word Aur meaning light.

The Ayin Sof is the ultimate infinite source of being it is the nameless, formless, eternal infinite source of which everything is from and is THAT.

Some may call this "God". It is Tetragrammaton the sacred four letter word as the "Name" of God. The non-pronounceable four-letter name Yod Heh Vav Heh. Referred to in Hebrew as Hashem—which just means, "The Name." It contains the sacred formula of cosmology in just those four letters.

The point is, if you are connected on the deepest level you know the ultimate source of your being and all of creation all of humanity all animals plants ,rocks stones pebbles sand. Sand that gets into your shoes, bees that sting mosquitoes that bite, snakes, bugs., Everything is from that source and nothing that is not.

Just get connected. And you will know what there is to know.

Tat Twam Asi — Thou ART THAT

- ॐ A drop of compassion deserves a wellspring of gratitude (Chinese saying)

- ॐ I do not know what, if anything, God had in mind when it created this world. But I am quite certain that what ever it had in mind was nothing like what we have in mind. And considering what most of us have in mind most of the time, it is just as well. Douglas Adams.

- ॐ "The more I learn, the more I realize how much I don't know." Albert Einstein

- ॐ The most important prerequisite for discovery of knowledge or research is ignorance. At this time we not seem to have a shortage of that resource.

- ॐ The only thing necessary for the triumph of evil is for good men to do nothing. Edmund Burke (1729–1797), Irish philosopher, statesman.

- ॐ "We know very little, and yet it is astonishing that we know so much, and still more astonishing that so little knowledge can give us so much power." Bertrand Russell

- ॐ He who angers you conquers you. Elizabeth Kenney

- ॐ An hour spent in hatred is an eternity withdrawn from love. Swami Satchidananda

Unwinding the Conditioning – Undoing the Default Setting

Much of the critical aspects of our character, our personality, who we think we are, how we relate and react to people and situations are set in place very early in life. This is the conditioning that the vast percentage of people are burdened with. It is what I also call "The Default Setting." It is this reactive mind that we fall back to in times of stress and critical situations. However, it is also one of the greatest obstacles to our Self—realization and understanding of the truth, living in that state of understanding rather than the reactive mind. It, therefore, is a priority to undo all of those layers of conditioning. Of course realizing this is fairly easy. However, the unwinding, undoing of all that conditioning and have actually reactive mind is quite difficult. It is possible through Paying Attention and redirecting that reactive setting of the mind. This can be done by the grace of Guru, as well as consistent practice of meditation.

If you are skillful and successful at unwinding, removing the layers upon layers of conditioning you will be free and your own true nature will shine forth. That is the reality, that is who you are, that is eternal. That is touching upon the Ayn Sof, The Absolute Truth, The Atman.

A Parable

Long ago, so far back that no one can say just when, there was in a little village of Poland, a very successful wealthy business man. He had it all. A lovely family with a beautiful loving wife, three delightful children, the most elegant home in the village complete with landscaped grounds, stables, guest house of course, but no swimming pool [they had not yet been invented—this was LONG ago]. He was always happy, always happy. People did admire him and paid him homage but they always felt he was happy due to his wealth.

Now after a while the market had gone bad, he stopped selling. He then lost his business. Debt collectors came took his elegant home, grounds, horses—the whole deal. He was forced to live in a teeny hovel. Of course, wife left and she took the beautiful children. But he was still happy, happy, happy. Now the people were very confused how could the Baron (that's the old way people there referred to the very rich) still be so happy.

So they sent a delegation to inquire.

> "Oh, honorable Baron—we saw that when you were very rich you were always happy, now you are dirt poor but still the same happiness exudes from you. Please explain."
> "Of course—you all have read the Bible?"
> "Yes".
> "Well it says there very, very frequently, 'And it came to pass.' It never says, and it came to stay."

The end.

- ॐ There is no "Getting god realized." There is nothing to "get".

- ॐ The real guru does not tell you what you must do. There are no secret words. None. The real guru teaches by example and just shows or rather subtly hints at what you must get rid of. Because he or she will tell you that you already have God. So there is nothing outside of you.

- ॐ You can learn great lessons from anyone, even some drunk guy on the street can be a guru. Sometimes Buddha will come disguised as a homeless man or woman, so be prepared. Gurus don't always come with a special attire or stand on a platform, or perform some ritual or quote scripture or come from India - nope. None of these makes one a saint. See the love, the heart, the openness and acceptance, You never know where you will find it.

Fundamentalism

When you believe that you know what is best for everyone else, it is a very short leap to the feeling that you have the right, if not the responsibility to impose on others the point of view you are so sure is not only correct, but even infallible. "It is for their own good", is it not?

If making the worshiper feel good is all you're after, and you don't care how you do it, the easiest way to do it is to assure him his prejudices are approved by God. Make him feel that he doesn't have to change because he's already arrived at salvation.

Fundamentalism almost invariably has a problem with science. Science is the process of starting with the hypothesis and gathering of the evidence to support that and proceeding to the conclusion that best fits the evidence, regardless of what that conclusion may be. Fundamentalism, on the other hand, starts with a conclusion and searches for evidence to support that conclusion.

When the "founders" of America wrote the Constitution they included the idea of freedom of religion they did not only mean freedom to worship, or not, as one saw fit but ALSO and more importantly freedom from any religious body or group from imposing their beliefs, idea or practice on everyone else. That is to say establishing a national religion. We have this problem when a group enacts laws as for example against same sex marriage, contraception or the right of women to choose. This is what is really meant by separation of church & state.

It is a very, very important tenet.

Jottings

When you go out to a desert and see the vast universe you may think, "Oh, my God compared to all this I am nothing, less than a speck, a zero." But that is not so. It should make you feel big. Because it is all inseparably connected with what you call You. This tremendous whirling energy is exactly the same that is looking out of your eyes, and breath, and making you talk. You are that energy. You do not die. What you call death is merely a pulse, a wave or perhaps a trough. Everything goes on and off. All things MUST go on and off. You would not know something was on if it did not occasionally go off.

You must have the courage to step out of your comfort zone, away from the protective shroud and unto new territory. There is nothing new. Be Still—first still the body, that is the purpose of hatha yoga; still the mind, the purpose of meditation—these are just tools. Finally quiet the restless thoughts and straight away, you will see what IS.

There is no "magic" thing; the guru is not there to give you some sort of "secret" to find out what "is". He is there to get you cleaned up and be strong to find your way. For us it was the way of service, but all that is only to rid ego. Eventually you have to figure it all out and not depend on anyone to give you the answers.

PAY ATTENTION

- ॐ What we agree upon as reality is not "THE Reality". However, without agreed-upon conventions we'd have no civilization.
- ॐ There is nothing worth getting upset about, that will not help, it only makes matters worse.
- ॐ Why has it taken so very long to learn these? However, I do see many young people today who really do get it. There is hope for the planet.

Some may ask if the mind is the source of cognitive knowledge, meaning all that we know comes by way of the mind—how can we know what is beyond the mind. Is that which is beyond the mind separate? This would then entail having: Mind and that which is beyond. This then is a dualistic state. Unless, of course, this idea of "something beyond the mind" is but another illusion created & sustained by misunderstanding and a great lack of clear thinking about what is. There is no separate being, mind is but a wave—it is so, however, that you cannot "see" the Self because the instrument by which you "see" is the same as that which is seen. That is one of the great paradoxes.

Belief & Religion are quite different from Experience & Spirituality. Religion is an institution with sets of rules and regulations. The most important tenet of all those religions, the only one you'll ever need to know is to do not do unto others what you would not want done to you. Better put as Hillel said, "Love your neighbor as your own Self." I put "self" in upper case. Kant said it as The Categorical Imperative, "Act as if the maxim of thy action were to become by thy will a universal law."

🕉 Belief is something that you would like to be true, experience is what holds the greatest validity for you. Spirituality is the path you are on. It is how you live Moment to Moment.

🕉 In all communities including spiritual community rules are needed. However, one often finds that there are a good number of people who rely upon rules. There are always some who are stringent in following them to the letter and expect everyone else to do likewise. They demand hard and fast documented rules for everything. This is universal. On further examination, however, I find that those people are often very insecure and they rely upon rules security. Because rules are written, reliable, and often absolute. Such reliance, however, misses the opportunity for creativity to solve the common as well as special situations.

Illuminations from Unexpected Places

Quite often there are great insights, miracles, teachings or illuminations that come to us when we least expect it, or from people whom we would never expect such wisdom. We need only remain open to the possibility and keep our attention to what is around us.

These events where recorded in my old diary found when cleaning out a box that was stored under my bed. They happened in San Francisco April of 1988.

Philosophy from an Unexpected Source

Encounter in a Chinese grocery/emporium in San Francisco's Chinatown.

I was on my annual trek to Chinatown to get my supply of Chinese incense. The kind they burn in Taoist & Buddhist temples, which are over a foot long and come in bundles weighing up to half a kilo. While examining the vast array of merchandise I espied a man who appeared to be the manager. He was a well-dressed man, suit, tie, spotless white shirt, who was tidying up the display that was already in perfect order.

I inquired.

"Sir, what is the difference between this large pack of low price incense and this smaller packet of the more costly kind?"

"Well this more expensive kind is stronger need only one stick, cheaper kind need many sticks. Some people when go temple like to burn many sticks. Much smoke." (I knew that he could speak English perfectly, he was doing this "tourist" English shtick only for the White visitors like me.)

"Ah, yes I replied, The Buddha does not need all that. One is enough."

"He really does not need anything at all." He said without hesitation.

"Yes, that is it. Nothing is required."

"Yes, he said "the reality is very simple. People don't see that, they want to think truth as complex."

Wisdom.

We are all miracles. If would but all realize that you would never do harm to anyone.

Encounter on the 22 Fillmore Bus

This very crowded bus goes from the Fillmore district to the Mission area.

This is exactly what happened, recorded in my diary at the time.

A "little old lady"—she really was little and "old" and what's more in Birkenstocks (NOT tennis shoes) was sitting across from me. She had a bunch of freshly cut flowers in her small, wrinkled hands. She was offering a flower to another passenger. The passenger smiles graciously but refuses the offer.

Little old Lady, "Oh, they are so pretty, aren't they? They bring such joy. Wouldn't you like one? You can have one." Finally she sees that she could not persuade the young passenger so she turns to a young lady and offers her one. "Would you like one?"

"Sure, thank you so much." The girl takes it in hand, full of smile and that light.

Little Old Lady, addressing the entire busload, "You know this is my whole joy in life. Just to give, give, give. It is what I live for. O.K., well goodbye."

And the Little Old Lady in Birkenstocks 3 sizes too large with flowers in hand gets off the bus. A very great light followed with her over her head.

ॐ Beauty happens every day. Teachings are all around us, we need just to pay attention.

Diary entry 6/8/75. - Keep the mind ever fixed at the seed of Gurudev. He will always protect you safely across the sea of Samsara. He is there to show you the Guru within. External guru is only a guide. He will always be with you in spirit, bless you, protect you. The Sat Guru will only speak truth. All that He says his truth but not The Truth. That cannot be spoken.

Walking Lessons

Climbing the steep hills of San Francisco I realized the number of steps is a finite number. I will eventually get to the top. It just requires perseverance. Much like all of life's tasks you'll get it done. What I do is look at a point, a marker such as a tree, that is ahead of me and I think all I need to do is get to that point. I get there I look at the next 200 feet ahead and get there, that way it is easy to get to the end which could be half a mile away.

ॐ There is a higher dimension of existence that pervades the universe,-- us, all things, all beings. This is the supreme energy which one may call Spirit, The Atman, Ayin Sof, the Supreme being of all, Yesh V' Ayin in Kabalah. Everything and nothing—No Thing—is without beginning or end - nameless, formless. It is not ever a separate identity that judges or punishes or issues edicts etc. It is that which is the that of Thatness. *Thatagata* in Buddhist terminology. When we drop all ego identification that is what remains is who we are. Maybe there is the "music of the spheres" there.

ॐ I wish I knew music like the brilliant masters of music such as Ravi Shankar did.

ॐ The path IS. It is where you are right now, being awake and mindful EVERY Moment. It is not something to "find" or "seek", or a series of methods, techniques or a school. Those are all very useful tools to help you get awake and stay awake.

One (or some "guru") can sometimes say the most trivial, platitudinous, clichéd, bumper-sticker bromide—but if you do so with the right gravitas and serious sonorous voice everyone will think you're at least a genius if not an enlightened being. Alternatively, if you have enough PR and a big enough church they will deem you a prophet and give you even more money. It works this way because people want something to believe in but have not the courage or energy to figure it out for themselves. Just because one can quote a lot of Scriptures does not make one spiritual. It's how you live that counts.

🕉 We come to this Moment each with a different set of experiences in life—hence we each form a different, yet valid in a relative sense, understanding and thus so many hypotheses of what Reality is. The Truth—who knows? So many ways of saying it. We would really like to know—and it is right there in front of us.

🕉 Only you can find your "Way" and it is only you who can change.

🕉 The understanding of this universe and our relation to it and to one another is very, very complex. A simplistic answer is for children.

🕉 Gratefulness is so important for one's wellbeing and growth.

A Poem

> The sands of time swallow mountains.
> What we build and build is so puny.
> Even our proud heaven-scrapers become scrap eventually.
> Discover what Is.
> The Suchness that is within you.
> You are that temple.
> No need to look for one man-made.

In a spontaneous conversation with a dear friend he said, in a self-doubting tone, "Someone told me, 'you're enlightened, I know you're enlightened.' Ha", saying it as if only the speaker knew the truth (implying that I was not enlightened). Indeed there is a vast gulf between the well-developed appearance of such a state and the actual knowledge and living in that state. There is that gap between Realization and everyday consciousness. Just what is it that created this gulf, or, put another way, this blockage? That is just the hard set of ideas about who I am. This is the identity which has ordered my life and from which everything is ordered. It is, in other words, my default setting. It is not what is apparent in public, not at all evident through the intricate web of personality projected in my teaching aspect. That is perfectly ordered and exquisitely presented through decades of practice and refinement.

Undoing the identity is not at all easy. It is what we are comfortable with and that which provides sustenance, security, support and is what we become to rely on for daily survival. So you can see we have a LOT invested in this identity, so one should not be too hasty to dismiss it. Such statements as, "let go of your false self", can often be too facile and are like spiritual bumper stickers. We often jump on such ideas without the proper understanding or working through all the psychological damages and traumas that have contributed to the identification and which often provide the only safe shelter. So let us not be too quick to dismiss the necessary but often painful unravelling of psychic damage. Not easy. Takes care, love and attention.

- ॐ It is that to which we give our attention, our energy, which defines our reality.
- ॐ The possession of too much cleverness makes the way difficult.

The instant you say—"this is the Now" it is gone. There is no point—in that infinite series of points of time which you can say is "Now". This is not just playing with words it's pure quantum physics. It is how the universe is organized. Many paradoxes. The old mind, does not change much. It is full of old reactions and belief systems and unless you have been very fortunate to be born to parents with highly advanced thinking processes, you were programed with all sorts of attachments and fears. What we need then is to make a very deep, deep transformation to root out that programing.

- ॐ Don't worry about meditation methods.
- ॐ In ACTUALLY doing the "idea" of doing it disappears. And I say, "Pass the salt" you don't think about "right method" you just do it.
- ॐ Prayer is not petition to "god" for something but refocusing your thoughts to increase the positive harmony vibrating in the universe. The cumulative effect of our thought waves creates the effect on the quantum level as well as the perceived physical level.
- ॐ Make sure your actions are in alignment with your words.
- ॐ Truth is always there, divine is always there. You just have to see it. There are indeed forces in this universe which are far beyond the rational mind, beyond what we can ever understand. That is the fundamental basis of the mystical world. I know this is so, I know that I have always been and will be protected. That there is a power, NOT a judging power, not a personal power, not something you can actually name—that is why I like the term Ayin Sof, Yesh & Ayin.

- ॐ If you have the resolve, if you put your mind to it you can overcome any obstacle or challenge or at least learn to accept it. Mind is the most powerful tool, use it well. I will be what I WILL to be.

- ॐ Sometimes silence can teach you the greatest lessons.

- ॐ We all have the same crap to deal with; some just get a bigger load. Sri Gurudev told me I am strong so He can be blunt with me. He would often do that and in public. But, He also would say the nicest things.

Sources of Knowledge

Within the vast framework of human knowledge, we have several sources or frames of reference for the acquisition of knowledge. They may basically be divided into two classes viz. that of rational scientific knowledge and then what we may call the intuitive frame of reference, we include in this set all the religious traditions, spiritual minded knowledge, creativity, the arts and so on. However, as was pointed by cosmologist Timothy Ferris in his book, The Whole Shebang, one cannot be mixing up these frames of reference. In other words it is poor scholarship to take points out of math or science to establish "Proof" for some spiritual or religious point.

There are other areas of knowledge which also rely on the higher dimension of consciousness which some call intuition this include the world of music. How else does one explain the magnificent works of such persons as Bach, Mozart and so many others too numerous to mention? Certainly when you see a great musician or artist at work you cannot help but think that they are tapped into that greater dimension. It must also be said that this type of thinking, this tuning in to a higher dimension, is not restricted to artists, or musicians but has consistently been reported by many of the great scientists from Newton, Leibniz, Einstein,, and the great Richard Feynman. Throughout history they have been such cases where individuals reported receiving a flash of understanding not always based on empirical evidence.

Spiritual knowledge, intuitive understanding of our purpose (if indeed we do have one) can also serve as a moral guide to our lives. Religions have also tried a go at this but as they for the most part created dissent, divisiveness and have brought upon humanity endless suffering and wars not to mention the invention of sin for the purpose of inducing fear in their followers and thus the ever-controlling tactics of guilt & fear have, for the most part, missed the boat. They did, however come up with the one solid guide to moral life—i.e. "Do not do unto others that which is hateful to you". That, as the great holy sage Reb Hillel said, is all you need to know all else is commentary." That was repeated by Immanuel Kant as "The categorical imperative"—"Act as if the maxim of thine action were to become by thy will a universal law of nature." Of course, he said it in German so it must have taken many more and much longer words.

- ॐ We come to this Moment each with a different set of experiences in life—hence we each form a different, yet valid in a relative sense, understanding and thus so many hypotheses of what Reality is. The Truth—who knows? So many ways of saying it. We would really like to know—and it is right there in front of us.

- ॐ We do not worry about the billions of years that passed before our loved ones were born why then do we worry about the few years that passed before us after they die? It is all part of the great cycle. What comes must go.

- ॐ Transformation and change a part of nature. All things become transformed. Nothing stays absolutely the same.

- ॐ It is best to do things for the love of doing them not for attaining a product or goal.

Over the years there have been many truly great and holy teachers, gurus and Saints. But, not everyone who calls him or herself a guru is really worthy of that honor. In our time, especially the early days, there have been many charlatans and opportunists and very minor players. Many who have come to take advantage of insecure and naïve youth. All of the people mentioned here were genuine, goodhearted, and highly evolved spiritual beings. I've been very fortunate to have been with so many great ones. I originally included very long list but deleted it thinking that this would be boring to most people. If you are interested email me and I'll send it to you.

I added the following segment because for so many years I have officiated the Chanukah service.

Chanukah Wisdom – The True Story

Introduction – Foreword – Prologue

I would like to tell the true story of Chanukah here but first it would be appropriate to inform you of these points. This story is not a secret it is well known to most scholars. And although we are going to tell you what really happened it in no way diminishes the spiritual lesson derived thereof. You should also be aware that Chanukah was originally was just a minor holiday much like Purim. This celebration is not based on a Biblical event such as Passover or Sukkoth; it acquired its current status relatively recently, that is to say at the end of the 19th and beginning of the 20th century's when it became something major due to modern influences such as the Zionist movement and the pure coincidence of its proximity to Christmas.

You should also know that Christmas is not the Christian version of Chanukah. That Chanukah actually antedates Christmas by some 200 years. It is just a coincidence of events.

Chanukah means dedication. In reference to the re-dedication of the holy Temple. There is i a ceremony amongst Orthodox Jews known as Chanukahat ha Bayit meaning "dedication of the house". This is done when people purchase a new house and move into it. At Yogaville we have a similar ceremony.

The History

We begin in the time of Alexander the Great about 350 BCE. He was a disciple of Aristotle as well as being much attuned to the Greek philosophies, arts and culture. He established five kingdoms (not an empire) in his travels and at the same time he allowed the indigenous populations to keep their own traditions, culture and religion. In Syria he established the Seleucid kingdom and in Egypt the Ptolemaic kingdom. We should note also that in Egypt he established the city named and after him, Alexandria, with the greatest library of the world of that time. It was really a great man.

At that time Syria had control of the land of Judea (It was not called Israel then) where many of the Jewish people lived. Contrary to what you may assume that population was not a united one, rather it was divided up according to clans. The capital of Judea was Jerusalem and a good number of the people living there were influenced by the Greek culture while not giving up the Jewish tradition they also adopted a considerable amount of the Greek culture. These were the so-called "Hellenized Jews". Some of those Hellenized Jews living in Jerusalem also were priests in the sacred Temple. A most important position. All went very well for 150 years until a certain king in Syria took over. This was Antiochus IV also known as Epiphanes. This man was your standard dictator, that is to say he wanted absolute power over the lands he controlled. He therefore issued an edict decreeing that the Jews may no longer practice their religion and he further ordered that the holy Temple be transformed into a Greek one. He therefore installed images of their gods. To the Jewish people this was a terrible desecration of the holy Temple.

Therefore, we had a situation where there were clans of Hellenized Jews living in Jerusalem each of which was fighting for the control of the Temple, plus the invasion and desecration of the Temple by Antiochus's armies. During that time there lived in the city of Modin the Hashmonean clan led by the patriarch Mathethias with his five sons: Yonathan, Yehudah, Yochanan, Shimon & Eliazer. They decided on two things, first to take out the Seleucid armies and second to take down the Hellenized Jews in control of Jerusalem. Yehudah (Judah—I'm using their original Hebrew ends here because that is what they were called) was the leader of this army who took on the name Macabee, which means "the Hammer" it is sometimes also defined as an acronym of the Hebrew letters defined as "Who is greater than you Lord our God."

In what is considered a short time, or at least that's how it is been recorded, Yehudah and his armies defeated the Seleucids and took down the Hellenized Jews in Jerusalem. Those events took place about 168 B.C.E. when they established the Hashmonean dynasty that lasted for at least twenty-four years. They also established a celebration of their victory, which they called Chanukah to remember the re-dedication of the holy Temple. In order to give this celebration greater authority they extended the time to eight days which is the same as Passover and Sukkoth.

What we had was a double sort of battle, first a rebellion against the Seleucid rule and second a CIVIL war against the Hellenized Jews. This is often forgotten. The military exploits are all recorded in the Book of Macabees I. This is in no way a part of the Bible. It is like the Book of Esther, an external historical account. If you read this book you will note in Maccabees 1:4—41—62 wherein they describe the re-dedication of the holy Temple. They describe how they gathered all the golden vessels, all holy objects, and lit the menorah and offered the ritual sacrifices etc. There is not an iota, not one word mentioned of any miracle, nothing at all.

This went along very well for about 200 years at which time the rabbis in Jerusalem thought that this holiday needed some spiritual aspect because just a rebellion & civil war are not enough. Therefore, they had a conclave where somebody, an unknown unnamed member of the group, had the brilliant idea of telling everyone in the population of Judea that what happened back then was a "miracle".

Thus was created from whole cloth the story of the miracle of Chanukah wherein a cruse of sanctified oil that was normally sufficient for one day lasted for a full eight days until they could obtain some fresh sanctified olive oil. None of this is recorded in the Book of Maccabees, which when you think on it is very odd.

The miracle story has thus continued to be told for well over 2000 years. Now this telling of stories about a special event is nothing new; the Old Testament is replete with such tales. You should recall that this was a desert culture, a tribal culture and a patriarchal one. It is quite common in such cultures around the world that stories are told about creation, about their history or just events that may or may not have happened. In some cases, they are just stories and in other cases they can be taken as metaphors, symbolic tales with deeply hidden mystical metaphysical implications. And that is how we may take this story.

The Spiritual/Mystical Purport

What I wish to explore is the mystical, inner meaning of this ritual and not just the "story". A story is good in that it is a way to get your attention, and it is sweet to hear but that is not a spiritual experience, not the inner teaching.

In the story that is told the miracle of the oil. The sacred oil is found only in the darkest little corner of the temple. It is well hidden. Likewise, when, in our own life, we are confronted with difficulties, with those who wish to destroy our faith, with those real hard tests—we are sometimes required to make a real effort and dig into the dark corner to discover that source of light. Sometimes it is in the worst darkness that we can discover the light. But it is there, it is there. No doubt about it.

By kindling the Chanukah lamp we generate light to elevate the material realm. Thus we unveil and actually can see the divine spark within every person and all of creation. Here is the reason for putting menorah by the window (that is the traditional practice)—it symbolizes bridging the private realm with the public realm. So the "light" generated in the home, that is to say the spiritual side, maybe shared with and transmitted to the material realm.

Now we present a mystical exegesis regarding the date which is the 25th day of the month. In the Hebrew Old Testament book of Genesis it says "God said, 'Let there be light.' "Of course it is not literal that God "says"—it is God and all that is required is just the "thought" but not on our level of the mind. Any way the Hebrew is "Vayehe Or"—and Or = light which is the 25th word in the Bible. Now this light is not the physical light by which we see with the eyes. Or is that mystical light, the pure consciousness that pervades the entire universe and is in all things, IS ALL things. It is said in the mishna that this is the light by which the first beings saw (Adam & Eve)—meaning they were fully conscious beings. That is a whole other story.

The inner purpose here is that we may get to that Original Light that enabled the original mind of man and woman to see from one end of the universe to the other. But on a much higher level is for one to be able to kindle that light in another person. The Soul of man is God's lamp Torah is the light—they can never be extinguished. When you see the Konica menorah one candle is a higher than the others. This one is called the "Shamash" its sole purpose is to like the other candles. It is not counted. It is much higher than the others for as it is said by the great holy Reb Hillel, "it is of much greater blessing to the one who gives the light of Torah to another than the one who receives it." This is a great, deep teaching. It is by this that we contribute to the spiritual light of the world.

Every Chanukah as the lights are kindled the hidden light within you is revealed your own true self. The Chanukah lights that burn in the darkest of night demonstrate that we can reach this level of Divine service not only during the daylight when Godliness is manifest but also at times when effort is needed to transform the darkness. So that we are not to resign ourselves to the darkness but to reach out till that dark is also lit.

This turns our home into a temple, right where we are. Jewish strength begins in the home, a dwelling place for God right here. Thus, we contribute to the spiritual light of the world. Flow from inside to out. It is lit only after nightfall—our purpose is to illuminate the darkness. The purpose is to affirm the supremacy of spiritual light over material; of Divine wisdom over human limitations. The way to eliminate darkness is to be rid of ignorance.

To shine, shine, shine. Even if darkness were to cover the earth you will still shine forth in God. Therefore, the light REAL victory is the transforming of darkness or more accurately of <u>EXTRACTING</u> the light FROM the dark. That's it. That is the real victory.

All the candles give light but know this God's Menorah is even greater. It is made up of people not candles. The story of Chanukah. Says light can burn even without oil. It is so. But that is just the littler miracle. The true miracle is that there is a place in each of us that can carry the light. God has made us this way. When He said let there be light he was speaking to each of us. He is telling us we CAN choose how it is possible to live. But one candle does not do much. He has made it possible for each to kindle that light in another. Passing the light along the way. That the light will shine forever. After many years I have found we often discover the place in us that carries the light only after it has become dark. Sometimes it is only in the dark that we know the value of this place. THERE IS a place in EVERYONE that can carry the light. This is so. May we discover that pure light which is hidden even in that darkest place. And may each of us have the love and generosity to pass on that light, to kindle the hope and faith in God's menorah which is greater than any other—which is all of us. The candle is just the external representation of "God's Menorah" which is each one of us. May that light of lights fill you, and may you and your family enter into its presence, may it fill your life, your home with peace and love.

Addendum: Something about Numbers

The Temple Menorah had seven lights. Seven is perfection of natural order, seven days, it has the potential of all situations, the Temple Menorah had but seven lamps, because God is manifest there. (Seven Dwarves, Seven Wonders of the World, seven tiles in Scrabble, Seals, Chakras, Samurai) But here we need to go beyond the nature and so we go one step above to eight. Eight is not bound by any limitations. The highest level of god is that which transcends the natural order; the INFINATE. Ayin Sof. Eight is redemption, ultimate transcendence to a higher reality, above the natural order. We need that power to illumine our ignorance.

A New Translation of the Blessings

A little explanation would be appropriate here. I have meditated on this deeply and it came to me that the traditional prayers and translations were no longer appropriate in this day. In the ancient days, tradition was that God was viewed as the King, a man or at least having masculine qualities and in the Biblical sense was somewhat of a jealous autocrat who would do well with a bit of anger management therapy. But that, as they say, is for another time.

But if you view the Kabbalistic tradition "God" is very much like the Vedantic concept; that is God is the Consciousness that pervades the entire universe without form or name and one cannot attribute human concepts to that. It is neither masculine nor feminine, nameless and formless, it pervades us and all things while at the same time being "everything and nothing (no thing)" as was so well expressed by Martin Buber. That is what is meant by the Ayin Sof and Yesh ve Ayin (Everything & Nothing—No Thing).

Those who are familiar with the tradition will also note that I've changed the order of these prayers. Normally first prayer which I put here is said last but to my mind it should be first because we would not be here had we not been nurtured protected and brought to the time. I also changed the translation of prayer about the lighting of candles in fact there is no such commandment light candles from any God rather one can consider it a privilege. In the translation of the occurrence of miracles in the original it refers to our "fathers" because in those days all of these traditions were very patriarchal and I do not think that appropriate in this time I therefore included the mothers.

Baruch ata Adonai ha Ayin Sof ve ha Yesh ve Ayin – shehechayanu, v'kiyamanu, v'higayanu la zaman hazeh.—Shalom aumein

We thank you oh divine universal, infinite, eternal, nameless consciousness that pervades the entire universe; the everything & Nothing—who gave us life, sustained us, nurtured us and brought us to this time.—Peace. Amen

Baruch ata Adonai ha Ayin Sof ve ha Yesh ve Ayin asher kidishanu, be mitzvotzah, vetzyanu lehadlick ner shel Channukah.—Shalom aumein

We thank you oh divine universal, infinite, eternal, nameless consciousness that pervades the entire universe; the everything & Nothing who has sanctified us with the privilege and has led us to kindle the Chanukah lights. Peace. Amen

Baruch ata Adonai ha Ayin Sof ve ha Yesh ve Ayin she asah nissim lavotenu, v' la emaot bahyamim hahem v'ba zeman ha zeh.—Shalom aumein

We thank you oh divine universal, infinite, eternal, nameless consciousness that pervades the entire universe; the everything & Nothing who has made miracles for our fathers and mothers in those days and at this time. Peace. Amen

Appendix II: A Very Few Movie Reviews

Just 4 out of over 400

A good friend suggested that I include a short selection of my movie reviews since this was a significant aspect of my life.

For many years, I have had a passion and love of cinema. In my obsessive manner I made lists of almost all the films I saw with ratings that I gave, −5 to a 10 with Gold Latkes. At this point I have a list of over 4020 films. During that time I also wrote over 400 reviews. It gave me an opportunity to exercise writing skills and simply as a way of expressing thoughts. I sent these reviews to various people who wanted them. It was great fun. Here is a small selection of some of the best films that I've seen and a one of the not so good. There is no necessity of agreeing with what I say. This is just how I saw it. As I have said a number of times in those reviews, "Opinions should not be confused with facts except when stated here".

As I see it, a well done film is akin to having a very fine meal in a fine restaurant. There are a number of elements that must work in harmony to make a good film. There must be good directing, writing of dialogue, plot or the arc of the story, excellent acting, of course. As it is a visual experience there must be quality photography. If CGI must be used it should be judicious not way overdone as is so common now. CGI is like the spice of a meal, the right amount is enhancing; overdo it and it spoils the enjoyment. That in brief is how I see it. There have been too many movies. If you would like my list of 250 best movies just email me.

I include the following essay, which I wrote on how I became passionate about films. (Note: the word maven is a Yiddish word meaning an expert in something.)

Birth of a Maven

This is a true story—names have not been changed to protect the innocent or guilty. I write film reviews under the name Movie Maven of the Western World (MMWW). Now, for those among you too young to remember; the title of this piece comes from the first feature film ever made, a silent movie, called Birth of a Nation by D W Griffith. Yes, kids, there was a time they made films without computers and F/X and you may not believe it, but it's the truth—they had no sound.

How I Became the Movie Maven of the Western World

(MMWW) – A True Story

In the summer of 1945, it was hot enough to bake codfish on the streets of N.Y. That was also two years before the greatest snowstorm in the history of that city—it snowed what was to me, and I'm not making this up, 8 feet. However, I was only 4 feet tall at the time so any measurement would be relative indeed.

In those days the movie theaters big draw was having air-conditioning. No person I ever knew had such a thing. AC for homes did not exist in our forlorn society. Actually, no one I knew even had a fan. So the cinemas advertised this fact by hoisting huge 17 foot long blue banners below the marquee proclaiming in big white "ice" dripping letters, "COOL INSIDE." That was the modern advertising of that age. They were never subtle. That was the summer attractor.

At other times, theaters would attract patrons by giving away free dishes. They were always either green or green. Never white. Women would go just to get the whole set. They did not care what the film was and if it starred Bette Davis or Paul Henride, or Robert Taylor or Cary Grant that was a gold star. Getting the gravy boat was like winning the lottery, it was the Holy Grail. It was second only to getting a ride with Cary Grant on that big ship. But at 25¢ a pop who cared. They could go, get a dish and have a good cry. What a deal.

But, I digress.

I was four years old when my Dad took me to see my very first film, The Wizard of Oz at the Ocean Theatre in Brighton Beach, Brooklyn. The Ocean Theater was right near the El (that's an elevated subway, an oxymoron). Why they put a movie house near a train shall for ever remain one of life's mysteries.

The monkeys were really scary.

I loved it.

I was hooked on film. (Of course, the poppies were not to blame. Right?)

At about age of eight I was allowed to go to the movies alone, or rather I just went alone anyway. Yes it's true; you could see an actual DOUBLE feature PLUS TEN or maybe TWENTY cartoons for 25 cents, two bits one quarter or a week's allowance (Well, it was either movies OR a double scoop ice-cream Sundae with, syrup, nuts AND ½ pound of genuine real whipped-cream—not from a can.) That was before inflation, oil embargoes and before sliced bread (If you always wondered what was the best thing BEFORE sliced bread?—those Sundaes were it!).

Kids always got in at a special price.

I managed to get in at Kid's price until I was 14 (12 was the cut-off point.) I blew it when the guy asked me when my birthday was.

The best thing was the long lines for really great sci-fi films when I would meet 100's of other kids who loved that movie.

Some of them would have seen it 3 or 4 times.

They always knew what would happen next and were always anxious to tell that to their pals in a real loud voice.

No one liked them.

They would grow up to be Trekies or programmers for Microsoft.

In those days movie houses were designed in the manner of the stage theater. It was complete with a magnificent stylish entryway, fountains, marble, lighting and all done up in elegant Art-Deco style. The very entry into the movie house was a welcome into another world. There was the marquee, which proclaimed the current shows in large bold letters that you can see from all the way to the end of the block. There were the gorgeously designed posters, placards and photos on the outside that gave you a teeny glimpse of what was held inside for you to see. There were balconies with heavy plaster moldings and ogees; and at their edges carvings of mysterious creatures. Beautiful Deco sconces, rather than 9000 watt amplifiers, lined the walls. And every screen had an actual CURTAIN; that is to say a giant REALLY HEAVY thick velvet maroon (always Maroon, never blue or black) colored curtain, the kind they had at the opera house; that would SLOWLY part at the anticipatory commencement of the presentations.

Needless to say there was just ONE screen per theater—no one would even conceive of those ghastly multiplex contrivances.

There were no video games.

After locating the perfect seat—exact center of the center aisle - the next strategy was acquiring the perfect movie snack. This took major consideration and profound thought, almost as difficult and arcane as the D-Day tactical planning. Now, popcorn with actual butter, fake butter flavor had not been invented, was 10 cents, but this was a poor selection— it would not last past the coming attractions (which is what they were called then and still should be—trailers are what you put onto the back of automobiles). No, a proper snack should be both tasty and last well past the first feature if not halfway into the second. There were a few possibilities. At a nickel a pop there was a good field to choose from: Root-Beer Barrels, Red-Hots, and Good & Plenty were top options followed by Necco Wafers, Jujubes, and Mary-Janes. (Trivia Master Contest-- for 10 points—what is the etymological origin of NECCO?) The latter three were, however, really too middle-class, Midwest, white-bread for me. No, I was a mainline Good & Plenty guy—I could make a nickel box last midway to the second feature. Red Hots and Root Beers were good second selections. On a rare occasion, when feeling particularly grandiose and wealthy, I'd pop for a bag of potato sticks (like chips but in stick form). These had exceptional taste and enough grease to lubricate an Army tank.

They would be consumed in 2 minutes flat.

But, they were REALLY delicious.

Seat and snack being secured I let go the ordinary mind and indulged in the wondrous world of fantasy and imagination. It was dark; there was no one else there but Ingrid Bergman and me. Harpo Marx, with baggy overcoat that could contain the world plus a four foot salami and me. Gary Cooper and I defending truth, justice and Grace Kelly. In color or black & white. Then came the gorgeous, lovely Julie Christie and Sophia Loren and Marcello or Cary Grant in some of the finest comedies ever made, Katherine Hepburn who never made a single bad film -- ever. The mellifluous voice of John Huston whom I always wanted to sound like and who also made some fantastic films and Sir David Lean who never made a bad film and whose every film stands as a classic.

It was all grand.

Movies carried me to the Wild West and the deserts, giant monsters that came from dark places that devoured whole cities in a single gulp. Even abysmally stupid Martin & Lewis comedies (which to a 9-year-old mind was really quite funny). Heckle & Jeckle cartoons (they were magpies or maybe blackbirds—I was not up on ornithology at age 6).The brilliant comedies of Sir Alec Guinness—who will always be the greatest actor of all time. The dark world of Robert Mitchum, the brilliant comedy of Judy Holiday. But let me say I never was and am not now a fan of the saccharine Disney genre. Enough of that.

To Continue

I was nine. I asked Mom if I could get a Hopalong Cassidy outfit. Total black and way cool. I loved Westerns.

> "Ma could I get this outfit—please, please!?"
> "No, you could poke your eyes out."
> "But, Ma it's a **SHIRT** and **pants** and **boots**—they don't even come near the eyes."
> I did not even think to ask for the cap-guns, no way.
> "No, you will look like a hoodlum."

(YES!!!)

I persevered.

Well Perry Mason could not have presented a better case. I got the outfit **and** the boots as well.

So from then on whenever I went to a big Western I could slog up the mountain huffing and puffing across the wild barren rock fields, whenever I had get to my horse or walk up the aisle to the candy-stand or bathroom. It was great.

I no longer have the boots and no longer slog up the mountain but it is still great.

Coda I: There were other films I went to see with my Dad. One was the "classic" sci-fi, The Incredible Shrinking Man." Those so-called "classics" were, by today's standards really pretty crappy films. Ghastly acting, shabby sets, lousy effects, dreadful dialogue—but we loved them and for that time they were actually good stuff. Shrinking Man was actually interesting. This guy on his little boat passes through a cloud of dust from an A-Bomb (Paranoia theme of any scientific advancement here). He was regular guy, Ozzie & Harriet family, suburban house, wore a tie every day etc. but shortly after the boat trip he discovers that all his clothes are five sizes too large. He continues this body diminution until he becomes really small, smaller than a fly. He ends up in the basement fighting a little mouse and escaping through the window screen. But he survives despite of all odds.

I asked Dad how he liked the film, what he thought. He told me this, "No matter what happens to you, however difficult it becomes, God will never forget you. You are never too small for God." I never knew he knew so much.

NB. Dad & I also went to numerous Marx Bro. films. We both loved the Marx Brothers especially Harpo and Chicko, "You don'ta believe in Sanity Clause, OK we cutta out Sanity Clause."

Casablanca

With: Humphrey Bogart, Ingrid Bergman, Claude Raines, Dooly Wilson, Paul Henreid, S Z Sakal, Leonid Kinsky, Conrad Veldt, Sidney Greenstreet (The Fat man), Peter Lorrie, Joy Page, Madeline Lebeau, Marcel Dalio.

The greatest movie of all time. Watching this is, on some level a religious experience.

The Maven has seen it at least 25 times. It has the two greatest scenes ever done in film (see below); it has fine casting; a great story; and lines that if you say just one of them; anyone who knows film will know from where it came. You could almost summarize the plot with those lines: -"Here's looking at you kid." "We'll always have Paris." "I was misinformed." "Watch, what watch?" "Play it Sam, play as time goes by." "Of all the gin joints in all the towns in the world she has to walk into mine." "I stick my neck out for nobody." "Round up the usual suspects" And of course -"The problems of three little people don't amount to a hill of beans in this crazy world". The dialogue has not lost any of its wit to this day. But it is also the perfect delivery that made it work. In the hands of lesser actors it would just be pap. Pay attention also to such greats as Sakal, Kinsky, and Greenstreet. Ahhhhhh.

It has it all:"action, adventure, bravery, danger, espionage, an exotic locale, friendship, gunplay, humor, intrigue, a love triangle, a masculine hero, a mysterious heroine, patriotism, politics (without being too political), romance, sacrifice, sentimentality, a theme song, a venomous villain, and war." (Whew!).

The opening scenes dance with comedy; the dialogue combines the cynical with the weary; wisecracks with epigrams. We see that Rick moves easily in a corrupt world. "What is your nationality?" The German Strasser asks him, and he replies, "I'm a drunkard."

The atmosphere (enhanced by the sterling black-and-white cinematography), that of encroaching gloom, is as palpable as ever. And the characters are still as perfectly-acted and three-dimensional as they were more than fifty years ago.

I have not reviewed it until now, imagine that. Well it's about time this omission was corrected. You will note I listed almost all the actors. You may also note that with the exception of just three of the principle actors, Bogart, Wilson & Joy Page, ALL the others are from various European countries, this is important because the film was made in 1942 at the height of the war and all of those people were, in a way, refugees. It is an amazing cast.

Bogart and Bergman. When anyone mentions Casablanca, these are the two names that come to mind. The actors are both so perfectly cast, and create such a palpable level of romantic tension, that it's impossible to envision anyone else in their parts (and inconceivable to consider that they possibly weren't the producer's first choices). Bogart is at his best here as the tough cynic who hides a broken heart beneath a fractured layer of sarcasm. Ilsa's arrival in Casablanca rips open the fissures in Rick's shield, revealing a complex personality that demands Bogart's full range of acting. As Ilsa, Bergman lights up the screen. We could speak about each of the major cast members and several of the minor ones at length but then this would become a book and we are not aiming for that—suffice to say that one from Raines, Henreid to Lorrie, Greenstreet & Sakal had all made a special contribution to this film.

Less known is Paul Henreid, a romantic lead who was on loan to Warner Brothers for this project. Most viewers know Henreid as "the other guy" in the romantic triangle, and, while his performance isn't on the same level as that of his better-known co-stars, Henreid nevertheless does a respectable job. Casablanca features some other well-known faces. Conrad Veidt plays the Nazi commander on Laszlo's trail, Peter Lorre is the man who steals the letters of transit, and Sydney Greenstreet is the city's black market overlord.

We all know the story, however, I would still like to point out the two great scenes plus one more. The first is when Ilsa asks Sam to "Play it Sam, Play as Time Goes By."And Sam feigns ignorance—but then there is the beatific smile and that perfect light. Who can refuse the request of an angel? Then the GREATEST scene in all of film - when Victor hears the Germans singing some sort of army song and he goes to the silent orchestra and tells them in a strong voice, "Play the Marseillaise." And Rick just gives a nod. And they play and all the voices rise up. No matter how many times I have seen this it never fails to explode in my heart. There is also a scene where Rick and Ilsa are seated on a couch and she just nestles her head into his shoulder. She is so very beautiful and so loving and he is just there. Who could not fall in love with Ingrid Bergman???

If Casablanca was made in today's climate, Rick and Ilsa would escape on the plane after avoiding a hail of gunfire (Rick would probably be doing the two-fisted gun thing that John Woo loves). There would be no "beautiful friendship" between Luis and Rick. Who knows what would have happened to Victor Laszlo, but he wouldn't have gotten the girl.

BTW—It is not true that Ronald Regan & Ann Sheridan were considered for the leads that was a false rumor planted by the studio. But they did consider Heddy Lamar—that would have been a disaster—no! The only one who could do Ilsa was Bergman. But it is true they did ask George Raft to play Rick and he refused.

The movie earned 8 Academy Award nominations, leading to three Oscars (Best Screenplay, Best Director, and Best Picture.

Well yeah, so many of the scenes are now considered cliché , like the driving happy along the back roads, or waiting in the rain for the loved one—and even that opener with the map and the line going along the map (Also used in Lost Horizon)– that was also used once for Indiana Jones— we loved it. And indeed its weakness is that it uses common film tropes, such as the doomed relationship between the dark, brooding anti-hero and the Madonna like heroine. The gaping plot hole—why would the Germans respect letters of transit signed by General de Gaulle?—is largely irrelevant. By the end your heart will be too big and your eyes too wet to notice.

"This is the beginning of a beautiful friendship."

MMWW

And for those .0000004% of people who never saw this:

Mainly it tells of a tough fellow named Rick who runs a Casablanca cafe and of what happens when there shows up in his joint one night a girl whom he had previously loved in Paris in company with a fugitive Czech patriot. The Nazis are tailing the young Czech; the Vichy officials offer only brief refuge—and Rick holds the only two sure passports which will guarantee his and the girl's escape. But the German-controlled local government, headed by Captain Luis Renault (Claude Rains), is on the move, and Laszlo has to act quickly to get the letters of transit he came for, then escape. But Rick loves the girl dearly, she is married to this other man(and was before when she met Rick)—and whenever his pianist sits there in the dark and sings "As Time Goes By" that old, irresistible feeling consumes him in a choking, maddening wave.

PS. Even though this was the greatest film ever the Maven would be remiss if he did not point out a few of the "dumb" things. Bergman's clothes—well first off she has a wardrobe for a queen, so many dresses. People who were escaping the Nazis did not have time to pack anything but their papers and most precious items like jewelry, which had real value. They are on the run; they cannot be encumbered with luggage. OK, she is gorgeous but then there was that "umbrella" hat, the big giant white one—it closely resembles those woven straw umbrella hats you see in all those ancient Japanese films, the sort worn by peasants 400 years ago. Then they have her wear with the hat the silly horizontal stripe jumper on top of which is that thick sleeveless white item (I don't know what to call it) but it is pretty dorky looking combo especially with that stripped jumper which looks like it came from an old prison uniform.. But she is gorgeous so she can get away with it. There is the airport scene—the fog is so thick you can barely see two feet ahead yet this idiot who calls the plane (No control tower in those day) says, "Fog ten feet visibility ceiling Unlimited" " good grief man that is NOT the weather in which even a jet would take off. Then there are just the **two** passengers—what? What is this a private flight? It's a small fortune to fly in those days, how could they afford to do that with just two people, especially since this is a bi-weekly trip?

PPS. Trivia

1. Many of the actors who played the Nazis were in fact German Jews who had escaped from Nazi Germany.

2. Of course we all know this - Rick never says "Play it again, Sam." He says: "You played it for her, you can play it for me. If she can take it, I can take it so Play it!". Ilsa says "Play it, Sam. Play 'As Time Goes By'". The incorrect line has become the basis for spoofs in movies.

3. Louie mentions at the end about an outpost in Brazzaville which is in the Congo in those days a colony of Belgium. Brazzaville is about 1500 miles from Casablanca. Were they planning to walk? Take a taxi? A private car? Whatever mode it would take several days to get there. A difficult and challenging journey.

PPPS. A curious thing about Casablanca is that hardly anyone ever talks about the director. It isn't as if Michael Curtiz is a journeyman hack who got lucky here. From the '20s to the '50s, Curtiz was one of the hardest working directors in Hollywood, helming over 100 films including White Christmas, Mildred Pierce, and Yankee Doodle Dandy. (Before that, he made nearly 50 movies in Europe, where he began his career in 1912.) Curtiz was a well-respected film maker and his work on Casablanca was first rate, but, for some reason, few non-cineastes associate his name with this picture.

One can only imagine that, in another fifty years, its position in the hierarchy of all-time greats will be even higher. (See also To Have and Have Not; also with Bogart not as good. Having a very similar theme, also stars a very young Lauren Bacall. It's the film in which Bogart falls in love with the gorgeous teenage Bacall. True.).

Dark Eyes

By Nikita Mikalkhov with Marcello Mastroianni, Elena Sofanova

In Russian & Italian with subtitles.

The Maven will now go out on a limb and declare that this is certainly one of the greatest films ever. It is on a very short list of 10's in the MMMWW'S rating system. In fact it is one of only 16 films on the 10's list that received the Maven's coveted *Golden Latke* award (as you would have figured out this a very special award among special awards.)

The Maven has seen this at least 7 times. In all that time it has never lost its charm, a good test for the quality of a film.

Just to see how Mastroianni pours a glass of water or light a cigar for his friend is to see a man who has perfected his art. It is a beautiful symphony. No note is out of balance, nothing is too loud, nothing too bright. He has an elegance and style that is quite rare in this field. It is a joy to behold. He is just sublime. There is no one else who can go into a mud bath to fetch a hat in the way he does.

This film is loosely based on the Chekov short story—"Lady with a Dog."

The story is about Marcello, who is telling the tale to a man on an excursion ship sometime in the early 1900's. It is about his life. Married into a well to do family in Italy that suddenly loses its wealth; he basically has been living off of their riches and has not much to do in life. This is exquisitely portrayed in one long scene. He leaves his domineering wife to just be roaming about Europe. Eventually he finds the love of his life only to lose it. He meets a beautiful married, Russian woman at a health spa and without intending to causes her to fall in love with him. But she must return to her husband in Russia soon after their meeting. Marcello follows her, but can never get her back. She is also really gorgeous!!! When he finally arrives at her home town he is greeted as the guest of the century. You will have to see it to find out exactly why that is and to see the man that she was married to. There is a lot going on here.

Eventually he ends up as the waiter on a cruise ship.

Just be patient as this films unfolds at its own pace. It is meant to be taken with fine food and not nachos. There are many subtleties, unlike most of today's Hollywood fodder which has to punch you in the gut to get your attention.

There are beautiful scenes of the countryside and an especially beautiful interlude with a band of gypsies. It is about dreams and how they come and go. It is about style and grace.

Dark eyes is a film to sink and luxuriate into. It has wonderfully gorgeous scenery, some delightful characters and mostly heart, oodles of heart. It is a movie with real soul. The spirit of Italy and the sad soul of Russia with a soupcon of irony at the end. And even though you may be able to predict the end it matters not for that too is gorgeous and touching. This is a film of pure art on every level—without any pretensions at all.

PS—Mikhalkov also directed the sweet film Close to Eden which won the Oscar. It is a modern parable about a Russian truck driver who gets stuck in the mud some place in Mongolia and how both he and the locals are transformed by their interactions. Terrific acting, beautiful scenery and a great story.

Dark City

With: William Hurt, Jenifer Connolly, Rufus Sewell, and Kiefer Sutherland.

Alex Proyas (Writer, director producer)

It is indeed a very "dark" city. Take equal parts film noir, science fiction, horror, German expressionist, mix in some Edward Hopper, a dash of Kafka, a pinch of Frtz Lang, a smidgen of Vincent Price, some Art Deco, Frank Lloyd Wright, Metropolis, Gothic, a dash of X-files and loads more. Is it the 40's (that's what the opening tells you) but then there are cars from the 50's and you spot a car from very early 1960. In reality it is none of these. But then what is the reality?

From the very opening shot you can see the brilliance and dedication to brilliant visual detail and gorgeous cinematography in this film. We see Kiefer Sutherland opening with a shot from behind wearing a gray Fedora and 30's style woolen overcoat doing a perfect Peter Lorrie. There is a very intelligent and judicious use of CGI here. Unlike most films this uses devices this uses it only to move the plot along not just to dazzle.

To some it may be a confusing plot but if you really stay focused and pay attention it is very clear what happens. Let us say that this is a good challenge to the intellect. And in this day of the really dumber that bent nails of most films, TV, and so on such a challenge is well needed.

This is a pre-Matrix movie that created many of the ideas which Matrix used. That is not to say Matrix stole these ideas but that they came here first and was not recognized as such. AND it is WAY better than the Matrix ever was. Yes it is for a more mindful, intelligent audience, OK. Perhaps that is why it did not gain the pop level of Matrix. There is alternate universe, created memories (as in Total Recall), reality perception, Invaders from Mars (a 50's sci-fi classic) horror, Gothic a seemingly drug addled universe. Oh yes and of course there are aliens who stop time and all life right at midnight, well of course. All of this may have been done before but Dark City has it over most all of them with style and panache. And it has Jennifer Connolly, what more would one want?

Rufus Sewell plays John Murdoch a sort of Everyman, but one who has powers he is not aware of. He is seen at the beginning of the film waking up in a bathtub with a drip of blood on his forehead, he is totally naked, he has no idea where he is or what happened. This is suggestive of a rebirth of sorts. And of course there is the dead hooker in the bedroom with the strange signs on her naked body. Of course. And, of course, he is staying at a sleazebag hotel.

The very beautiful Jennifer Connolly plays the 40's style chanteuse with pitch perfect style. She is Sewell's wife, or is she? But he is lost someplace and is accused of being a serial killer. Worth seeing just for her.

William Hurt is the cop (or should we say "gumshoe") named "Bumstead" (What!! That is Blondie's Husband—played by ____? You have to guess.) who never takes his big hat off, perfect film-noir type cop. Well there is a whole lot more but we do not wish to spoil the viewer's discovery of what this package contains.

Kiefer Sutherland as the hyperkinetic, duplicitous doctor suggests a punked out Peter Lorrie with Vincent Price overtones. Oh Yes and Ian Richardson plays, with pure delight, the proto-Fascist alien head of the group of aliens known as the "Strangers". But the Maven has already said too much.

It would be worth seeing more than once just to catch the parts you missed the first time. It sometimes has a bit too much cruelty for this viewer's taste. But it does have some very cool action stuff at the end. Oh and did I mention it has Jenifer Connolly?

After Life

Japanese with subtitles

What happens to us after death? What happens to our thoughts, our memories? This has been a subject of great interest to philosophers both of the professional and the university stoned sophomore type as well as countless religious discussions. In the past there have been several attempts at producing films on the subject. Hollywood often failed in this, producing such treacle as It's a Wonderful Life and Here Comes Mr. Jordan or sentimental pap like What Dreams May Come, that's Hollywood. But here is a film on that subject which really works.

This is perhaps one of the most difficult films for which the Maven has had to write a review in a very long time. Its concept is most original and bold. It is one of the most thought provoking films the Maven has ever seen.

It's quite simple really—the story opens, as what we are told, Monday morning. We see a small band of workers coming to work to a very drab building. It could be an abandoned school building. It is a cold fall day. Their job is most unusual. They are to interview a group of people—one per person—to ascertain what their most fond memory in life was. They will then make a film of that memory. Simple, yes? No, turns out all these people are very recently deceased. Yep they are all dead and that includes the people who work there. But the ones working there do not age. The ones working there are there because they never selected any memory. And when one selects the memory then he or she leaves to go on to the next level (whatever that is). They go one with that memory for eternity. So they have to think carefully on what they select. After all they can choose but ONE memory and they will have the film of it for ETERNITY while all other memories are gone.

[side bar] And you know Eternity is a long time. A very LONG time. Think about it. It is more complex than you would suppose. As is the whole concept of infinite universe. (See: The Infinity Book by John D Barrow, an interesting in depth exposition on the subject.) Does it really exist, and what are the consequences of an infinite universe? It's not as simple as you may think. There is an excellent reason why St. Augustine avoided the whole question. It's in the book.

They have just 3 days to select the memory, Turns out that this is not an easy task. And it also turns out that in following the interviews the Maven was also trying to figure out what memory would he select.

Because there is very little action on screen one would think this would be a very boring film. That is not so. It is very character driven. There is the very sweet old lady who smiles a beautiful smile, it will just light your heart. Her fondest memory was the time she was a little girl in a red dress, which she draws for the filmmakers. It is the time she learned to do a certain dance. She has a bit of difficulty in dredging up that complete memory.

There is the very beautiful young girl who wistfully recalls her visit to Disneyland but then changes her mind.

There is the very old lady who speaks little but goes out to collect little leaves and acorns and asks if the trees ever bloom here. She misses her cherry trees. There is the young teenager who refuses to select any memory. And so on. The central character is an elderly business man, Watanabe, who worked all his life for one company as an office manager and got married later in life by an arranged marriage. He has the greatest difficulty in finding a good memory. His story is very important in that it links to someone else there (and we will not spoil the surprise by telling you).

All this is done with a delicate, transcendental beauty. It does not try to impose any doctrine or preach any moral. It just presents these peoples' lives in a clear way. Now what is most amazing is that the way this is all done. The beauty of each character pulls you in. And most astonishing is how it will get you to contemplate on what is your own most precious memory.

After each one selects his or her memory the workers there will make a film of that memory. They use the very lowest of tech methods. They also play very low tech Christmas music. And even though they are not too good musicians, it is lovely.

And here is where the Maven would love to be fluent in the language so that the subtleties that cannot be translated can be felt and understood. But even without that ability the film is so well done, the actors so refined and skilled that one can really feel what is going on. So it does not require a massive over-production or acting that hits you on the head.. This is a film that also requires the viewer's participation (i.e. ATTENTION).

There are some difficulties in watching the film. The technical quality is poor. One wonders, for example, why any director would aim his camera directly into a desk lamp light. The whole method of filming was on an amateur level. The film stock was also rather grainy. He may have done that on purpose to reflect the way the characters in the film did the filming of memories.

Take special notice of the symbol they use which is first seen on a teen brooch worn by the young female worker the displayed on their flag—very interesting.

What memory would you choose?

Atonement

This is presented so you do not think that every movie I've seen was spectacular.

Opinions are not facts, except as expressed by this writer.

Despite the cameo (around 5 minutes) of the magnificent Vanessa Redgrave at the very end of this epic this contribution from the UK remains what the maven calls a VBB—Very Boring Brit. It is Masterpiece Theater meets The English Patient. Turgid and pretentious. The critics will all love this because they must. After all It is British. Of course that means they do not wish to be charged with being unsophisticated boors. Never.

Well, yes it does have great visuals.

They begin with your average British manor estate. You know the setting; 400 year old 96 room stone manor-house, stables, numerous out-buildings, 7000 acres of perfectly manicured lawns, impeccably arraigned trees, flowers, and fountains. There are the residents, who change clothes 14 times a day and the hordes of servants, maids, gardeners, footmen (whatever that is), cooks, and dressers who manage to change clothes every 14 days. They smoke lots and lots of cigarettes. They always drink at any time of day and have loads of freeloading relatives.

They have way cool cars.

AND way cool clothes.

Even the men.

Kiera Knightly is the eldest daughter who, in her usual gauntly mode, falls for the son of one of the servants. We all know he is just a servant's son and not one of the upper class people because he has but one name. Rod. Class people always have at least three first and three last names—George Philip Arthur Spencer Chapman Wilberforce is very acceptable. No guy in these films is ever called Joe or Mike or Pete. Never.

As we stated the eldest sister of the manor falls for the gentle son of the housekeeper. He is absolutely bonkers for her. Events follow that are seen from two points of view; as they actually happen and as viewed by the younger sister, a budding brat and prepubescent scribe. The little brat is stricken jealous. Because, even though she does not have a clue what sex is all about she has a crush on the man. So when a wretched crime occurs on the estate she accuses the young man. She even claims to be an eye-witness to the event. Thus begins the ruination of the innocent young man and the downfall of the lady of the manor.

The story then shifts 8 or 9 years into the future. WWII is on full blast. The perfidious brat, neophyte writer is now a young lady. (Note to those under 25: the device they use to put words onto paper in this film is called a typewriter. It was a most clever invention that did away with cumbersome things such as pens and quills—look it up.)

Anyway the young girl is now a war-time nurse. With nice starched uniform. You can tell the underlings because the supervisor always calls them by their last name (Tillis, is her name). The entire middle section is occupied by the events during the war most notably is a terminally boring very extended tracking shot (over 7 minutes long) of the guys walking the fields at the Battle of Dunkirk. It is a disturbingly surreal scene of death and despair as these guys along with our hero are seeking their company and rest. Sometimes this scene has the feel of a dream and that is how this viewer understood it to be.

All the time young sister is trying to make up for the lies she told. She knows she did wrong and is trying to right the wrong, or in this case write the wrong. If this were a fantastic Martin Scorsesse film she would be in a church confessing to the Bishop pounding her breast and saying a thousand rosaries. That is not the case here.

At the near end of the war the younger sister, who has made many vain attempts to meet with her sister and to set things right and confess her wrongdoing finally does meet up with the sister in some drab apartment in London where our young hero is also to be found united at last with his one true love. Although we observe the couple to be reunited there is simply no observable chemistry between them.

BUT—now here it comes ---------- we discover at the very end that all the foregoing center piece is just part of the younger sister's novel called, of course, Atonement. We meet her as a much older woman played by the most luminous Vanessa Redgrave. Furthermore we are told that not all of what was depicted actually happened. What appears to be truth was in large part made up. So even when she is trying to tell the truth she resorts to imaginary events. Alas this film about the heart lacks that very thing, it is all a gathering of smoke & mirrors. And that is that.

NB: No matter what she does, we always love Vanessa.

Coda: One may wonder why such period films are so popular. Well it is not so much the era in which they take place but the fact that they are British and most importantly that they are about the really rich people of that time. What woman would not want to have scads of elegant dresses? Who would not want to have cook whip up a batch of scrambled quail eggs and truffles at any time of day, served up with a nice carafe of Champagne? And never have to worry about getting fat. Women were always reed thin. Men did not have to ever have a real job plus their trousers fit perfectly, their shirts were always well ironed, they had way cool cars and did not have to ever worry about money. They had a constant supply of great food like scrambled quail eggs and truffles and nice dinner jackets. The only thing they worried about was whether to have a girl-friend or boy-friend.

If they did require a "career" it was always in the "foreign service "or some sort of ministry or other falderal, where they could be in some exotic locale, wear white suits and eat a lot of good food at lawn parties. If they had to work in the secret service, or MI5 as they call it, they were frequently gay. Which was actually true.

And of course they speak perfect English and have terrific accents.

Now one should not conclude from the aforesaid that the Maven has any dislike of Brit film. On the contrary there are 100's of very great films from the UK and numerous very great actors as well. Any film by Sir David Lean is great (NEVER made a bad film) and any Film starring Sir Alec Guinness (who was the star of most of Sir David's films) is fantastic; as would be any film with Sir Anthony Hopkins, Sir Ralph Richardson, Ian Holm, Ian McLellan, Most films of Jeremy Irons, Dames Maggie Smith, Judy Dench, and Joan Plowright, as well as Vanessa Redgrave, Richard Harris, Christopher Lee, the oldies like Edmund Gwen, Peter O'Toole, Sir Charles Laughton, many more.

MMWW

There have been too many great ones. Perhaps a whole book of reviews should be done. But, there are so many books.. I've written over 400 reviews in that time. Obviously I could not put them all here so this was just a selection if, however, you'd like a few more sent to you just email me and I will make a small selection for you.

Appendix III: A Bit of Humor

Herein is a short selection of my humor bits. I have enjoyed doing stand-up for some 34 years here. It has usually been done on two of our major holidays on Guru Poornima, which takes place around the full moon of July, and Jayanthi, Sri Gurudev's birthday, the weekend on or before December 22. Some have been used on those occasions, some appear here for the first time. Enjoy. Much of standup comedy does not read well on the page, as it is dependent upon the inflections and method of delivery by the performer.

- ॐ Sometimes, when I'm depressed I get a pregnancy test so I can say, "Well at least I'm not pregnant."
- ॐ Things I'm grateful for:

Never been caught doping at Tour de France. Never had to give up any of my Olympic Gold and did not slip up at the Nobel Prize speech. I did not put the mirror in backwards in the Hubble space telescope. So much to be grateful for.

- ॐ Back in the day when I was hitchhiking a hearse stopped once I said, "No thanks, I'm not going that far."
- ॐ Whenever you feel anger in public, you should repeat, "May I be free of this anger!" This rarely works, but talking to yourself in public will encourage others to leave you alone.

I have coined a new word—Foodamentalist—someone who insists that his/her diet is the only one to follow and all others are false and will lead to death not to mention: acne, arthritis, lumbago, sciatica, anemia, and death. They tell you not to eat so many things be it gluten or Parmesan cheese and to have just agave sprouts and oak bark and mashed yeast over pumpkin seeds. I used to call them The Vegan Taliban. But that was too specific. So This foodamentalist is covers all varieties and subspecies.

> Losing one glove
> is certainly painful,
> but nothing
> compared to the pain,
> of losing one,
> throwing away the other,
> and finding
> the first one again.

ॐ After all is said & done there's more that's said than done

The good thing about living in such a small community is that when I don't know what I'm doing—somebody does

ॐ Enough of this focusing biz—I'm gonna spend my time (well some of it) in pure dawdling, with some staring at bees drinking from the moss, with occasional mumbling strange incantations to myself.

Aphorisms Plus

The Easy Path is Hard Enough.

The road to nowhere is also a path

If you don't know where you are going you are not lost

Truth is one—Mistakes are many

Even if you are on the right track, you'll get run over if you just sit there.

The sooner you fall behind the more time you'll have to catch up.

Christmas: What other time of the year do you sit in front of a dead tree and eat candy out of your socks?

The moon may be smaller than the Earth, but it's much further away.

The Problem with doing nothing is you don't know when you are done.

Artificial intelligence beats real stupidity any day.

In the beginning there was nothing. Then God created light. There was still nothing but we could all see it.

Only when you know you are nothing do you really become something.

Reality is the major cause of stress.

Depressing thought of the day, my inner child is now middle aged.

What is the penalty for killing time? Or shooting the breeze? Are they capital offenses?

When is it that a brilliant insight is transformed into a trite cliché?

Everything makes sense to someone.

The future is like the present only longer

We all must encounter bad situations from time to time.

The way to deal with a bad situation.

You have 2 choices:

> A. Decide to do something about it—or
> B. Ignore it and move on with life.

If A what you want, then you have two options:

> A. Determine the cause—or
> B. Discover that the cause is impossible to determine—in which case:

You just ignore it and move on with life.

If A can be done then you have 2 courses of action:

> A. It is important to solve and you must solve it—or
> B. It is far too trivial—in which case

You just ignore it and move on with life

If A is true then you have 3 options:

> A. It is possible to solve.
> B. Totally impossible to resolve
> C. By this time you have spent so much time with this thing

That either the problem will have gone away on its own, or another even more horrid and trenchant problem will have come into your life.

In which case the best thing to do is—

—Ignore it and move on with life.

Cartoon idea: Bunch of Guys in an office with glass door—on the inside of door you see the words backwards "**Waiting Room**" guys wearing tee-shirts with logos.

>Waiting for Godot
>Waiting for Lefty
>Wait Till the Sun Shines Nelly
>Waiting For the Robert E Lee
>Just You Wait.
>Wait 'ill next year."

What I say, "No Pain—Good!"

>Thinking about the past is a great excuse to waste the present and forget about the future.

Just remember tomorrow—today will be yesterday.

>The problem with people who worship themselves is when they get together their religions conflict.
>So quiet you can hear a mouse dropping

>A day without food is like a day without food.
>Food is an important aspect of a balanced diet.
>The road to health is paved with good intestines.

>The bite is definitely worse than the bark.
>Be grateful to Edison for inventing the light bulb or we would all have to be watching TV in the dark.

>The nice thing about having nothing is you don't have to worry about losing it.
>That was Zen this is Tao.

>There is less than meets the eye.
>I'm only the self of my former shell.
>Sign in sporting goods store, "This is the discount of our winter tents."
>Money talks, but does it tell the truth? And can it give you directions to China-town?

>Rampant Apathy [Newage oxymorons]
>Active leisure

From my master list of metaphysical mixed metaphors. You'll have to figure out the connections on your own. Some of these have multiple layers of meaning.

>Skating on hot water.
>Don't count your chickens before they cross the road.
>The Early bird gets into the bush.
>Hitch your wagon to a rolling stone.
>Like the bland leading the bland into a den of inanity.
>I have a bone to pick the mote out of your eye.
>You can always tell a book by the company it keeps.
>I didn't see the book but I read the movie
>It's an ill wind that grows the grass greener on the other side.

The chicken crossed the road because the grass is greener on the other side.

>A fool and his money...Never the twain shall meet. Because they got in a twain weck. —Elmer Fudd

>Early worm gets the fish.
>Surfing on the horns of a dilemma.
>Don't cry over spilt beans.
>He who hesitates misses the boat waiting for his ship of fools to come in.
>Sign in our library: Watch what you say here. This is a house of "wordship".
>Loose lips do a prison make.
>A miss is as good as no cigar

>I'll see it when I believe it.
>Give them and inch and they will take the whole nine yards..
>Truth is one; Mistakes are many.

Appendix IV: Story of the Yogaville Library

Sometimes things happen in the most unusual way.

A friend recently suggested that I write up the story of how the Yogaville library came to be. Here it is.

The Beginning: Part One – First Preamble

Around 1984 Swami Ramananda asked me to create a library for what was then our Vidyalyam (Yogaville School). It was then full up with students and they had decided to get official Virginia accreditation. Ramananda, who was then president of the ashram, explained that one of the requirements for this was that school have a functioning library. I told him that I knew nothing about how to do that. He came back saying you're probably the only one who could figure it out. At that time, they had many shelves of books, in the basement, in no particular order.

At one time, in my distant past, I worked in a university library. Scratching my brain and trying to remember what the classification system was. I discovered that I really did not know much. I eventually obtained one important book; the abridged Dewey Decimal system and used that as a guide. After reading the introductory chapters, I still had no idea what most of it was about. I also needed some sort of computer program to enter all the data. At that time card-catalogs were still in limited use. A program was needed to print those out as well as labels for the books. I went to the Buckingham high school to inquire what application they used. The woman in charge told me of some program made by the publisher, Follett, which was then the major publisher of middle and high school texts. I asked Swami Sarvananda what kind of computer I could get at that time. What they had was the most primitive Apple Computer in existence.

This was very tedious work especially considering that I didn't know much. Furthermore, the program I was using from Follett publications was so primitive that it did not allow storage on the hard-drive; instead, I had to store all the data on those ancient 5.25" floppies. I called the company to complain saying, "What's the point of putting it on floppy when you can't look anything up?" They had no proper answer. I went along with it anyway. Printing out thousands of cards. On that point, I had no drawers to store the cards. So on a whim I called the main library in Richmond knowing that the Virginia library system was all interconnected. I inquired whether there was any library switching over to computerized cataloguing where I could get some cabinets at a good price. They told me of the library in Herndon, Virginia that was doing just that. I called them to inquire with the status of their card cabinets was and they informed me that they had them free of charge available right away if I picked them up. Serendipity sometimes comes at strange times and places. It just "so happened" that there was a couple living in Herndon who was very closely connected with us. He and his wife had been associated with the organization for many years. It also "just happened" to be that he had a pickup truck to transport all the cabinets. It also just happened to be that they were coming down the next weekend and he was happy to go pick up the cabinets, no problem. There were three complete sets. Just out of curiosity, I looked up the price in the library supplies catalog that I had and they were over $8000. A pretty good deal I would say. After about one year, with some assistance, I completed the project.

The Beginning: Part Two – Second Preamble

When the Vidyalayam was finally completed, it was suggested that I do something similar for the ashram. I thought, "Well, that would be okay but this time I would want a proper computer and proper program." One of our members happened to have a computer store in Charlottesville and he obtained the PC, which at that time was the basic DOS 3.3 system made by Ultron, a since long-gone company. DOS 3.3 was one of the earliest OS's available. It was quite intimidating, as I knew nothing about the command line entries etc. I purchased THE manual that was the official Microsoft user manual. This was written for programmers and people trained in that very arcane language. It was fortunate that we had a few friends who could interpret this for me. Once I understood the basics that was easy-going. I also obtained a more user-friendly manual from Microsoft for free. I then went to the Charlottesville high school find out what program they were using for the library and purchased that. At that time, it was very crude and basic. However, it could put all the data on the hard drive, which was a very useful feature. At this point, the program was still stuck with printing out cards. It took a tremendously the long time to print out so many cards and have someone help me sort them out. Later on I got the next version of the program it did away with cards (it did provide the option of doing that if one wanted) I could now print out an index on paper that could be, subject, title, or author. I did away with the whole card catalog. Eventually all printouts were done away with and we had all data on the computers.

In any case, the card catalog is very cumbersome, inefficient and time-consuming method. I cannot imagine what it was like in the pre-computer days. Imagine having to type it up thousands and thousands of cards on a clunky typewriter. Having to determine all the subjects and write it according to the very rich and specified format and then having to sort them out alphabetically. That was truly a daunting task.

As we had no building for the library, I commandeered what we call the "multipurpose room" (MPR). I requested our able-bodied carpenter, Swami Daasananda, to build several bookshelves according to my design, which was practical except that they were quite heavy and were not modular; that is to say, the shelves were fixed in place and could not be reconfigured. We had thousands and thousands of books stored up in one of the attics in Sivananda Hall. I sorted the books out as best I could. Selecting what I thought would be suitable. I worked in the attic sitting on the floor with the computer on a very low table and entering data, one book at a time with my very crude method of typing. I really did not know how to type. It was, as you might surmise, quite a daunting job. Or to put it another way, totally insane

After a very long time I completed the project. I was at it all day, every day.

54. Inspecting book on opening day.

Gurudev Story 26

I put all the cards labels, books shelved in place etc. everything done. I thought it was time to invite Sri Gurudev to come for the first viewing. One fine day He came. Very slowly, He looked at the books and picked one out, blew the dust off, and said, "This was one of my books." Wouldn't you know, the one dusty book that He pulled out was one that belonged to Him. Just my luck.. Gurudev then asked me,

> "Are these all the books you have?"
> "No sir, there are thousands and thousands more in the attic. There's just no more room here."
> "Well, you need a building."
> "Yes Sir."
> "Where would you like it to be?"

I was a bit stunned, never expecting Him to say such a thing directly to me. This was a private conversation no one else was in the room at that moment. I pointed to the spot opposite Guru Bhavan. I said, "That would make a nice quadrangle. It would be very harmonious and symmetrical."

I knew Gurudev loved symmetry and balance.

> "Sure, we'll do that."

The Serious Bits

I thought to myself, yes many things have been said about something being built. That that does not mean it will actually happen. I, therefore, dismissed it from my mind being content to stay with what I had done. However, three months later Mitra Metro came by saying they were having the groundbreaking for the library and would I do the puja. He also asked me if I would make a design for what I wanted. Of course, I agreed to do the puja but I had absolutely no experience in designing anything, not even a bulletin board. However, I went along drawing out a little bit of the design. What I wanted was two floors top for adults lower for children I thought that would be nice. Eventually they completed the building I got the top floor. The lower level was divided into two sections. Three quarters used for Gurudev's dining room for Him and His special guests, and a smaller section for kitchen storage. This eventually became what we call the "Boutique".

Now began the serious work of properly classifying and cataloging all those books. I finally got some sense and decided that the attic was not a good place for me to work. I, therefore, enlisted the aid of some strong guys to help box and hauled down all those books from the attic to an empty room in the monastery. I also obtained a few sets of empty shelves that they had in storage which although flimsy would serve as a temporary device.

While the building was being constructed, I contacted the local manufacturer of industrial grade shelving. I had already determined the size and number of shelves. I called them with the order and they suggested various parts that would be very useful such as end pieces, braces etc. I had never done anything like this before consequently I ordered far too many parts. I also for the first time in my life, made a contract with a large company that sold library products, mostly to elementary and middle schools. They were easy to work with polite people from Minnesota, of course they were polite. I made a deal wherein if ordering a certain amount per month I would get an additional 20% discount. They sold every imaginable product for libraries. This was very exciting for me, doing all this.

I also ordered every possible book I could find on library classification, cataloging, as well as the American Library Association (ALA) rulebook. Within that exceptionally large tome I read only two or three chapters. Which was quite enough. All of these rules, systems and methods of classification were completely alien to me. I may just have well been reading Etruscan. However, by and by I managed to figure it out.

[FYI the term "classification" refers to the assigning the correct Dewey number to a book. While the term "cataloging" refers to the terms used to identify the book such as subjects, author(s), title, or any other terms that may be indexed searched for and then some.

The new program was fantastic it did not take long to learn it but it did take long to set up the printer. In that spare room of the monastery would be ranks of books and day after day, classifying and cataloging one book at a time with my very amateur typing method.

Eventually the building was completed and we got going on installing the shelves. I wanted everything to be super secure. That is to say, nothing should fall down on anyone, no catastrophes. So along with tying two sets of 7 foot shelves together with back-braces & end-braces I bolted 2"X1"lengths of wood to the wall and bolted the ranks of shelves on top and bottom to those lengths of wood. Now, nothing will move those shelves. Except maybe an elephant. I determined the distance between the ranks of shelves with the book cart plus a person standing between it and the shelves. I just figured this made sense. Years later while looking in the library supplies catalog I saw some diagrams of shelves rank plans, and wouldn't you know it the measurements I made was exactly the same as suggested in the catalog.

Years before someone had donated thousands of vinyl albums of Opera and Classical music I obtained those along with the custom-made shelves for them and created a music section with three old couches along with a Persian rug. We also set up a children's section. For that I set the shelves down to 4 foot height cutting the uprights to that level. There was a separate little rug for that. Gurudev had also given me a beautiful record player for LP's, along with an amp and two high-grade speakers.

With everything neatly in place. We were ready for the grand opening. "Ta daaa". I arranged for a date when Gurudev would be able to attend. We did a puja. I got around to saying a number of mostly very silly things. What got into my head to say such things? I do not know. In any case, it was all done nice and neat.

The Long Hard Climb

I proceeded to set up an office space with a beautiful wooden desk, made of real wood none of that fabricated nonsense. I did acquire a fabricated computer desk that served well. Now came the very long period of classifying and cataloging all the rest of the books. The job that took so many years. I also became a bit of a computer geek. Aside from classifying the 25,000 items that comprised the library I created a special system for the Hindu Scriptures section. The official Dewey system did not know of so many Scriptures and therefore did not include them. My system was infinitely expandable and was able to include any Scripture that may come along.

In the original construction of the library there was no cooling system. As the climate here turns to very high humidity and heat in the summer, I knew that this would be quite harmful for the books. What to do? I thought it would do no harm to post a little notice saying that we would like to raise $2000 to purchase two AC units. Shortly thereafter a lady came to me while I was at the reception desk saying that she would be happy to donate the entire amount with one small condition. She would like this to be in the memory of her mother who was a librarian and asked if it be okay for me to get a small plaque stating that it was in the memory of Mrs. Edna White, Librarian. Of course, I could do that. I ordered two top-level window AC units from Lowe's. We put them in after cutting out the openings in the wall, and putting a wooden frame around them. Our electrician installed the 220 line and wall switches. These were indeed the very top-level, highest power AC units. Even though they were very noisy, they did cool the entire area. An interesting point was when Gurudev saw the units, He asked if He could have one. Of course, I said yes and gave him one and purchased another.

There were many times that I would go down late at night to check on the process of a computer program that I initiated just to be sure the computer wasn't burning out. I did print out the indices of subjects, author & title. They took up three very large specialized binders for dot—matrix printouts. You don't see this sort of thing around anymore.

[Sidebar note.] It is worth noting that along the way we had many old-style hardware. For example, when I acquired the Windows 95 computer (Micron) I wanted good backup system. At that time the top-level was a tape backup that could be built into the computer. So I had a "Colorado tape backup" that was very slow and cumbersome. When the Windows 98 (Dell) came along we got an external drive. First, there was The Jazz drive that was very expensive and had a limited capacity. Following that, we got the more efficient much less expensive Orb drive; it also featured a much larger storage capacity. My terrific ultra-advanced windows XP (HP) came. It featured two CD reader/writers so I could copy one CD to another. I was able to use the CD writer to do my backups now. There were specialized programs for this purpose. We later obtained an external hard drive that was 200 Gig. Considered to be, at the time, a massive storage space. It was a very large unit. There was no such thing as a terabyte hard drive then. External portable hard drives coming in at 8 TB are now available. I now use automated software that creates a clone to an external solid-state hard drive. We used a lot of old technology back then. It is constantly evolving state. [Thus endeth the tech geek sidebar.]

One day one of our schoolteachers (Satya) came by to inform me that the school was not going to get accreditation after all. They proceeded to bring about 90% of the books that I had previously classified etc. It was then necessary to retype every book in to the system. Furthermore, many of the books were incorrectly classified so they needed to be redone anyway. More work. On and on it went.

Most of the thousands of books originally came from the old Connecticut ashram. Included among those volumes was a beautiful and large collection of art books, most of which were quite rare. There was a complete collection of Shakespeare as well as beautiful volumes of fiction, reference books, and of course many books on yoga, Hinduism, Buddhism, Christianity etc.

This was a very long tedious, most challenging task. We had hundreds of boxes, literally HUNDREDS of boxes. I went through them one at a time. Determining the classification number sometimes extended out to 5 or 6 digits. Making thousands and thousands of labels fitting everything nicely on the shelves. I invented my own system for classifying about 2000 LPs.

In library jargon, we had some 25,000 "holdings". This refers to all forms of materials held by a library that could be in the form not only of books but; manuscripts, periodicals (magazines), digital and analog recordings on tape, VHS, CD, and DVD. We had all of these. We have a complete collection of the Integral Yoga magazine. And a complete collection of the Divine Life Society publications. The latter came under many names over the decades. We are also in possession of the first edition (1893) of Swami Vivekananda's Raja Yoga. This is kept with our antiquarian collection. There is also a very large reference and Special Reference sections the latter containing many of the books donated by Sri Gurudev. In that section there also signed editions of books such as the biography of His Holiness the Dalai Lama who made an inscription in Tibetan on the title page. There is also a signed copy of the biography of Charles Shultz. So many wonderful books I cannot name. We also have very large collection of National Geographic magazines the first one dating from 1914 but it is not a complete set, there are many gaps.

We have books in a great many languages. This includes:

Greek, Japanese, Chinese, Tibetan, Pali, Farsi, Hindi, modern Tamil, Bengali, Arabic Italian, French, Spanish, German. Sanskrit, Hebrew, Latin, Aramaic, Russian, Literary Tamil (rather different from standard spoken it is an old form reserved for ancient Scriptures and writings. It is more difficult to understand. Sri Gurudev was fluent in this).

Great Occurrences

A few of the more memorable events..

I. One day we received some 14 extremely large boxes of books. I did not recognize the name of the person who shipped them. These boxes contained books mostly on Buddhism and Hinduism. Among which were the 42-volume set of the Pali Canon in the Pali language. This is the essential Scripture of Buddhism as laid down in India. We also received the 22-volume set of Tibetan Scripture that were a facsimile of the original Palm leaf writings. This was a beautiful boxed set in perfect condition. There were also volumes on Buddhism in French and German as well as a set of the magazine published by the Buddhist Society in England just before and during the war (WW II) a good percentage of these magazines were edited by Alan Watts.. Included in this collection was a complete set of the works of Sir Arthur Avalon a.k.a. John Woodruff—they included the Serpent Power and all his other books on Shakti. They were all first edition books. My assumption was that this came from a retired professor of Buddhism perhaps one who passed away. Several times, I wrote to the person whose name was on the boxes asking her to call me so that I could personally thank her for this collection. She never did call. I asked everyone here who had been around for a long time if they recognized the name. No one did. It remained a mystery.

Gurudev Story 27

II. Over the years, Gurudev would send occasional small boxes of books from his own collection. However, in the winter of 2002 he called me up asking if I had room in the library for some more books. I said, "Yes, of course Gurudev. I have room." (What was I going to say, "No Gurudev I have no more room"? I was not that much of a fool.)

"Well, come over them. Bring some boxes."
"Yes Sir, I will do that."

I went with a friend in a van with many empty boxes.

Gurudev was sitting on the floor in his reception area. In front of Him was a very long coffee table. On top of which were hundreds of books. At one point while handing me books he said, "This was from Gurudev." Meaning from Sri Swami Sivananda. Of course, they were all in perfect condition. We then came to books about which he asked me if I knew the author. I would say, "Yes Gurudev I know that person." Or "I know that book." Then came a Moment; He pointed to the cover of a small paperback book sitting there. "C K Ramaswamy?"

After a long pause I said, "So sorry, Gurudev I do not know that person."

He then laughed well, "That's me." Oh my God, I forgot that was his original name. It did not console me that my friend also forgot and did not recognize His birth name. He had signed his name in very tiny, neat letters on the cover as well as on the title page. It was a book from 1934 by Mahatma Gandhi on health and diet. In excellent condition except cover was torn off. I had it restored by a professional book restorer whose services I used. In that book He also put in the margins some very teeny, teeny notes in Tamil usually two or three words. I have thus far not found anyone to translate them.

Among the treasures was a three volume, leather bound, folio size, works of Shakespeare circa 1860 with a number of steel engravings. It was a magnificent set. I had that restored as well.

He gave us thousands of books and had to purchase a full double set of extra shelves to accommodate so many books. Included was his entire Tamil collection, the complete works of Ramalingam, many copies of the principal Tamil Scriptures, hundreds of pamphlets in Tamil including some of Gurudev's father's treasured poetry which were done in a Yantra form. Also a great many of the old pamphlets by Sri Swami Sivananda from the 30's and 40's, most of which were published before Gurudev met Sivananda. There were the books on Ayurveda, Sanskrit. Grammar, numerous translations of the Ramayana, sets of many Hindu Scriptures and Puranas. Finally half a dozen books about classic American automobiles. Some were signed editions. Some signed by Gurudev, some by the authors. We have all of these in our library. There were several such visits over a period of 3 to 5 weeks. At the end of each visit, we always had some tea and biscuits. That was so nice. It was deeply personal.

It is worth noting that these transferring of His books took place some eight months before his Mahasamadi. He had planned it all out well ahead of time down to the Moment, to the minutest detail.

III. Many years later, thanks to the diligent work of our own Swami Chidananda we obtained an entire collection that was in Gurudev's ashram in Sri Lanka. Many of them were moldy and riddled with the effects of bookworms (the insect variety not the human). I called the man who did the book restoration for us. He gave me some simple remedies for these infestations. Some of them were signed by Swami Sivananda with inscriptions to Gurudev. Many signed by Gurudev.

IV. One day while visiting our beloved Swami Tyagananda at his home, he told me that I may take any of the books that he had in his library. He really meant it. So I checked out what there was and took a number of the old books most of which were from 19th century and one from 18th century. These are the antiquarian book collection now in the library. Number of these had covers broken so I took them all to our book restorer in Charlottesville and he lovingly rebound them and labeled the spines. All beautifully done. It is interesting to note the English usage that was prevalent in 19th and the 18th centuries. Included in this collection is the oldest dated book in the library, a British publication from 1795 "Little Women's Magazine". An anthology of articles from that magazine. (Not a magazine for "little" women. It was the name of the magazine, not the women)

V. There were also many anonymous, unsolicited donations just to name a few.

1. Meyer Baba society in Myrtle Beach, South Carolina sent us the complete 12 volume hardbound set of stories about him written by his disciples. This arrived volume by volume, one per year

2. The Society of Friends, publishers of Quaker books, sent this a complete set of their books.

3. Some unknown person from a group of Kabbalistic studies sent us a one volume Zohar in Aramaic. So far nobody has been able to read it.

4. One day we had the gracious visit by Grandmother Doris an elder of the Matapanai Native Americans. She was known to be a much respected and venerated storyteller of her people. I got into a conversation with her about preserving the stories and language of the people. I related to her that I also was a storyteller. It was a most beautiful encounter. At the end of our conversation I got up to go when she stopped me and handed me a large bag containing a five volume hardcover set of the Encyclopedia of the Native American Peoples. This is in our reference section.

5. I received in the mail a signed copy of a book on movies by Roger Ebert. He signed it to me. Probably because I wrote him a couple of handwritten notes telling him of the errors

we made in his very fat book on films with capsule reviews by him.

6. One day I got a phone call from a gentleman whom I did not know. He lived in Florida. He was in charge of The Sivananda Yoga Center (DLS). They were closing up their center. He wondered if I would like to have a number of Sivananda Divine Life Society publications. I really didn't know what to say. So I said, "Sure, send them I will put them in the library." I received about eight or nine boxes containing many publications and little booklets by His Holiness Sri Swami Sivananda.

7. Over the years, we received subscriptions for many magazines. I have some of the more unusual ones there. When we had to do the reconfiguration (see below) I gave away many of these. That was quite difficult.

8. Early on, someone donated the very beautiful and interesting set of 29 VHS tapes, World Music and Dance along with booklets about the music and dance. It is a fascinating study. Am now attempting to sell this on eBay.

9. Among the other interesting sets that we have our: The Great Books of the Western World (56 volumes), The Centenary Celebration of Sri Aurobindo (29 volume), the Siva Purana. The Sikh Scripture, Sri Guru Granth Sahib (two versions), the Mahabaratha (two versions), and many versions of the Ramayana given by Sri Gurudev.

There are just too many wonderful books. There is just not the space to list them all.

It is worth noting that during the long years of dealing with the library holdings and system I did a few other things. Most notable among which is the creation and completion of the SASTRI Project. This is the master database of text of every talk Gurudev ever gave in English that I could find. This project took 23 years to complete. It is the master reference from which comes many of the booklets, articles, and talks people give at satsang. As well as answers to questions, people have had from all the world about what Gurudev said on many subjects. For persons living here it is a free service. For people living outside the ashram a small charge of $35. Which is quite small considering that it took over 23 years of very hard work to complete and many thousands and thousands of dollars invested in equipment.

On the side I also registered the domain name "yogaville.org". I developed the first website. It was plain and simple just using pure HTML code. Pure coding no fancy apps. Very down-home simple style. Some pages were colored; there were many, many photos of the ashram and people. There were also program listings, Satsang summaries, mantras that you can hear, and even one time a little attempt at a humor page. My favorite page was called Meet the People. The purpose of this page was to present the profile with photo of people who did service. They were not recognized or in the limelight. I got the idea when there was a big Hooha celebration for one of the most prominent people in our organization. It occurred to me that there were other people who did great service. They were not recognized or given a big celebration. During that time, I also acquired a couple of beautiful cameras from Gurudev. They were early digital cameras. I remember well the first one was a very big one that could also do videos. I knew it cost a fortune.

For some 24 years, everything went very well. Then came.

The Great Reconfiguration

As the ashram grew in popularity programs multiplied consequently the numbers of guests and people coming increased tremendously. We all knew that more space was needed for teaching classes and conducting programs. Several times administrators wanted to reconfigure the library to accommodate these classes. The proposal was to remove at least half the books and put in a nice classroom. I resisted this a number of times pointing out how we have a beautiful children section, music listening section etc. However, eventually we came to realize that it was necessary to take this space and reconfigure it. An agreement was made as to how that was to be done with demarcation points of this change. We removed half the shelves (and of course half the collection).

Instead of the ranks of shelves being perpendicular to the walls they would be flat against the walls. A new carpet and new draperies would be installed, as well as new HVAC, and new lights in the center. The extremely difficult task of selecting which books were to be taken out was up to me. It took a number of weeks to go through the entire collection of 25,000 items and take many things out. This was extremely difficult on many levels. I also had to give away our beautiful and valuable collection of LPs. (Also very difficult), while the music cassettes, video tapes, movies, so many books. Finally, I had to remove about 10 years' worth of the more recent National Geographic. Giving away the music section was really a very difficult experience.

The Carpet House came to install the new carpet and draperies. The company that did the HVAC came and installed ductwork and all the heavy equipment and an entirely new HVAC system.

Is now been several years since this event. We have many classes, and programs here. Everyone who comes speaks on how beautiful the place is. It is beautiful. The books are neatly arranged along the wall. There are two special handmade wooden bookcases on each side of the altar.

The place is full. It is beautiful. It is peaceful. It is well used.

Appendix V: The Story of SASTRI

The Master Archive of all of Sri Gurudev's Satsangs

55. Satsang under the tree CT, the classic way of teaching. This is the cover to the SASTRI CD.

After 23 years of some very intense and challenging work, I have completed this project. I thought it would be nice to relate the backstory, its history and development.

The last satsang was imported at 11:30 AM, 24 November 2018. This database has been used for many of our publications, books, the Integral Yoga Magazine, searches for lecture topics and searches for individual personal interests. (See below for policy on how this is done.)

Acknowledgements

So many people were involved in helping with transcribing that I cannot remember all their names. Of course none of this would be possible without the supreme dedication and love of Sri Gurudev. It is to Him that we owe the greatest gratitude.

Many people typed the original transcriptions. Foremost among them was Swami Hamsananda who over so many years was the sole person transcribing. She was very dedicated to this.

There have been many people who came forward. Among them are: Fiona Ream, Lisa Dean Hawkins, Anthony Haro, Ananda Radha Andre, Sundaram Gross, Donna Strumm, Barbara Dhyana Stiefel, Cindy Nichols, Lynn Mukti Meffert, and Candy Lavender.

SASTRI is an acronym that stands for—Satchidananda Automated Satsang Text Retrieval & Indexing. Sastri is also a Sanskrit word meaning—one who is versed in the Sastra (Hindu scriptures).

Here is the story, offered with gratitude and love.

Sometime in 1994 I was given charge of our reception desk and bookshop. Things went rather well for a bit until it did not, that is to say it got crushingly dull. I decided to quit this post and take on something more interesting. In my way of thinking, I could not just quit rather I had to propose a new job to focus on. So I put a set of proposals to the administration. These proposals included getting on the maintenance crew and learning electrical work (only slightly absurd, as I had done stuff for them previously) and some other things that I have forgotten. One suggestion was that I create a system for cataloging all the satsangs of Sri Gurudev. I observed that, up to that point, all of Gurudev's public talks were typed up nicely, printed, and then put into an enormous set of three-ring binders and those binders were neatly shelved into the archives, locked and forgotten. It then occurred to me that this wasn't really that useful in that there was no practical way whereby one could retrieve anything on a specific topic. What good is even the greatest teaching if one cannot access what one is interested in?

Shortly after I had put my proposals to the Ashram Board, Swami Karunananda let me know that while the other ideas had merit this what jumped out to them.

However, I had NO IDEA how to do this, none whatsoever, except that there must be a way with computers. Sometimes knowing nothing is good.

Then, a tiny light blinked in the mind. I had heard about a new project at the University of Virginia (UVA) known as the Electronic Text Project. Through one friend I found out who was in charge and where this project took place. I then boldly went there to see the man in charge, David Seaman. He had a teeny set of offices in the Clemons Library. David was a very proper, posh Brit, always in tie, blue blazer, and khakis, very proper indeed. I presented my idea to him and he said the best words of all, "Yes, this can be done; we are doing that very thing here." And he then showed me in detail how it was done : hardware (flatbed scanner, automatic doc feeder, a good computer, proper back up system (Jaz drive, later an Orb drive and then a tape backup), etc. plus the most up-to-date OCR software. It all looked pretty straight-up to me. Well in truth I had half a gazillion questions all of which he answered quite patiently. Well all, except for one item, he could not tell me of a practical data-base software because they all used university licensed software which is REALLY expensive. Now remember this was 1995—and there was no really good internet, so I did my search in the only way I knew, by checking the micro-fiches (you youngsters will have to Google that) of old PC mags which I knew had reviews of all sorts of computer stuff including software. I had no idea what to really look for. But in about an hour I hit on a product that looked perfect and at a great price. The company was called Ask Sam, a small company in the Florida panhandle. It looked like the perfect application.

Having gotten some preliminary data I composed a brief outline of my idea with a very basic "guessstimate" of its cost and sent it off to the Board members and Sri Gurudev. A week later at the end of satsang there was the usual massive crowd surrounding Sri Gurudev, being rather shy I just stood there in the middle of the crowd when I felt someone just push me to the front right near Gurudev. He then turned to me and said, "That's a good idea, but it sounds costly."

"Yes Sir, but it's worth it." I whispered.
"Good, you should do it then."

Gurudev Story 28

I next compiled a very detailed list of every item I would need along with: merchants, exact prices and so on; I then wrote a synopsis of my proposal, submitted this to the Board with a copy directly to Sri Gurudev, and proceeded to play the waiting game. About three or four weeks later while in the library (my second home) fiddling with the smoke detectors when the phone rang, I jumped off the ladder it was Sri Gurudev calling. A rare occurrence.

> "Murugananda?"
> "Yes, Gurudev."
> "What are you doing?"
> "Right now I am working on the smoke detectors Sir."
> "No, I mean what are you doing about your project?"
> "Ah, well Sir, I am waiting for the Board to approve it."
> "Yes, yes—why do you wait? Tell them I approve."

Yikes, wow—That was the exact the conversation word for word. I was set—The Master gave me the go.

> "Wowee Zowee"—I said out loud where no one can hear. I straight away called all the companies made about a dozen orders for all sorts of hardware, software, etc. Total cost about $1,900.

The Project Begins

Stuff started arriving soon after along with all the invoices (no e-mails in those days). Soon all that I needed arrived. It took about three to five days to assemble all the hardware and install the software. In those days there were no USB's and no CD's, so all the software was on floppies (youngsters look it up) and the scanner and other big hardware got hooked up via SCSY (pronounced scuzzy) cards (Yep kids, you know what to do) so it all took longer than it would now. Installing the SCSY cards required opening the computer attaching cables restarting and figuring out the settings for each device and installing the software for each device. (There were several devises on the system, in a chain. Having to do all of this ONE item at a time, and using those floppy discs it took a long time.

Now I was ready to go. Almost.

Well I needed a name for this project. What to call it? What to call it? What to call it? The question kept repeating itself. OK, I took a bit of paper- well obviously it had to have the name Satchidananda and naturally the word Satsang would be in there---after a bit I included the term Automated. I wanted a snappy acronym, because in this age that is what folks do. All of a sudden without any further thought the whole name came and there it was SASTRI. Kazam.

The next step was to get the key to the archives building and retrieve those 3-ring binders a few at a time—there are about 80 of them—each holding some 190—250 pages. Then came the heart of the project itself. Using the automatic doc feeder (ADF) attached to the flatbed scanner I was able to scan a full Satsang in about 15 min, then do the OCR (Optical Character Recognition—I used the top-rated OCR app.—Omni-Page Pro) and created a Word doc in 10 min. BUT since even the top-level OCR program was far from perfect there was always a massive amount of editing of errors for each talk. I discovered that there were a number of common errors consistent across all the docs so I created a short set of macros to correct them at one stroke by simply pressing a key letter + Ctrl. This bit saved a major amount of time. Next step was importing the completed doc into the search engine—Ask Sam Pro.

[N.B. A few weeks prior to all this I traveled to DC to meet a fellow who used this app so that he could walk me through the whole process. That took about thirty minutes. Now I was set.]

So it went: Scan—edit, edit—import;Scan—edit, edit—import;Scan—edit, and edit—import—on and on and on. During this time I also managed the library, classifying and cataloging many incoming books, doing inventories, and all that was required there.

In my spare time I got our internet connection started; got our domain name registered; created our first web page and kept that going for three years and also dealt with a series of major medical issues. That carried on for a long, long time.

Every year or so we updated the software and after five years we got a new computer.—Hooray.

At some point I came to the very early talks (1966-1970) almost all of these were transcribed on very poor typewriters or the ink had simply faded out. In any case none of them were fit for scanning. I then had to make copies and found a good friend to retype them all. That took a few more years.

When all the scanning was done, I thought that was it,—I'm done,—WAHOO! However, that was not to be. It came to me that I had to check the archives, you know; "just in case I missed something, just in case". Checking the archives, the archive logs & Shakti.com logs I started finding hundreds of talks that were never transcribed and when I combed through the archive's boxes & boxes of cassettes I found even more. I ended up with over 350 tapes. What must I do?—Digitize. But, just how do I do that???

Well, **that very day** (Jung called this "Synchronicity") my dear old friend Ramanan Shultz "just happened" to show up and it "just so happened" that this was his very job at UVA. I asked how to do it, and he told me. "Well you need a tape deck, and this software that you can get for free, plug it all in install software and you're good to go." I did all that. But as you know you must do this in "real time"; there is no short-cut. I also gathered up boxes and boxes of our special sannyas meetings, "Family Meetings", all sorts of things including talks done in other countries etc., etc., etc. Thus began the next phase.

Then—Digitize to MP3, create CD's to give to transcribers

In between there was still the library and more medical stuff.

Step by step by step though we are getting closer.

Now I had to find people who have the typing skill, can understand Sri Gurudev's accent, have the time and who had the willingness to transcribe all this. Many, many were involved.

Gurudev Story 29

At some point during this process, after I had done 800 or so satsangs, I invited Sri Gurudev to see what was happening. Swami Vidyananda also came by to video this meeting. I showed Gurudev the program and all its parts.

He then said. "Very, very good. **You were born to do this**."

> "Does anyone else know how to use this?"
> "No, Sir."
> "So what will happen when you are gone?"

"Well, Gurudev I have been requesting for someone to train."
"You should not just request you should insist!"

This was put on video I don't know where that recording is.

Since then, I have trained several people in the basic methods of searching and have written a complete manual. However, I have as yet to find an apprentice to train on how to do everything. Alas

The digitizing of all those tapes took a long time. Finding people to transcribe also took a long time—all this took years and years. Added to everything else was the major reconfiguring and renovation of the library that added eight to nine months to the project.

Coming to the end there were tapes that were so degraded that no one would be able to understand them. However, as I am quite used to hearing what Gurudev said, have excellent hearing, and a fine sound system, I undertook to do those files. I purchased the Dragon Naturally Speaking and was, thus, able to do transcribe the damaged tapes.

Finally, at 11:30 AM on 24 November 2018—the last Satsang --27 March 1975 was imported into SASTRI.

OM TAT SAT

Search Policies

For any subject please put specific topic (be as specific as possible not just something like "hatha yoga") send an e-mail to Murugananda@yogaville.org with subject in body of letter. Only one search per letter. I will then compile a doc with all pertinent citations which will include date. It usually will take 3-4 days to get the document back to you—so plan ahead. Service is gratis for IY publications and all IY workers, for IY lectures & talks. There is a $35 charge for individuals not living in an institute or the Ashram, this fee goes to support our Ashram library.

Appendix VI: My Big Book List

An Abbreviated List of the Most Inspirational Books in My Life

[Other than Sri Gurudev's books.]

This is not in any kind of order [nor is it a list of "big" books]. This represents a small percentage of what was inspiring in my journey. I am sure you can add many others. We each have our sources of inspiration and this may change as we travel the road.

1. The Book: *On the Taboo Against Knowing Who You Are*, by Alan Watts. His best among many books. A bit of a rant, but inspiring nonetheless. One of my first.

2. *Be Here & Now* by Ram Dass. One of the most inspiring books I ever read. Got this near the beginning of my journey. Try to get the original with the blue cover. Note: This was not actually the way it originally came. It came with three little booklets and a set of cards with photos of great Saints. All of his books come from the heart and are so inspiring. I knew him before meeting Sri Gurudev.

3. *Raja Yoga,* by Swami Vivekananda. Decades ago while living in Sri Lanka Gurudev gave a radio interview when asked what books he reads he stated that all his life he carried with him four books. The first of these was Raja Yoga by Swami Vivekananda. It was while reading his book on Mount Shasta in California that I decided to become a disciple of Sri Gurudev many decades ago. The other books that Gurudev recommended were *Thirukkural* by Thiruvaluvar. He quotes from this book many, many times. He always had the traditional Tamil Saivite books [Thirumantram & Thiruvachacam] these are very esoteric, difficult to understand books for one not well versed in that ancient tradition. He references these many times as well as the work of St. Ramalingam. The latter is also a complex work on Tamil Saivite religion. Thirukkural is the collection of great wisdom written by a simple householder. Divided into various sections such as blessing of rain, duties of a householder, health etc.

4. *The Thirukkural,* by Thiruvaluvar (sometimes spelled as Tirukural) many editions, Rajagopalachari is good, as is P.S. Sundarm.

5. *How to Know God,* by Isherwood, Christopher & Swami Prabhavananda. This was the first book Gurudev recommended to us prior to His publication of Yoga Sutras. This is a retelling of swami Vivekananda's book in a more Americanized English version. Gurudev also recommended the book Yoga by Ernest Wood.

6. *How Can I Help,* by Ram Dass. More from Ram Dass's beautiful heartfelt thoughts.

7. *Only Dance There Is,* by Ram Dass. An early work, beautifully devotional.

8. *Miracle of Love,* by Ram Dass. Stories about him and his master Maharaji.

9. *Maitri Vani* (3 volumes) by Maa Anandamayi Ma. Anandamayi Ma was a true fully realized being one of the most remarkable of the 20th century Saints. Many would consider her as an avatar. She was a pure bhakti. There are many small books with her words. A few lectures to disciples but mostly taken from transcripts of her responses to questions by disciples. There are several biographies most are out-of-print. Her chanting may be found on YouTube in home movies.

10. *Words Anandamayi Ma,* by Anandamayi Ma.

11. *Mother as Revealed to Me,* by G. Dasgupta. A rare but well-written book on the life of Anandamayi Ma.

12. *Collected Works of Ramana Maharishi,* by Osborne, Arthur. Osborne was the major chronicler of Ramana's life & teachings. I was introduced to this great St. at the same time as Ram Dass. Just looking at his photo, I was enthralled. He didn't actually write things they were just transcribed from his talks, which were very simple and direct. He was a great master of Jnana Yoga, the path of self-knowledge.

13. *Discourses* (5 volumes) by Meher Baba. I was introduced to him by Ram Dass who mentioned him in a talk I heard back in 1965 telling us about this St. who kept silent for 30 years. He was a Sufi master from India. His books are very dense, filled with a lot of arcane terminology and rather difficult to follow. However, once you understand it, it's inspiring.

14. *The Forth Way,* by P. D. Ospensky. Early disciple of Gurdjieff. Went on to found his own school. Very interesting, rather intellectual.

15. *The Aquarian Gospel of Jesus,* by Levi. A book I read very early on, still have the original copy in my own library. Allegedly a "channeled" book. Beautifully done. Tells His teachings and the story what Jesus did in His middle years wherein He supposedly traveled to Egypt and India.

16. *Wisdom of the West,* by Bertrand Russell. Russell was an early inspiration for me. Brilliant mathematician, logician, philosopher and antiwar thinker.

17. *Self-Reliance,* by Ralph Waldo Emerson. Read this in high school, ignited independent thinking process. He was a Transcendentalist.

18. *In My Own Way,* by Alan Watts. Autobiography. Interesting insight. He started out as an Episcopalian priest.

19. *From Man to Godman,* by Ananthanarayanan. One of the best biographies of Sri Swami Sivananda. Many beautiful photos.

20. *Gurudev Sivananda,* by Swami Venkatesananda. Written in his unique style.

21. *Way of a Pilgrim,* by French, R. M. The personal account of a devoted seeker for the truth & how to keep God in his heart 24/7. Russian Orthodox tradition. He found a holy man who gave him a simple mantra. [The Jesus Prayer].

22. *Pilgrim Continues His Way,* by French R. M. A continuation of the above.

23. *Tao Te Ching,* by Lao Tzu-Trans—Feng Gia-Fu. One of the greatest books of wisdom. Simple and elegant. This is one of the better of many translations.

24. *I Ching: Book of Changes,* by Wilhelm, Richard. I read this book and the Tao on a daily basis at the beginning of my journey. This is the best translation. It is THE standard. Introduction by Carl Jung. Note: James Legge's is also a good translation.

25. *Chuang Tsu Inner Chapters,* by Chuang Tsu—translation by Feng, Gia-fu & Jane English. Beautiful verses on Taoism. There are several other books by Chuang Tsu worth reading.

26. *Upanishads,* commentary by Sri Aurobindo. Very deep if a bit dense and intellectual but well written.

27. *Upanishads,* commentary by Eknath Easwaren. Easier to understand than the one above. It Is said that the essence of Hindu philosophy is contained in the Vedas, the essence of Vedas is the Upanishads and the essence of Upanishads is Mandukya. That is but one page long. Easwaren has a keen way of interpreting. He has several other books, all well done. A 2 vol. Gita is one.

28. *Valmiki's Ramayanna,* translated by Sastri, Hari Prasad (3 vols.) best literary translation. One of few that is complete.

29. *Mahabharata,* translated by, Subramaniyam, Kamala. Best translation.

30. *New Testament,* translated by Lamsa George M. Taken from the original Aramaic. Interesting translation.

31. *Island,* by Huxley, Aldous. Huxley was one of the most brilliant thinkers of the 20th century. His father T H Huxley was a renowned biologist. Best known for his other novels such as Brave New World, This book, in the form of fiction, but is really a philosophical treatise of Vedantic thinking. He along with his friend Christopher Isherwood were members of the Vedanta Society of Southern California in Los Angeles. Disciples of Swami Prabavananda.

32. *Wisdom of the Desert Fathers,* by Merton, Thomas. A brilliant and truly inspirational Trappist monk who inspired me very much to become a monk. He was designated by the church to do a lot of writing which he first did in strict accordance with Church Policy. He was later exposed to Eastern philosophy, which he absorbed and on which he wrote. It is those books that are inspirational. You can skip his autobiography Seven Story Mountain instead, if you're interested in his life story, read the one by Monica Furlong.

33. *Merton, a Biography,* by Furlong, Monica –Best one.

34. *Way of Chuang Tsu,* by Merton, Thomas. Interesting insight.

35. *Thoughts in Solitude,* by Merton, Thomas.

36. *New Seeds of Contemplation,* by Thomas Merton. Close-up look on the monastic life.

37. *Hasidic Tales,* by Rabbi Rami Shapiro. I just love this book so much. Beautiful simple stories from the Hasidic tradition with a lesson. There is deep devotion in this tradition.

38. *Open Secret: Letters of Reb Yerachmiel ben Yisrael,* by Rabbi Rami Shapiro. First book of his I ever read I was taken by the simplicity and the very yogic Vedantic expression. He is a Rabbi who was a disciple of Zalman Schachter Shalomi. Founder of the Jewish Renewal. I have known Rami for many years. His background is quite eclectic, having studied Buddhism & Vedanta.

39. *Way of Solomon: Finding Joy & Contentment in the Wisdom of Ecclesiastes,* by Rabbi Rami Shapiro. A Taoist understanding of this book from the Old Testament.

40. *Sometimes a Great Master,* by Eli Wiesel. Collection of Hasidic tales told in his personal style. Beautiful.

41. *Sadhana,* by Sri Swami Sivananda. One of Sivananda's best books. It Inspired me the most. There are some 200 books by His Holiness so it is virtually impossible to choose just one but this was the one for me.

42. *The Golden Thread,* by Father Bede Griffith—A humble and holy man I met in India. He was an English Catholic priest who combined and blended East and West in a beautiful way. His ashram, Ananda Ashram, in Tamil Nadu India was a truly holy place. Father Griffith also attained full Realization.

43. *Message of East & West,* by Father Bede Griffith. Expressing the bridge of two great streams of religion.

44. *Return to the Center,* by Father Bede Griffiths.

45. *The Patanjali Yoga Sutras,* by Swami Venkatesananda. One of the most brilliant Raja Yogis of our time. Among the many translations of the Sutras, this ranks at the top. Venkatesananda was Swamiji Sri Swami Sivananda's personal secretary for many years. He established a Divine Life Society in South Africa as well as a center in Australia. Produced

dozens of books. Most are out-of-print. I had the good fortune of knowing him well. Always a man good cheer and humor.

46. *Condensed Yoga Vaisishta,* by Swami Venkatesananda. One of the classics on Vedantic teachings. Probably the best translation and most accessible.

47. *The Idea of I,* by Swami Venkatesananda. Talks on Raja yoga. Rare, out-of-print book.

48. *Foundations of Tibetan Buddhism,* by Lama Govinda. He explains the meaning of the great mantra Om Mane Padme Hum and Padmasambhava. Lama Govinda was a German born scholar who moved to Tibet before the invasion by the Chinese. He was a humble man who was infused with the great Buddhist wisdom. I had the honor of meeting him in 1972.

49. *Way of the White Cloud,* by Lama Govinda. Story of his life in Tibetan Buddhism. Also on Padmasambhava & Bodhisattva Mantra.

50. *Cutting Through Spiritual Materialism,* by Trungpa, Chogyam. This is a very well done book, quite interesting cuts right to the point. Worth reading, despite the authors idiosyncratic and controversial character. I heard him speak in 1971.

51. *Dali Lama's Little Book of Wisdom: Essential Teachings,* by His Holiness Dalai Lama. Exactly what it says. Beautiful wisdom. I have had the honor of meeting His Holiness several times including once at a conference in Bangalore.

52. *Kindness, Clarity, Insight,* by His Holiness Dali Lama. An essential book.

53. *Zen Mind, Beginners Mind,* by Daitatz T Suzuki Roshi. Basic manual on Zen Buddhist thinking. Suzuki Roshi has written many books, all are accessible.

54. *The Sufi Message,* by Khan, Hazrit Inayat. He was a clear writer also a musician. This is a set of 10 volumes. All are worth reading. Volume 9 Unity of Religious Ideals, V. 4 Alchemy of Happiness, V. 2 Mysticism, Sound, Music...He is written many other books all in harmony with the ultimate source.

55. *Way of the Peaceful Warrior,* by Millman, Dan. Some may think of this book as "pop" spirituality. True, it is simple and easily accessible; however, there is great wisdom in this book as in the entire series by Millman.

56. *Johnathan Livingstone Seagull,* by Bach, Richard. A fiction version expressing similar philosophy of Millman's books.. See also Bach's book One.

57. *Illusions: Adventures of a Reluctant Messiah,* by Bach, Richard. Beautifully done. He has an easy way of putting it. The teachings herein are consistent with any spiritual practice I'm familiar with. It doesn't take sides on any religious debates, so it's not likely to offend or upset anyone. It's just a quick bit of entertainment. It always leaves me feeling a little happier and a little more in touch with life.

58. *Major Trends in Jewish Mysticism,* by Sholom, Gershom. On the Jewish mystical subject of Kabbalah. It is virtually impossible to give to give a comprehensive list on this vast subject, let alone single basic book. This is one of the classical entry-level books with some good scholarship by a well-known writer on the subject.

59. *Zohar: Book of Enlightenment* (literal trans. - Book of Splendor) by Matt, Daniel. One of the most ancient books on the subject..A foundation book on this great mysticism. Matt is probably the best translator and expositor on this subject. He is in the midst of producing a 12 volume set of translation of the ancient Zohar. A text with emphasis on Genesis. It is profoundly mystical and extremely difficult to follow as it is written in a highly symbolic language. Purposely hidden.

60. *Zen Flesh, Zen Bones,* by Paul Reps. Collection of several classical Zen texts including: Zen stories, 10 Bulls, & Centering Gateless Gate. Met him in 1971, interesting fellow.

61. *Siddhartha,* by Hesse, Herman—This is a classic. Almost forgot this most wonderful author—read all of his books. Demian, Narcissus & Goldmund, Magister Ludi etc. His thinking & philosophy was quite unusual for his place & time.

62. *Yantra,* by Kahana, Madhu. A deep extensive exposition on this important subject. Gives a full explanation of the root Sri Yantra and all the variations, iterations and adaptations thereof. Fully illustrated. Long out of print, it is once again available.

63. *The Essene Gospels of Jesus* (all volumes) by Szekely, Edmund Bordeaux. As well as a Essene Gospel of Peace. All beautifully inspirational.

64. *At the Feet of the Master,* by Alcyone (name on title page is actually J. Krishnamurthy) one of the many publications by the Theosophical Society. A somewhat beginner's guide to spiritual life. Theosophical Society published a great many books a whole list can be compiled just from that. Krishnamurthy was discovered as a young lad by the leader of the society Annie Besant in the beginning of the 20th century she declared him their Avatar. He remained so for many years but later renounced the whole idea, spoke vigorously against the whole idea of guru as commander of one spiritual life. I had the opportunity to hear him speak in 1967 I did not understand a word.

65. *God Is a Verb,* by Rabbi Cooper. David Nicely written, very accessible on ancient, Kabbala. It incorporates Rabbi's personal slant on it, which is quite interesting.

ADDENDUM

The many things I forgot to put in.

They are nice.

Summer Recollections: A Little Memoir   November 17, 2022

[This really should have been in my biography, but I just never thought of it until now. So here it is an addition —outside the book. An important lesson derived from these is that one never knows what experiences in early life is prescient to how one acts, or responds to what happens in adult life.]

When I was a wee lad one of the things I got every summer was a new kite. The kite itself was made of paper and came with two bamboo sticks to shape it into a sort of diamond shape. Also came with four little string hooks to attach the sticks. I first laid out all the parts neatly on the bed and then proceeded to assemble. I just loved assembling it and eventually I got pretty good at doing that and innovating a tail made out of an old cotton bedsheet. It also came with a large ball of very thin twine. One has to be careful with this as it could snap at any moment.

They were only 10¢ then so every year I would get a new one. It would come very neatly wrapped up all the parts some kind of cellophane wrapper which I would open excitedly and assemble very carefully. Making sure all the sticks and hooks were very tight. Then came the fun part of attaching long twine by which you flew this thing. One must not to forget to attach the tail that would add balance. I believe that practicing this very well would later allow me to develop considerable computer skills. (One never knows the whole story behind what went into shaping the person.). There is nothing better than flying that at the beach and learning the skills to move it about. It was lovely.

I loved summer days. Going to the beach, running into the ocean and splashing in the waves, which sometimes would come and pin me down to the rough sand below. Then of course, there were wonderful delicious *kinishes* always carried by a very fat man with long trousers and a singlet. Carried big brown shopping bags with handles. They were only 25¢ compared to $.15 charge at

Yonah Shimmel's. But, the man had to make a little profit and the work was excruciating, it was right to give him a break. There are but TWO varieties of knish, i.e. potato and kasha. That was it!! None of those wimpy blueberry, chocolate, cranberry (yeech), raspberry-watermelon-pomegranate or whatever concoction some imaginative guy (or *goy*) would dream up. No! It was like bagels there were just these few varieties, plain, pumpernickel, salt, and maybe onion no such thing as tomato or "everything" or God-forbid —pumpkin-spice as wretched as the coffee with the same name. That was a simpler time.

There were great rock jetties that went out into the ocean about 300 feet. I surmised that it was for controlling waves. The water was sometimes a bit cold but I loved it. It was dreadfully salty. I believe the water at our beach in Coney Island-Brighton was far saltier than any other beach on the planet.

I learned to work the sand pretty well digging holes putting the sand in the tiny bucket and making sand piles.

I lay out in the sun a lot and as expected became quite red every year frequently developing big blisters, that would peel off neatly. I rather liked doing that. Made me feel like a grown-up. Eventually, however, all the redness and blisters disappeared and I was just permanently tan. I like that.

One time I recall there was a small group drunken men under the boardwalk fighting. I saw two big guys punching each other out. It was so scary I could never understand why they were doing that. It was very, very scary. I promised myself to never get drunk. Of course, in college I did just that but only on a rare occasion. It was fun for just a short time. I would always go to some neighborhood pub have a few beers maybe meet some guy there, have a stupid conversation. Then go to the local pizza place and have a square slice for 15¢. YES, fifteen, cents. That was it.

There was of course something to drink. Pepsi, which I always favored over Coke simply because Pepsi was "12 full ounces that's a lot" or so, went the jingle. Dad, on the other hand, was a big fan of 7-Up. A clear fizzy lemon lime. Their slogan, "You like it —it likes you." I tried it for some time and did like it. No doubt, the lemon lime came from soon dreadful chemical concoction. Coke on the other hand was far too sweet and was only 6 ounces. What a rip-off. We would, of course, collect the empties for the two-cent deposits.

With which we could acquire a nice ice-cream pop, or "Mellow-roll", I do not think you can that get now. It was ice cream in the shape (3x2") of solid piece of pipe mounted on a wafer cone pretty good. Even better was a big pile of real homemade whipped cream atop a bit of sponge cake held firmly in a tube white cardboard. This magnificent creation went by the unusual name of Charlotte Russe. How it acquired such an unusual name I do not know. (Must look it up). Just the best!!

While on the subject of ice-cream....... You could go to the local corner store of course where cones and pops were available. But, in summer, the ubiquitous ice cream truck came around any time of day. There were just two brands that I can remember. There might have been more I remember just two. There was of course the ever-present Good Humor whose headquarters were actually in Brooklyn. I remember that because that is where I went to get my very first job. The very dreadful carrying of a 700-pound box of ice cream on the beach. That job lasted maybe 15 minutes. There was also the Bungalow Bar. It did not matter which one came out that moment we just got what was available. "My favorite was the "Walkaway Sunday" [it was ice cream cone vanilla with chocolate coating a big bunch of chopped nuts on top] or the coconut pop. I would also get chocolate. Now I believe it was Good Humor or, it may have been Bungalow, who offered free ice cream to any kid on their birthday. Thus, every kid in the neighborhood for miles around had his or her birthday in the summer. I'm not making this up. You heard those ridiculous bells for blocks. On the truck was there the man who was very pleasant and friendly always giving out the ice creams with a smile. All the ice-cream men had a white uniform and hat with a very cool change dispenser on their belt NO credit cards then. It was always one dime 10¢. Speaking of ice cream a two scope Sunday with hot-fudge sauce, real whipped cream nuts etc. local candy store was 25¢ a quarter. One of the places always set down a little glass of seltzer free. Speaking of which a two scoop malted milk with real malt resulting in a 2 ½ cups delicious drink that was also just a quarter.

To be quite honest I was not a fan of any Nathans' products I tried some. Did not satisfy me in any way. It was also way too crowded. Nothing like the hot-dogs we had at our local deli.

The big rip-off was the Italian ice, which was just shaved ice some very cheap funky syrup poured over it. Dreadful. Good, meh. For some stupid reason we would get it. There it was and we just went along with the gang. I figure it was all that sugar and the unusual ritual that went with it.

Back in the early days, we lived in a disgusting, dreadful apartment that was near Brighton Beach. The only advantage to this was that we could walk to the beach and in the summer sit on the boardwalk in the evening watching the fireworks once a week. They had boats out in the ocean with some sort of "cannons" that would shoot off fantastic, delightful fireworks. I just loved it.

Unrelated to the summer is a recollection I very clearly have of that place in Brighton. Across the street from us directly opposite our building and down several concrete steps was most amazing place. It was two long rows of horse stalls. These were the horses used to haul carts where a man sold various things or did certain services. There was a man who sold fruit, one who sold flowers, and one who sharpened knives and others things like that. Each had his "shout". The flower man would say, "Whoop flowee". That's what it sounded like to me. Watermelon man would say, "Waaartermelon..." Loved the horses. Is was on those concrete steps down to the horse-stalls that I learned to climb steps.

I recall, quite well, around 1945 when they had a big parade on VE Day with hundreds of veterans walking along many with crutches, missing legs. There were many vehicles decked out with banners and flags. I did not understand any of it, but it was quite fantastic.

Later on, I loved certain rides at Coney Island. Which you could get for just a quarter, two bits, 25¢. My absolute favorite was, of course, the Bumper Cars. That was my sole opportunity to "drive" something. It was great fun. I truly could not stand the carousel. Just got me dizzy. Also, because I was so short and quite visually impaired thus could not see anything I would never get the brass ring. Not for me. I did try the gigantic Cyclone, our roller coaster; it was exciting and got me very nauseous. I could not understand why some people kept riding it. It was too stimulating.

One of the pivotal little moments of my life was when I learned how to blow a bubble with bubble gum. Now this may seem like something too trivial to even think about but to me it was a very big deal. It took me months and months of practice. When it finally happened, it elated my mother to no end; she was so happy that I could finally do this. I loved that completely. I spent endless hours and much money on bubblegum. And, by the way, this did occur one of those early summers whilst residing in one those shacks in the Catskills, described below. By far, the top best gum was—Double Bubble. Came in a long thick roll. Tons of gum AND a comic. Super terrific deal. At 5¢, wow!

WAY back in those very early days we would often rent a country cabin, a very funky place. It was, of course, in the Catskills. I do not recall what town. I do remember the place had a little canteen to get snacks and treats and for grown-ups they had something called, my shoddy memory pulling it from the ocean of ancient tales, The "Hotcha Club". My guess is that it was kind of nightclub. I was just a tiny, tiny kid then so I did not mind the funkiness of the place. One of my favorite personal games was to roll up in the blanket in bed, then roll onto the floor by the door wrapped in the blanket. I thought that was fun. I don't know why. I kept a Dixie-cup lid collection (those were a little cup of ice cream) the underside of the lid had pictures of cowboys etc. I do not know what I was doing or why I was attracted to that. I kept my collection in a shallow box that I stored under my bed, away from prying eyes of other collectors who might have been jealous. Bizarre mind of a four year old. I recall a few days when we went blueberry picking. I had a little bucket into which to put pickings. It was great fun. One day while looking into the can, I discovered a big bug no doubt it was just a grasshopper. It scared me so much that I dumped the whole thing. It is a vivid memory. A great waste of blueberries.

Several years later, we rented a more appalling room in Rockaway Beach. A question, why did we always get such crummy places? Most important how did living in such very bad environments affect my life growing up and what influence does it have to this day? These are important questions not considered previously.

It was not really that far away from Brooklyn so I don't know why we went through all the trouble of renting the room. I was a little bit old maybe 5 or 6. The cool thing was the boardwalk. They had actual "penny arcades" where you can get and do things for pennies. My favorite game was Skee ball —this was a game we took large wooden bowl rolled it up and incline to where they were concentric holes middle hole was a high score of 10 points other holes had lesser points. I got pretty good at this. Loved it. So many other games that I do not remember but I loved running around playing. I guess that is how video games became popular. BUT, the very best things were dispensing machines of picture postcards. [Note to younger ones: A postcard was kind of mailing thing you did when you had actual physical mail and it was, just a card on one side was a photo on the other side was a space for the address and your brief message.] However, those that we collected were not meant to be postcards for mailing they were 3 x 7"with sepia tone photos of athletes, cowboys, movie stars etc. I just loved collecting them. And, only a penny each. I went wild over that. One day I found the big stash of them that was behind one of the machines. It was like discovering gold. At this very ramshackle rooming house the bathroom etc. was in the hallway and happen to be just opposite our room.

In those days, we had radio and I was very fond of many shows not just ones for kids like Capt. Midnight [more on him later], Lone Ranger, Superman etc., I also really loved so-called "scary" shows. They were, Suspense & Inner Sanctum. The opening gambit of those shows some variation of very squeaky door opening and show by a very spectral voice saying something like, "Welcome to the Inner Sanctum." Followed by that awful what was supposed to be scary laughter but was just silly. [Very recently, I explored what is known as the radio archive, on the web, where they keep thousands of these shows when I listen to them today they are really terribly done. Poorly scripted, very poorly acted. This even includes, hard to believe, The Shadow, FBI in War and Peace, and even Gangbusters.] One time I will not forget. It was early evening, yet dark. One of the shows I loved was on (either Suspense or Inner Sanctum) was on. I turned off the lights, turned on the radio and hid under the table. I invited little brother Milton (Moishela) but he declined. Anyway, it was a narrated tale told by the protagonist. He was stranded on a little Island with an old defunct lighthouse. This was over a hundred years ago perhaps around the mid to late 19th century. He was there alone for a very, very long time, almost no food. Fish was getting harder to catch. Naturally, he was constantly on edge searching for a vessel that may come and save him. He'd say, "I'm going to the top of the lighthouse as I do every day. Peering out into the vast ocean hoping to see a ship come and rescue me from this horrible situation. I have long ago lost my trusty spyglass, alas, so must rely on these old bare eyes. Just today, a rather stormy day, I see a ship far in the distance sailing this way. It is a three-mast, heavy ship. It is coming closer. I can see the sails they are bright red. They are not simply billowing out in the wind but rippling. Red sails constantly moving and rippling. I have never seen a movement like that in sails. I see no man on the ship. No one at the wheel. It is very unusual. It comes quite close now I see on the sails they are not sails, and those are not sails but swarms of red rats. That is why there is no man on the ship. They have come for me how am I to escape? I run up the lighthouse they know where I am. They know my smell......." I think it just ended like that. Loved it.

As mentioned above I searched for that episode on the radio archives website but could not find anything. I did listen to a number of different episodes of different shows and they were altogether dreadfully produced. Script, acting, the whole deal was amateur hour.

Now as promised above reference was made to Capt. Midnight. The story in brief. Midnight was what one might call early American action hero. Coming from the War (II), he was a pilot. Naturally, being American he was white, good-looking, clean white teeth and spoke well. Do not recall if he had any sidekicks, I imagine he did. Anyway, I liked listening to the show. The sponsor was Ovaltine, which I love to drink. It was a powder mixed with milk usually warm and had cocoa powder, lots of sugar, barley malt, which was the most important flavor, malt. That's what I loved. As with all the other action characters on radio they gave the opportunity to join their "Secret Club". All it required was sending in the top liner of the Ovaltine jar and a dime 10¢. For that you received; the membership card, naturally, AND most important—The Secret Decoder Ring. With this in my tiny hand I could decipher secret messages that were given in the middle of the show. Pretty soon a little bulky packet came to me. Since that time I love ordering stuff that would come in little bulky packets. I think this is the secret of so much success for Amazon. I thought to start a special service or society for small annual fee get every month in the mail a special bulky packet that would contain miscellaneous stuff. That aside when I got my packet I signed the membership card, which in actuality was not worth anything. I had my secret decoder ring on my little finger awaiting the show and the part in which they gave the very secret message. What excitement! As it turned out secret decoder ring is worth about as much as the membership card. *Bupkis*—which means nothing in Yiddish. I loved wearing it anyway. Funny how certain little things give us pleasure when we are young this pattern repeats itself when we are older you look at it is very small larger context of the Universe.

There is another recollection from way back quite the same time. And not necessarily related to the summer but was not in the book. For a brief time I watched a fellow on TV who did hairdressing. I thought to myself, "That's easy. I can do it." I guess I was about 11 or 12 for a period of time I would brush my mom's hair. The first I volunteered but then after that she actually asked me to do it all for her. I sort of style and follow up and just made it look nice. She loved it. I really like doing that it was something requiring attention to detail. An attitude that I carried on all of my life. It is informative and interesting on some of the habits and inclinations that cultivate in our early life carries on and develops for the entire life.

As I was telling someone about my recollections of making kites it reminded me of something else I did which probably informed how I worked in my adult life. Growing up mom was very self-sufficient she would, for example, make her own dresses every year. She would just zip it out. Put some cloth on the pattern and cut, cut, cut then sew, sew, sew and was done. Bada bing bada boom. Now, she would even wallpaper the kitchen and maybe the living room and paint the stucco outside walls. She let me help her with this as best I could. I got very intrigued with the details of wallpapering. This is how my orientation towards doing detailed work came. I would try my best to get paper onto the wall with no bubbles I also loved removing the old wallpaper. It was hard labor but I enjoyed it.

There were a few other skills I picked up along the way. Like cooking. I watched my dad made foods and I just would do what he did. Then I picked up a few on my own. One of these actually came from watching Julia Child. This was eggplant Parmesan. It was quite intriguing to me. So I followed it exactly and made it. Mom totally loved i. She would frequently ask me to make that dish for which she did not know its name. Now, speaking of eggplant we had a traditional dish which is a basic simple eggplant salad. To properly prepare the eggplant by taking out the water and bitterness. This was accomplished by first blistering in the oven for 30 seconds making the skin easily removable. This is very necessary. I would then take the oven rack place and on top of a cookie tray or something similar. Then cut the eggplant into 1 inch thick pieces, thickly spread with kosher salt, emphasis on the kosher part because it did the job best. Then place another cookie tray atop the eggplant place a heavyweight item atop the cookie tray, let it sit for about an hour. All the water and bitterness would drain down into the bottom cookie tray. I would then wash off the salt. Now comes the secret part. We had these big wooden bowls and special knife that was more or less a horizontal half circle about 5 inches in diameter. Atop the semicircle was a large handle (Mezzaluna), which you can fit your whole hand in and would make chopping things very nice I would take red onion, skinned cucumber, a lot of garlic and the eggplant & salt I would then chop, chop, chop it all. Then drench with white vinegar and Wesson oil (now I'd use a very fine tamari or modest amount of balsamic & extra virgin olive oil). That's what we knew then. Marinade for about an hour. It was quite good served with crusty rye bread. That is how we got bread at the baker on the "Avenue" made that very day.

My very first experience with gardening: this is a most wonderful fond memory. This was at our nice home in Brooklyn. We had the practice of purchasing raw sunflower seeds in the shell for a wonderful snack. I loved piling up seeds on the plate and eating a bunch all at once. I thought what would it be like to plant the seeds; just one to see what would happen. I took a single seed while still in the shell. I knew zero about gardening. Keep in mind these were untreated raw seeds. Not roasted. Well I dug a little hole with a trowel in the small strip of earth in our backyard. I applied generous amount of water waited to the next day. Nothing came out. I would watch it every day without fail. I was totally dedicated to my plant. It eventually started to sprout. Very it quickly began to grow and grow and grow. Quite soon, it became as enormous plant that produced a giant flower filled, filled with seeds. I waited a long time before picking them out. Well, four days. Naturally, I had to try one immediately, it was quite soft and moist. I think I picked them too soon. Regardless, it started me on the path to becoming a gardener and learning all about how to do plants properly.

Finally, I loved helping dad in his *Shul* (Yiddish word for synagogue) I will mention two of them, which when thought on now were quite ordinary tasks. One was a cleaning, of which I recall mostly dusting all the benches plus straightening out the prayer books. The latter was far more important than you would imagine. According to strict Orthodox Jewish code prayer books (Siddurim —Hebrew word) and Bibles (Chumashim) or any book with God's sacred name are very, very holy and in no case should they put upside down or on a bench or chair or in the bathroom. This is how I learned great respect for books. Anyway, I did this on a regular basis and it was very satisfying. The second task came infrequently and that was to do the Shul's mailing. Back in those days we used a machine called "Addressograph." This is machine where you had metal plates upon which was embossed the name and address of the recipient and the slot for the envelopes there was also a section for inking the metal plates. I would stack a whole batch of these plates plus a big stack of standard business envelopes and fire away. There was great fun running the machine. Something that I have never done before. That felt very grown up. It was a delight. I loved helping dad.

One of the obsessions I had as a young pre-teen and in my early teen years was collecting the latest pop music record, which back then were 45's, singles. Now for you mostly younger folk those were plastic records that played on a "record player" [go look it up] at 45rpm. They had a giant hole in the center which required either an adapter for the spindle or a plastic insert for the disc to make it fit the player spindle [[OK now really look it all up and get some photos]]...

All About the Cover Photo

Very important point that I skipped was to put in a little bit about my cover photo. This is a photo I took my on my trek in Nepal in 1998. It is one of the many, many bridges we had to cross. Always swinging always made of bamboo wood with slots missing. Sometimes very precarious to cross these bridges but we made. We always made it. This photo is a metaphor of my life. Has always been dangerous precarious moments, bridges, bridges, but I always made it. I somehow managed to survive so many precarious really dangerous moments. It was quite amazing.

And so it went. And So it goes.

I have been very selective in what I put down. I left out all the bad stuff. That would've been a very large tome, very large indeed. Not worth recording.

Ahh, Nostalgia—not what it used to be.

"And that's the way it is."—Walter Cronkite

Made in the USA
Columbia, SC
11 January 2024